MARKET FAILURE, GOVERNMENT FAILURE, LEADERSHIP AND PUBLIC POLICY

Market Failure, Government Failure, Leadership and Public Policy

Joe Wallis
Otago University
Dunedin
New Zealand

and

Brian Dollery
University of New England
Armidale
Australia

First published in Great Britain 1999 by
MACMILLAN PRESS LTD
Houndmills, Basingstoke, Hampshire RG21 6XS and London
Companies and representatives throughout the world

A catalogue record for this book is available from the British Library.

ISBN 0–333–73423–8

 First published in the United States of America 1999 by
ST. MARTIN'S PRESS, INC.,
Scholarly and Reference Division,
175 Fifth Avenue, New York, N.Y. 10010

ISBN 0–312–22186–X

Library of Congress Cataloging-in-Publication Data
Wallis, Joe
Market failure, government failure, leadership and public policy /
Joe Wallis and Brian Dollery.
p.   cm.
Includes bibliographical references and index.
ISBN 0–312–22186–X (cloth)
1. Economic policy.   2. Social policy.   3. Policy sciences.
4. Intervention (Federal government)   5. Political planning.
6. Business cycles.   7. Economic stabilization.   8. Leadership.
I. Dollery, Brian.   II. Title.
HD87.W354   1999
338.9—dc21   99–18650
                                                CIP

© Joe Wallis and Brian Dollery 1999

This book is printed on paper suitable for recycling and made from fully managed and
sustained forest sources.

10   9   8   7   6   5   4   3
08   07   06   05   04   03   02   01   00

Printed and bound in Great Britain by
Antony Rowe Ltd, Chippenham, Wiltshire

In loving memory of Vicki Rowena Francis
(1953–1996): lover, friend and life's companion.
Mane me in caelo, carissima

Brian Dollery

Contents

List of Tables

List of Figures

Preface

The role of the state in advanced market economies and the attendant problem of appropriate public policymaking remain intriguing and unsettled questions. This is undoubtedly due in part to the complexities of the policymaking process in contemporary developed economies. But it is surely also attributable to the fact that until fairly recently social scientists approached these questions from within the analytical confines of their own disciplines. Thus economists, policy analysts, political scientists, sociologists, theoreticians from public administration, and others, have found their attempts to provide positive explanations for observed policymaking processes and their efforts to formulate normatively prescriptive frameworks for optimal policymaking inevitably constrained by the limitations of their own disciplines. Certainly in our own attempts at analysing and explaining the policymaking process we have often felt inhibited by our own disciplinary strictures, despite the rich array of analytical tools available to economists.

Other economists have expressed similar feelings. For example, although in a somewhat different context, in his recent 'distinguished lecture on economics in government' Henry Aaron (1994) gave expression to some of the unease even mainstream economists experience when they reflect on the adequacy of their tools in dealing with complex social issues. Aaron confessed that after reading about the 'interlocking web of social pathologies' in communities facing a daily diet of 'illicit drugs, random violence and murder, unemployment, truancy, theft, abandonment and despair' he was left feeling 'stunned'. He found that he could not avoid asking the following questions (p.4):

> Are the methods we economists use adequate to the task of evaluating how policies affect such communities? For that matter, are they adequate for evaluating how policies influence other major social problems including violent crime, out-of-wedlock births, or poor school performance? To put the matter more aggressively: are we even making any progress in answering these questions?

In this book we have sought to move beyond conventional disciplinary frontiers in our analyses of the role of the state and policymaking in representative democracies. In particular, we have attempted to augment contemporary economic discourse on policymaking by developing an economic theory of leadership. Our theory of leadership draws on a long tradition of

xiii

theorizing about leadership in the social sciences which has been ignored by economists. One way of conceptualizing this project is to view this book as an attempt at creating an alternative approach to dealing with the pervasive problem of 'agency failure' in public sector hierarchies. In contrast to the current dominant paradigm, which is encapsulated in the doctrines of what can be termed 'generic managerialism' and its derivative school of thought known as 'New Public Management' (NPM), like commercialization, competitive tendering and contracting out, corporatization, deregulation, and privatization, our economic theory of leadership provides an alternative solution to the problems of public sector agency failure. We argue that effective leadership can modify the endogenously determined preferences of civil servants and others in the governmental process and thereby at least attenuate the degree of agency failure.

This book represents the outcome of longstanding friendship and research collaboration between the authors which goes back to the Department of Economics at Rhodes University in Grahamstown, South Africa in the early 1980s. Following literally dozens of informal discussions over thousands of cups of tea and glasses of beer, our first formal paper published in the 1985 volume of the *Journal of Studies in Economics and Econometrics* dealt with various problems associated with the deregulation of the South African transport sector. Since that time our research collaboration has blossomed into a regular flow of articles as we have steadily developed a theory of leadership perspective on policymaking and policy reform. Joe Wallis' move to the Department of Economics at the Otago University, Dunedin, New Zealand in 1987 and Brian Dollery's subsequent relocation to the Department of Economics, University of New England, Armidale, New South Wales, Australia, in early 1988 proved especially fruitful as we were able to observe at first hand the astonishing policy reversals associated with 'Rogernomics' in New Zealand and the rather more sedate pace of 'microeconomic reform' in Australia. Much of our thinking on the importance of leadership derives from the observation of these policy changes and their associated policy paradigms.

Joe Wallis would like to express his sincere appreciation to Pat Cosgriff in the Department of Economics at Otago University for her expert secretarial assistance. He would also like to thank his colleagues in the Department of Economics at Otago University for providing a supportive and encouraging work environment, with special thanks to Brian Easton for thoughtful comments on Chapters 5 and 8. He would also like to extend his gratitude to students in his Economics 308 (Public Economics) class for acting as gracious guinea pigs for some of the ideas of this book. Most of all, Joe would like to thank his wife, Kim, and daughters, Caitlin and Jessica, for their love and fun times, and God for renewing his strength.

Brian Dollery would like to thank collaborator Joe Wallis for an exhilarating friendship and research partnership. He would like to express his appreciation to Mrs Rosalie Hall of the Department of Economics at the University of New England for her help in getting the final manuscript into shape. Brian would also like to thank various colleagues for their help and encouragement in the preparation of the book, especially Dr Greg 'No Go' Smith and Michael 'Kortto' Kortt of the University of New England and Andrew 'Wortho' Worthington of the Queensland University of Technology. He would also like to extend his appreciation to recent generations of students in his Economics 306; Australian Microeconomic Policy and Economics 352/452; Public Economics, for suffering earlier versions of this book in good spirits. Most of all, Brian would like to extend his heartfelt gratitude to Grahame and Betty Francis for their love and support following the tragic death of their daughter Vicki Francis. God bless you both.

1 Introduction

It is widely recognized that the formulation, implementation and evaluation of public policy in contemporary advanced market economies is an extremely complex process and often contains idiosyncratic elements not readily amenable to the abstract reasoning typical of the social sciences. Nevertheless, scholars from a wide range of disciplines have long been intrigued by the policymaking process and have developed a number of positive theories about how policymaking actually works and several normative models offering conceptual guidelines on how policymaking should work. Our book lies within this broad tradition.

The past two decades have witnessed a state of flux in both the conceptual frameworks which inform the process of policymaking and the institutional milieu within which public policies are formulated and implemented. While the primary focus of this book falls squarely on shifts in the theoretical paradigms underlying policymaking and changes in the policy paradigms influencing policymakers, these transformations have taken place against a background of fundamental and ubiquitous institutional change in the nature of public administration of developed market economies. It is useful to at least mention some of these changes as a means of placing our subsequent discussion of shifts in theoretical paradigms and policy paradigms in context.

INSTITUTIONAL CHANGE

Peters (1996a, p.4) has identified 'six old chestnuts' on the 'old model of public administration' which have assisted in aiding 'our thinking about the public service and governance'. Three of these shed considerable light on institutional transformations currently underway in contemporary civil administration. Perhaps the most enduring assumption about twentieth century governance has emphasized the principle of a politically neutral civil service offering impartial policy advice to the elected government of the day. However, despite this longstanding stress on the depoliticization of the civil service, especially characteristic of Anglo-Saxon industrialized democracies, the increasing importance of public servants in the process of policy formulation and implementation has become clear (Plowden, 1994). Moreover, some commentators have argued that this trend is desirable insofar as it improves the quality of policymaking (Terry, 1995). The sensitivity of civil servants engaging in the delivery of policy advice to elected governments is highlighted by growing public demands for accountability and transparency in contemporary governance. The resultant conundrum has been outlined by Peters (1996a, p.6) as follows:

> The problem then becomes how to structure government in ways that recognize the reality, and even the desirability, of the significant policy role for civil servants while simultaneously preserving the requirements of democratic accountability. This is a difficult balance for designers of government institutions to achieve, especially given the historical legacy of thought concerning the neutrality of the civil service and the current reality of public demands for enhanced accountability.

A second important feature of the transformation of modern governance resides in the decline of the 'traditional sense of permanence in public organisations' and an attendant 'realisation that many significant social and economic problems currently exist within the interstices of public organisations' (Peters, 1996a, p.9). This has led *inter alia* to a search for new alternative institutional structures within which to conduct the policymaking process, including task forces, interdepartmental committees, official commissions, and even 'virtual organizations' linking people in numerous disparate places.

Thirdly, the Weberian model of civil administration, with its insistence on procedural rules and hierarchical managerial structures, no longer enjoys predominant status as the quintessential methodology of governance. Alternative administrative regimes have been adopted for a growing range of governmental activities, notably market-based delivery systems and interactive or participatory structures. A significant consequence of the demise of the Weberian model has been to '... make the role of civil service managers even more difficult than it has been and leave the role of civil servants within governments more ambiguous' (Peters, 1996a, p.8).

PARADIGM SHIFTS

Much of this book revolves around the question of theoretical paradigm shifts and policy paradigm shifts and the causes and consequences of these shifts. Accordingly, it thus seems appropriate to briefly to consider the metatheoretical underpinnings of the notion of paradigm shifts and place this concept in the broader context of the history of the philosophy of science. In his pathbreaking treatises *The Logic of Scientific Discovery*

(1959) and *Conjectures and Refutations* (1963), Karl Popper sought to develop a fundamental methodological criterion to differentiate between science and non-science. The rule he proposed was the so-called 'principle of falsifiability' which specified that the scientific status of a theory lay in its capacity for falsifiability, and not in either its verifiability or its irrefutability. Whilst falsifiability denotes the 'line of demarcation' of science, this need not imply that a single refutation provides sufficient grounds for the dismissal of a theory, nor does it imply that empirical falsification is the only criterion, for rational falsification is also possible. A scientific theory is thus retained for as long as it remains unfalsified, and once it is falsified, it should be replaced by a new theory which is also capable of falsification. Consequently, the advancement of a scientific discipline is not dependent so much on ideological and institutional influences as on the universably applicable criterion of falsifiability.

Despite its intuitive appeal, Popperian falsificationism has largely been abandoned (Callebaut, 1993), even in the physical sciences. Its applicability to the social sciences was always severely circumscribed largely due to the fact that the social sciences and natural sciences are intrinsically different. Elster (1993, p.202) has observed that '... to study the logical structure of theories is certainly feasible in physics and, I guess, in biology; but there are no general theories comparable in scope, rigor, or precision in the social sciences'. Similarly, McCloskey (1983) has pointed to a long tradition in economics of using rhetorical devices to persuade audiences rather than any strict deference to '... the lordly demarcations of yesterday's philosophers as to what is and what is not scientific...' (Maloney, 1994, p.253). But perhaps Hayek's (1970, p.23) argument has come closest to identifying the fundamental distinction between the social sciences and the natural sciences:

> Unlike the position that exists in the physical sciences, in economics and other disciplines that deal with essentially complex phenomena, the aspects of the events to be accounted for about which we can get quantitative data are necessarily limited and may not include the important ones. While in the physical sciences it is generally assumed, probably with good reason, that any important factor which determines the observed events will itself be directly observable and measurable, in the study of such complex phenomena as the market, which depend on the actions of many individuals, all the circumstances which will determine the outcome of a process, for reasons which I shall explain later, will hardly ever be fully known or measurable.

An alternative explanation for the progress of scientific thought was advanced by Thomas Kuhn. Kuhn (1970) posits the idea of a 'paradigm' which is a conceptual framework of 'disciplinary matrix' within which the problem-solving work of 'normal' science takes place. Thus, the ruling paradigm delineates and defines the scope of the so-called 'research agenda'. The ruling paradigm will only become endangered should it leave unexplained certain important empirical events or 'anomalies'. When this is so then science is said to be in a 'crisis'. But a crisis is not a sufficient condition for a 'scientific revolution' or a 'paradigm-switch': there must also be present an alternative paradigm which can incorporate the anomalies more successfully, for 'to reject one paradigm without simultaneously substituting another is to reject science itself' (Kuhn, 1970, p.79). The revolution and subsequent alternative paradigm provide in one stroke a solution to the anomalies, a different conceptual framework, and a new research agenda; normal science can therefore resume its problem-solving course. In juxtaposition to Popper's internalist explanation of scientific progress, Kuhn lays stress on the influence of external factors. Truth is relative and dependent upon factors like institutional structure and culture. In addition, while Popper sees progress taking the form of a continuous dialectical interplay between conjecture and refutation, Kuhn's theory holds that scientific progress is discontinuous and disjointed, occurring in the form of revolutions.

In what may be seen as an attempt to synthesize the metatheories of Popper and Kuhn, Imre Lakatos (1976) proposed his 'methodology of scientific research programmes'. Deane (1978, p.x) has outlined his approach as follows:

> This approach, which brings normative methodological criteria to the fore, interprets the history of science in terms of a continuous competition between alternative research programmes, rather than as a succession of conjectures and refutations on the one hand, or of total paradigm switches on the other.

Lakatos (1976) argues that any given science is made up of a series of research programmes each comprising a number of interdependent theories which make some sort of organic unity. A scientific research programme consists of a 'hard core' or 'negative heuristic' of basic postulates not open to falsification in the Popperian sense, and a 'positive heuristic' which 'consists of a partially articulated set of suggestions or hints on how to change, develop the "refutable variants" of the research programme, how to modify, sophisticate, the "refutable" protective belt'. Lakatos (1976) distinguishes between 'progressive' and 'degenerating' research programmes. A research programme may be theoretically progressive when theoretical alterations have independently testable content and empirically progressive where substantiating evidence exists for this testable content. On the other hand, a degenerating research programme is one which survives only by *ad hoc* additions to itself which allow for the accommodation of potentially damaging new facts. Scientific progress is made possible in this schema because a degenerating programme can be replaced by a rival progressive programme which 'explains the previous success of its rival and supersedes it by a further display of heuristic power' (Lakatos, 1971, p.104).

THEORETICAL PARADIGMS AND POLICY PARADIGMS

The metatheories presented by Kuhn (1970) and Lakatos (1976) can assist us in developing the crucial distinctions between theoretical paradigms and policy paradigms. Theoretical paradigms in the present context refer to the social science variant of the Kuhnian paradigm: that is, a conceptual framework or intellectual map to guide researchers and practitioners alike. For example, the market failure paradigm discussed in Chapter 2 provides intellectually rigorous criteria for government intervention in a market economy. Similarly, the government failure paradigm examined in Chapter 3 represents an alternative conceptual apparatus for prescribing and evaluating government involvement in a capitalist society. These paradigms or research programmes have mutually exclusive negative heuristics, with the market failure paradigm conceiving of state intervention as essentially benevolent and motivated by considerations of the 'public good' whereas the government failure paradigm views government intervention as fundamentally malevolent and premised on self-interested intentions. Moreover, the research agenda of the market failure theoretical paradigm focuses on identifying and remedying instances of market failure whilst the government failure research programme is preoccupied by an emphasis on policy failures and the unintended consequences of state intervention.

By contrast, policy paradigms derive from theoretical paradigms but possess much less sophisticated and rigorous evaluations of the intellectual underpinnings of their conceptual frameworks. In essence, policy advisers differentiate policy paradigms from theoretical paradigms by screening out the ambiguities and blurring the fine distinctions characteristic of theoretical paradigms. In a Lakatosian sense, policy paradigms can be likened to the positive heuristics surrounding theoretical paradigms. Accordingly, shifts between policy paradigms will be discontinuous, follow theoretical paradigm shifts, but occur more frequently than theoretical paradigm shifts since they do not require fundamental changes in a negative heuristic.

Moreover, while theoretical paradigm shifts will occur in the face of 'crises' contingent upon unexplained 'anomalies' characteristic of 'degenerating' research programmes when alternative 'progressive' paradigms appear to be able to accommodate these 'anomalies', policy paradigm shifts are much more responsive to the sociological status of the particular exponents of specific policies. Policy paradigm shifts will thus usually be less gradual and more frequent than their theoretical counterparts.

Implicitly adopting our concept of policy paradigm shifts, various writers have sought to explain two phenomena characteristic of the policymaking process. Firstly, the observed long periods of policy stability have attracted the attention of a number of theorists, not least the advocacy coalition framework presented by Sabatier (1988) and Sabatier and Jenkins-Smith (1993). And secondly, sudden episodes of dynamic policy change also typify the policymaking process and require explanation. Various arguments have been advanced to account for this aspect of policymaking, including the agenda-setting literature (see, for example, Baumgartner and Jones, 1993 and Kingdon, 1995) and work on the politics of ideas (see, for instance, Derthick and Quirk, 1985 and Wilson, 1980). In this book we develop an alternative leadership model of the policymaking process to explain radical policy reform associated with policy paradigm shifts.

OUTLINE OF THE BOOK

The text itself is organized around the key concepts of theoretical paradigms and policy paradigms. Thus, whereas Chapters 2, 3 and 4 are centrally concerned with the market failure, government failure, and 'new institutional economics' theoretical paradigms and shifts of these paradigms, Chapters 5, 6, 7 and 8 focus on policy paradigm shifts.

Chapter 2 is devoted to a detailed analysis of the conventional market failure paradigm and we examine both the 'narrow' version of this paradigm which defines market failure exclusively in terms of allocative efficiency and the 'broader' version more relevant to policy analysis which also includes equity considerations. We discuss the growing scepticism evoked by the application of this paradigm to real-world economic and social problems. Moreover, we address the major methodological flaw associated with the market failure paradigm, namely the 'nirvana fallacy'.

Chapter 3 begins with a discussion of various alternative conceptions of the state which are contrasted with the idealized model of government encapsulated in the 'public interest' approach adopted by the theory of market failure. Attention is then focused on the government failure paradigm which developed as a consequence of disaffection with the market failure paradigm. The examination of the literature on government failure deals with both the positive theories of government, namely the Chicago approach or 'capture' theory of regulation and public choice theory, and normative theories of government failure, including Wolf's (1989) theory of 'nonmarket failure', Le Grand's (1991) theory of government failure, and Vining and Weimer's (1991) theory of 'government production failure'. In the light of the antithetical market failure and government failure paradigms, we evaluate the appropriate role of government in a market economy, including conceptions of the 'enabling state'.

Chapter 4 examines the nature and implications of 'new institutional economics' (NIE), especially its agency theory and transaction costs strands, for the analysis of problems in a public sector context. We then investigate 'generic managerialism' (GM) which consists of a particular stream of management theory that has been applied to public sector organizations. Discussion moves on to 'New Public Management' (NPM) which refers to an amalgam of NIE and GM from which a policy paradigm has been constructed that supplied the principles and doctrines that have been used to reshape the public sectors of many countries since the early 1980s.

Chapter 4 can thus be considered a bridge between the theoretical and policy-related sections of the book. Chapter 5 deals with the broad issues that have arisen as economists and political scientists have sought to explain the radical reform processes launched in many countries since the early 1980s. These have encompassed the parallel processes of liberalization, stabilization, privatization and commercialization. A puzzling feature of these reform processes is that while they have generally sought to address pervasive problems of government failure, government failure theorists neither predicted that they would be implemented nor recommended that they should be advanced in such a radical, discontinuous way. Extensive reference is made to New Zealand's recent reform experience as this chapter tries to explain the punctuated equilibrium pattern these reform processes have been observed to follow in terms of the institutional and political risks associated with paradigmatic policy change and the opportunities for the emergence of new sources of policy leadership that can arise during periods of radical reform.

However, leadership is a phenomenon that has been relatively neglected by the economics profession. Chapter 6 considers the issues of the sigficance, distinctiveness and legitimacy of leadership that have been repeatedly raised in the broader interdisciplinary literature on this subject, taking a somewhat philosophical approach. The particular relevance of these issues to the political economy of policy reform is demonstrated and the comparatively isolated attempts economists have made to model leadership are discussed.

The economic theory of leadership that is applied in the remaining policy analysis is based on Elster's (1998) dissonance theory of the emotions. It treats leadership as being collectively supplied by networks within which member interaction serves to build up the hope and counter the disappointment experienced in relation to shared commitments. This concept is then used to explain how a 'progressive leadership network' maintains its cohesion as it seeks to penetrate, break up and reconfigure the fragmented structure of policy networks that have been observed to characterize many governance systems.

Chapter 8 then considers the type of impasse that can arise when a reactionary leadership network has generated resistance of sufficient strength to counter the forward momentum of a reform process set in motion by a progressive leadership network, and the pragmatist remnant of the policy community is genuinely puzzled about the future direction in which policy should develop. In this situation, the rhetoric of the protagonists can take on a repetitive pattern with reactionaries advancing what Hirschman (1991) calls 'jeopardy', 'perversity' and 'futility' arguments and progressives countering them with 'imminent danger', 'desperate predicament' and 'futility of resistance' counter-arguments. The incidence of this pattern of argumentation in the debate over the implementation of the NPM is considered as well as the way each argument is used to affect the dissonance the various leadership networks experience in relation to their policy commitments. The intransigence of the rhetorical positions the protagonists can take in this type of situation points to the need for a moral leadership that strives to forge a broader understanding of the public interest through an 'autonomous politics' that leaves participants with the impression that they have been the subjects of a reasonable process.

Chapter 9 ponders some of the important implications the preceding analysis. It examines areas of overlap between governance theories and the theory of policy leadership developed in this book, but argues that the focus of leadership theory will typically be broader. In addition to a concern with whether policy can be steered in a coherent direction, it will also focus on how cohesiveness can be established within particular leadership networks and the question of whether it is possible for a leadership network to internalize good politics without losing its distinctive identity. The leadership paradigm developed in this book then attempts to lead policy theorists back to a consideration of the important tradition in political thought that seeks to develop a normative understanding of discursive or participatory democracy. It also develops a distinctive concept of *homo politicus* that recognizes that political agents have both private motives and public reasons for their commitments and that rhetoric matters since it affects the hope that these agents invest in political interaction.

2 Market Failure and Government Intervention

2.1 INTRODUCTION

The appropriate role of government in contemporary advanced industrial democracies is a complex and controversial question which remains unsettled. A vast research effort has been devoted to resolving this question. Social scientists, including anthropologists, economists, policy analysts, political scientists, public administration specialists, and sociologists, have devised numerous approaches to the study of the nature and role of government, with varying degrees of success. One of the more successful approaches to the analysis of the state has been developed by welfare economists in the form of the theory of market failure. In essence, the market failure paradigm examines the operation of the economy and prescribes government intervention when markets 'fail' on the grounds of either economic efficiency or equity.

Although the origins of the theory of market failure may be traced back several hundred years in the history of economic thought, the contemporary version of this theory owes much to William Baumol's (1952) *Welfare Economics and the Theory of the State*, Paul Samuelson's (1954) famous paper on 'The Pure Theory of Public Expenditure' in the *Review of Economics and Statistics*, and Francis Bator's 1958 article entitled 'The Anatomy of Market Failure'. Notwithstanding the success of the market failure paradigm in providing a rigorous conceptual framework to guide policymakers in the design of public policies, from the beginning it contained several serious limitations. Mitchell and Simmons (1994, p.xvii) have described these problems as follows:

> Because no human institution is perfect, it is easy to find imperfections or 'failures'. It is even easier if, like the welfare economists, you only concentrate on the economy and do not recognise the effects of the political system on the shape, direction, and rules of the economy. It is also easy to call for government intervention if you have no corresponding theory of how government functions.

The present chapter focuses the nature and limitations of the theory of market failure as an explanation for the appropriate role of government.

9

The chapter itself is divided into five main sections. In section 2 we examine the meanings which can be ascribed to the concept of economic efficiency, which forms the analytical core of the theory of market failure. The market failure paradigm is discussed in detail in section 3. The growing scepticism with both the effects of the application of this paradigm and the theory itself, not least its implicit assumption of the benevolent and omnipotent state, are assessed in section 4. A major methodological flaw in policy design based on the prescriptions flowing from the market failure paradigm, known as the nirvana fallacy, is examined in section 5. The chapter ends with some brief concluding comments in section 6.

2.2   THE MEANING OF ECONOMIC EFFICIENCY

Economics is said to be founded on the acultural and ahistorical principle of relative scarcity. In this sense, relative scarcity characteristically refers to the universal relationship between limited means and unlimited wants representative of the human condition. Available means or resources are thus scarce relative to the various ends to which they can be devoted, which necessarily implies economizing in both the allocation and use of scarce resources. If means were unlimited, or human wants limited, then efficiency in the use of resources would not be necessary. But given the pervasive existence of relative scarcity in the real-world, the efficient employment of limited productive means to fulfil unlimited consumption wants becomes a critical issue. It is thus clear that the concept of efficiency plays a central role in economic analysis and economic discourse.

Interaction between 'rational maximizing economic agents' occurs within the context of exchange relationships with the market mechanism acting as the basic co-ordinating structure. Although economics focuses on voluntary interaction in exchange relationships, it is important to emphasize that other co-ordinating mechanisms coexist with exchange relationships in human society. Kenneth Boulding (1978) in his *Ecodynamics* distinguishes between three broad groups of social organizers. First, the 'threat system', based on interaction of the type 'you do something I want, or I will do something you do not want', underlies the existence of organized government thus providing for the existence and enforcement of property rights and other legal entitlements and obligations. Secondly, the 'integrative system' embraces such things as love and hate, altruism, affection, and so forth, and consequently generates social structures like the family, community and nation which serve to foster and legitimize the operations of the threat and exchange systems. Finally, and in direct contrast to the threat system, the 'exchange system' is based on mutual gain epitomized by interaction of the type 'you do something for me, and I will do something for you'. Exchange or market relationships are thus premised on the twin notions of voluntarism and mutual benefit.

Given the historical existence of market interaction involving the voluntary transfer of property rights between buyers and sellers, economic theory must explain why exchange relationships arise and endure. In essence, it is argued that rational maximizing economic agents exchange property rights through the market mechanism because they benefit from such exchange. Mutual benefits occur due to the gains from trade accruing to all market participants as a consequence of the law of comparative advantage. The law of comparative advantage holds that individuals, firms and nations can raise their incomes by specializing in that sphere of economic activity where they possess a greater degree of relative (and not absolute) efficiency, and exchanging property rights for their output for the output of other economic agents specializing in areas where they in turn possess a greater degree of relative efficiency.

While microeconomic theory is centrally concerned with the behavioural implications of the universal existence of relative scarcity, microeconomic policy focuses on measures designed to reduce the extent of scarcity and to alter the burden of scarcity among members of society. Put differently, microeconomic policy seeks to diminish the degree of relative scarcity by improving economic efficiency, and redistribute the burden of scarcity by modifying income differences between individuals. For example, the programme of privatization in the United Kingdom, public sector reform in New Zealand, and airline deregulation in Australia all represent cases of efficiency-enhancing microeconomic policies. By way of contrast, federal government efforts aimed at the equalization of the financial capacities of the various states and territories in Australian fiscal federalism, drought relief programmes in Southern Africa, and unemployment benefit systems in western Europe are all instances of microeconomic policy interventions directed at redistributing the burden of scarcity among different individuals and groups in society. Thus, whereas microeconomic theory attempts to explain how markets work, microeconomic policy deals with how well markets can work.

Productive Efficiency

Economic efficiency is defined in three main ways in economic discourse. Firstly, technical or productive efficiency refers to the use of resources in the technologically most efficient manner. Obtaining the maximum possible output(s) from a given set of inputs, or technically efficient production, was first defined with precision by Farrell (1957) and approximates what lay people commonly conceive of as 'best practice' in production. A somewhat looser term, covering both the social and technological dimensions of productive activity, was subsequently developed by Leibenstein (1966) and took the name 'X-inefficiency'. Leibenstein (1966) argued that although X-inefficiency (sometimes also termed organizational slack) derives primarily from a lack of motivation by productive agents, factors such as the incomplete specification of labour contracts, incomplete knowledge of production functions, and the lack of complete markets for some inputs, including market information, can also explain the existence of X-inefficiency.

Regardless of whether we accept productive efficiency or the broader concept of X-inefficiency, this notion of economic efficiency alone is an insufficient measure of economic efficiency since the efficient production of goods by itself does not consider the consumption desires of society. It is pointless to produce goods efficiently if people would rather consume some other combination of goods. Accordingly, additional measures of economic efficiency are necessary.

Allocative Efficiency

The second measure of economic efficiency, known as allocative efficiency, refers to the efficient distribution of productive resources among alternative uses so as to produce the optimal mix of output. In the jargon of economics, under conditions of 'perfect competition', the optimal output mix arises through consumers responding to prices which reflect the true costs of production, or 'marginal costs'. Allocative efficiency thus involves an interaction between the productive capacity and consumption activity of society.

Historically, economic theory has been chiefly concerned with allocative efficiency, and only in recent times has attention been focused on productive or X-efficiency. Perhaps the main reasons for this is the central position traditionally occupied by the perfectly competitive model in neoclassical theory. Under perfect competition, market forces ensure an absence of X-inefficiency since, with decreasing returns, firms must produce at the minimum point of long-run average cost. Any producer which exhibits X-inefficiency will thus not pass the 'survival of the fittest' test.

Pigouvian Approach

A major accomplishment of economic theory resides in the establishment and refinement of the properties of allocative efficiency. Two approaches to the problem of allocative efficiency have been developed. Firstly, the partial equilibrium or Marshallian approach represents the primary method of studying particular markets in isolation. This technique examines the equilibrium conditions in a single market on the assumption that the prices of all other commodities and factors of production are given. It is evident that a partial equilibrium approach does not allow for feedback effects between markets. In practice, the partial equilibrium or Marshallian approach is especially suitable for markets whose output is not a significant item in total expenditure nor highly substitutable for any other single commodity.

In terms of the Marshallian approach, the conditions for allocative efficiency were first specified by Arthur Pigou (1920). In essence, Pigou argued that allocative efficiency occurred when the benefit to society of consuming some good or service exactly equalled its cost to society. In technical language, allocative efficiency for private goods occurs where marginal social benefit equals marginal social cost; that is, no divergence between private and social benefits and costs exists. In intuitive terms, this means that the resultant price and quantity accurately reflects the degree of relative scarcity for this good or service.

Paretian Approach

The second major approach to the problem of allocative deficiency is the general equilibrium or Walrasian approach which examines equilibrium conditions in all markets simultaneously. Since all markets are analyzed at the same time, interrelationships between markets and feedback effects occupy a central position in the general equilibrium approach.

Whether a partial or general equilibrium approach should be employed depends largely on the problem at hand. For instance, if the primary concern is a proposed policy change which has a direct impact on many sectors of the economy simultaneously, then a general equilibrium approach is clearly appropriate. An example of this kind of problem would be the introduction of, or modifications to, general sales tax. On the other hand, if the main concern is a proposed policy change which has a direct effect on only one sector, then a partial equilibrium analysis would probably suffice. Excise taxes on items such as cigarettes and alcohol constitute examples of this type of problem.

In terms of the general equilibrium or Walrasian approach, the conditions for allocative efficiency are somewhat more complex. In fact, allocative efficiency in the general equilibrium context requires the simultaneous concurrence of three conditions. Firstly, economic efficiency in production must occur such that no intersectoral reallocation of resources can increase the output of any economic good without decreasing the output of some other economic good. In economic jargon, this means that the marginal rates of technical efficiency of input factors must be equal in all production sectors at current factor market prices. Secondly, economic efficiency in consumption must occur such that no interpersonal reallocation of commodities can increase the wellbeing (or utility) of some consumer without decreasing the wellbeing of some other consumer. In technical terms, the marginal rates of substitution for all goods and services must be equal for all consumers at prevailing market prices. And finally, overall economic efficiency in both production and consumption requires an optimal conformity between economic efficiency in production and economic efficiency in consumption, such that a change in the composition of output cannot increase the utility of some consumer without decreasing the utility of some other consumer. In technical language, a given set of market-determined prices will equal both the marginal rate of transformation in production and the common marginal rates of substitution in consumption. If these three conditions are met, then society is said to have achieved high level optimality in the sense that allocative efficiency occurs in all spheres of economic activity.

Walrasian general equilibrium is said to be Pareto efficient in the sense that it is impossible to improve anyone's welfare by altering production or consumption without impairing someone else's welfare. The concept of Pareto efficiency derives from the work of Vilfredo Pareto (1848–1923) in his 1906 *Manual of Political Economy* and forms the basis of much of contemporary welfare economics. A central proposition of neoclassical welfare economics holds that if all prices are market determined, then a Pareto efficient general equilibrium will ensure. In other words, the operation of competitive markets in a capitalist economy automatically ensures that allocative efficiency will occur in all markets. No corrective intervention by governments can improve upon this outcome since it is already Pareto efficient.

Dynamic or Intertemporal Efficiency

Dynamic or intertemporal efficiency represents the third way of defining economic efficiency. The notion of dynamic efficiency can be traced back to Joseph Schumpeter's (1943) emphasis on innovation and his argument that the perfectly competitive conditions of allocative and productive efficiency were not necessarily the most conducive to long term innovation and economic growth. In contrast to both productive efficiency and allocative efficiency, dynamic efficiency is a much less precise concept with no universally agreed formal definition. In general terms, dynamic efficiency refers to the economically efficient usage of scarce resources through time and thus embraces allocative and productive efficiency in an intertemporal dimension. Sometimes the concept of dynamic efficiency is given more specific meaning in the literature. For instance, the macroeconomic debate on the optimal rate of saving, or the decision to postpone some part of current consumption to a future date, has been referred to as intertemporal efficiency. Similarly, the comparative institutions approach, often associated with New Institutional Economics, focuses on the efficiency of alternative institutional arrangements at exhausting the welfare gains attendant upon exchange relationships (Vira, 1997), as we shall see in Chapter 3.

2.3 THE THEORY OF MARKET FAILURE

The Doctrine of the Invisible Hand

The notion that the pursuit of rational self-interest by individuals engaged in the exchange of property rights through market institutions results in socially benevolent outcomes represents one of the most important insights of economics, and can be traced back to Adam Smith's famous doctrine of the 'invisible hand' in the *Wealth of Nations* in 1776. In essence, this argument holds that maximizing behaviour by individual economic agents in market relationships generates a socially rational use of scarce resources under certain defined conditions. Moreover, the voluntary exchange of goods and services through the market mechanism is itself a positive sum game for all participants since exchange enhances mutual welfare. Because the behaviour of *homo economicus* leads automatically to Pareto optimality in consumption and production, this eliminates the necessity for active policy intervention, and thus creates a strong case for the role of government to be limited to the definition and enforcement of property rights.

The doctrine of the invisible hand has not only proved to be extremely durable but it has also been very influential. For instance, in the great nineteenth-century debates surrounding free trade Smith's arguments had largely carried the day, at least among economic thinkers. Paul Bairoch (1993, p.17) has put the matter as follows:

Book IV of Adam Smith's *The Wealth of Nations* is essentially a defence of free trade at the international level. Smith's book (published in 1776) became the leading work in economics at the end of the eighteenth century. In England eight editions were published before 1800; and before 1796 it had been translated into almost all European languages. The direct successors to Adam Smith, which means, for most economists, all the founding fathers of modern economics, adopted a liberal position on international trade.

Similarly, Smith's views on the role of government in society became widely accepted in the nineteenth century, and this acceptance was mirrored in the limited nature of government intervention in the economy during this period, at least in Great Britain and the United States.

Since Arthur Pigou's momentous *Economics of Welfare* in 1920, modern welfare economics has been largely concerned with the development and refinement of the conditions necessary for the effective operation of the invisible hand: that is, the underlying conditions which must be met for a perfectly competitive or decentralized system of price determination to efficiently allocate scarce resources among alternative ends. The discovery of these necessary and sufficient conditions for economic efficiency led to the systematic identification of generic instances where markets 'failed' to produce allocatively efficient results. In essence, the existence or absence of several factors can prevent the rational self-interest in exchange or market processes characteristic of the invisible hand from generating socially desirable outcomes. This phenomenon is termed market failure and provides the intellectual basis for extensive government intervention aimed at achieving economic efficiency in market economies. Market failure in this sense refers to the inability of a market or system of markets to provide goods and services either at all or in an economically optimal manner. Market failure is thus defined exclusively in terms of economic efficiency in general, and allocative efficiency in particular. The market failure paradigm for microeconomic policymaking assumes governments intervene in the public interest to restore economic efficiency. The market failure paradigm is thus a normative theory of government intervention insofar as it prescribes how governments 'should' behave. As we shall see, the market failure paradigm can be extended to include distributional or equity elements, and its policy implications can be modified in the light of a positive theory of government intervention, namely public choice theory.

Sources of Market Failure

Economists have identified numerous sources of market failure and indeed instances of real or perceived market failure are probably limited only by the imaginations of the economic theorists. However, text books typically emphasize six main forms of market failure which we will discuss below.

Firstly, for Adam Smith's invisible hand to operate properly markets must be competitive rather than monopolistic or oligopolistic. Various reasons exist for the absence of competition in some defined market. Geographic factors such as large distances or isolated locations can mean limited competition. For example, the vast outback of Australia contains numerous small communities often serviced by a single retail supplier. Similarly, limited ownership of some natural resource can confer monopoly power on a producer. Governments may often create monopolies through the legal system. For instance, patent laws grant monopoly rights to inventors for specified time periods. Similarly, gaming operators are usually given exclusive control over casinos in particular jurisdictions. However, perhaps the most significant in the present context are barriers to entry into an industry which arise from increasing returns to scale. This necessarily implied decreasing average costs over large volumes of output and the potential for natural monopolies to arise. Because of the technological nature of production in industries of this kind, competition simply cannot exist. This source of market failure is most commonly evident in the provision of services like electricity, water, railway networks and post offices.

Traditionally government policies towards competition as a potential source of market failure have taken two general forms. Firstly, laws have been promulgated which seek to prevent collusion and other defined types of anti-competitive conduct among producer groups. And secondly, public policies have sought to deal with the problems associated with natural monopoly by either nationalizing the industry in question, historically the preferred approach in Western Europe, or by regulation, and especially rate of return regulation, the policy instrument most favoured in the United States.

A second source of market failure resides in the existence of positive or negative externalities involving an interdependence between consumption and/or production activities, and resulting in a divergence between private and social costs and benefits. In essence, the problem posed by externalities is that the resource allocation yielded by markets will not be efficient because market prices do not reflect the full costs and benefits involved, and accordingly will not generate socially efficient levels of consumption and production. Literally, thousands of kinds of externalities exist. Perhaps industrial pollution is the most widely cited example of a negative production externality. By contrast, industrial agglomeration along the lines of Silicon Valley represents a positive production externality where separate economic activities reinforce each other and lower production costs. A myriad of consumption externalities can be readily identified. Drinkers in a bar enjoying listening to a juke box constitutes a positive consumption externality, whereas tired neighbours attempting to sleep alongside a rowdy party signifies a negative consumption externality!

Conventional policy responses to externalities have almost always resulted in government intervention. Two generic forms of intervention can be identified. Firstly, direct intervention sought to supersede markets and embraced direct government production and regulation. Thus governments often impose standards of food hygiene, water and air pollution, and so forth, and provide vaccination and other medical services in the event of epidemics. Secondly, indirect intervention attempts to work through the market mechanism by means of taxes and subsidies. For instance, because education is supposed to confer benefits on society at large in addition to those bestowed on the recipients of eduction, it receives large subsidies from the fiscus.

However, in principle at least, the problems posed by externalities need not necessarily require government intervention. The so-called Coase theorem, which stemmed from Ronald Coase's (1960) brilliant paper 'The Problem of Social Cost', demonstrates the validity of this proposition. In essence, the Coase theorem holds that if nothing obstructs efficient bargaining between parties affected by an externality, then people will negotiate until they reach a Pareto efficient outcome. Accordingly, no government intervention is necessary. However, for the Coase theorem to work requires the invocation of several heroic assumptions including the existence of costless bargaining with no transaction costs. Coase (1992, p.717) himself has eschewed any practical significance for the Coase theorem:

> The significance to me of the Coase theorem is that it undermines the Pigouvian system. Since standard economic theory assumes transaction costs to be zero, the Coase theorem demonstrates that the Pigouvian solutions are unnecessary in these circumstances. Of course, it does not imply, when transaction costs are positive, that government actions (such as government operation, regulation, or taxation, including subsidies) could not produce a better result than relying on negotiations between individuals in the market. Whether this would be so could be discovered not by studying imaginary governments but what real governments actually do. My conclusion: let us study the world of positive transaction costs.

A third kind of market failure stems from the inability of private markets to produce public goods. Numerous public goods exist which cannot be provided through the competitive market process due to their particular characteristics. Pure public goods are said to be both nonrival in consumption and nonexcludable in consumption. Nonrivalrous consumption occurs where one person's consumption does not reduce the good's availability for consumption by others as, for instance, in the case of national defence. Nonexclusion means that producers of the good are technologically and/or economically unable to prevent individuals from consuming the good as, for example, in the case of radio and television transmissions.

Given these characteristics, there is no incentive for private firms to provide public goods and accordingly they must be furnished collectively through either private voluntary arrangements or through government agencies. If public goods are provided through the public sector, this need not necessarily imply public production, but may simply mean public provision through contracting. Thus, whilst some public goods, like law and order, are produced directly by government through justice and police agencies, other public goods, like highways and water reticulation systems, are provided by governments, but constructed under contract by private firms.

The efficient operation of the invisible hand implies that markets will provide all goods and services where demand is sufficient to cover the costs of supplying these goods and services. Where this does not occur economists argue that incomplete markets have resulted in market failure. It is often argued that this form of market failure is especially evident in insurance markets and capital markets. In many countries governments intervene to provide loans (or at least guarantee loans) to categories of home mortgage borrowers, small businesses, export industries, and farmers in the belief that private credit markets would not provide capital in the absence of such intervention. A related form of market failure due to incomplete markets focuses on the purported absence of complementary markets. Complementarity between markets is said to occur where activity in one market is dependent on the existence of other, related markets. For instance, large scale property redevelopment in modern cities typically requires extensive coordination between local authorities and many private firms, which is often provided by government development agencies on the assumption that the necessary level of co-ordination would not be forthcoming without public intervention.

An additional source of market failure resides in the fact that economic agents on one or both sides of a market may possess incomplete information, or available information may be asymmetrically allocated among market participants. Akerloff's (1970) famous analysis of the market for used cars is a good illustration of this source of market failure. In advancing the concept of adverse selection, or a situation in which those on the informed side of the market self-select in a way that harms the uninformed side of the market, Akerloff (1970) argued that in used car markets sellers typically possess better information than buyers. Since sellers are more adept at picking 'duds' or 'lemons' than buyers, buyers will realize the possibility that they may inadvertently purchase a 'dud' is high and offer only 'discounted' prices to reflect this perception. In turn, sellers will be unwilling to part with good used cars and will sell only 'duds' or 'lemons'. The final outcome will be an adverse selection process where 'lemons' crowd out good used cars. We take up the phenomenon of adverse selection again in Chapter 4 in the context of transaction costs economics.

Market failure due to information failure has lead to widespread government intervention in developed market economies. Much public policy-making has focused on measures to protect consumers, especially product labelling and the disclosure of product content. But direct government intervention has also been evident. For example, weather forecasting is usually produced by public agencies as a means of disseminating information on weather patterns.

A final source of market failure is often argued to exist in the macroeconomies of market societies in the form of the business cycle. Periodic downswings in economic activity result in unemployment and falling incomes, whereas upswings in economic growth may generate inflationary episodes. Macroeconomic instability of this kind is usually met with government intervention in the guise of macroeconomic policies intended to flatten the business cycle. Typically these macroeconomic policies seek to increase economic activity during recessionary periods and decrease such activity during boom periods.

Scepticism about the capacity of governments to improve welfare through interventionist policies has spilled over into macroeconomic theory. Following the formulation by Lucas (1973) of a rational expectations model of aggregate supply in which changes in the growth rate of the money supply could only affect the real level of GDP if they were unanticipated, a number of 'new classical' macroeconomists have sought to provide 'real' or non-monetary explanations of the business cycle. In a survey of this literature, Plosser (1987) has referred to the way real business cycle models that assume continuously clearing markets and treat the annual growth rate of technology as a stochastic variable can generate predictions of cyclical fluctuations in real variables such as output, employment, consumption and investment that correlate impressively with actual real-world time series data. The clear implications of these findings would seem to be that cyclical fluctuations are largely equilibrium phenomena and not instances of market failure. It follows that countercyclical macroeconomic policies are unnecessary and could potentially be destabilizing.

Ethical Considerations

Thus far we have only considered market failure from the perspective of economic efficiency. If markets failed to yield Pareto efficient outcomes, then we have seen that a *prima facie* case for government intervention can be made on efficiency grounds alone. But even if markets do generate economically efficient outcomes, additional ethical arguments may still be invoked to justify a role for public policy. This of course requires a somewhat broader definition of the meaning of market failure. Wolf's (1989, 19–20) observation that '... markets may fail to produce either economically optimal (efficient) or socially desirable (equitable) outcomes ...' is a good example of such a broader definition.

The introduction of equity or fairness considerations into economic analysis brings with it complex issues (Kolm, 1993), not least the fact that a virtually inexhaustible range of plausible standards for judging equity exist. Wolf (1989, p.82) has listed just a few of these possible standards:

> ... Equity evaluated as equality of opportunity; equity as equality of outcome; equity as perfect equality of outcome *unless* departure from equality is an essential precondition for securing advantages for those who are least favored; equity as a categorical imperative specifying that no personal or individual action is fair unless it can be applied as a general maxim to govern the behavior of others; equity in the sense of horizontal equity (treating equally situated people equally); equity as vertical equity (treating unequally situated people in appropriately unequal ways); equity as Marxian equity ('from each according to ability, to each according to need'); equity according to the Old Testament ('an eye for an eye'); or equity according to the New Testament ('turn the other cheek'). (original emphasis)

Quite apart from the difficulties raised by the existence of the myriad of possible equity criteria, further complications arise when different methods of approaching ethical questions are considered. For example, in its 1987 *Government Management: Brief to the Incoming Government,* the New Zealand Treasury provides a useful distinction between approaches to equity which focus on distributive processes, opportunities and outcomes respectively. Thus an approach which emphasizes distributive outcomes might call for equality between all individuals. But this would ignore the procedural aspects of distributive outcomes. For instance, it is entirely conceivable that unequal distributions could be fair if they are the result of fair processes of exchange. By the same token, an approach which embraces procedural fairness to the exclusion of outcomes would allow massive income and wealth differences to occur. Moreover, both the outcome and procedural approaches neglect initial endowments enjoyed by individuals in society. But considerations of equality of opportunity require complex interpersonal judgements on the inherited abilities of people and their socioeconomic backgrounds. It is clear that the adoption of any of these three generic approaches to fairness involves tradeoffs between processes, opportunities and outcomes, not to mention more general tradeoffs between equity and efficiency.

Not withstanding these complications, three common ethical arguments are often used to support government intervention. Firstly, widespread support exists for the contention that the distributive results of efficient markets may not meet socially accepted standards of equity, or accord with a desire to reduce extremes of wealth and poverty. Moreover, practical politics tends to emphasize distributive issues. Wolf (1989, p.30) has put the matter thus:

> [M]ost public policy decisions are usually even more concerned with distributional issues (namely, who gets the benefits and who pays the costs) than with efficiency issues (namely, how large are the benefits and costs).

Equity-based distributional arguments along these lines have been used to justify massive redistribution programmes characteristic of the modern welfare state. Specific programmes range from targeting beneficiaries, like the Aid to Families with Dependent Children programme in the United States, to universal coverage, such as the Medicare system in Australia.

A second line of argument is based on the notion that people do not always behave in their own best interests. For instance, unless compelled by law some citizens might not send their children to primary school or wear seatbelts. Others might ingest dangerous narcotics or watch violent pornographic movies. Arguments against these kinds of behaviour are based on the concept of merit goods, and not on distinctions between private and public goods. Merit goods are defined '… as goods the provision of which society (as distinct from the preferences of the individual consumer) wishes to encourage or, in the case of demerit goods, deter' (Musgrave and Musgrave, 1984, p.78). Thus government intervention in the form of, say, subsidies to the performing arts, or prohibitions against marijuana smoking, can be justified.

A further common (if highly contentious) ethical argument for public policy intrusion into economically efficient market outcomes is based on the idea of equal economic opportunity. It is sometimes claimed markets resort to ethnic, gender or racial stereotypes as a filtering device in labour markets, and that these biases are reflected in employment patterns. Exponents of these arguments call for government intervention in labour markets in the form of equal opportunity programmes and affirmative action laws to improve the job prospects for minority groups.

These efficiency and equity arguments for public policy intervention in market economies, sometimes termed the 'public interest' school of thought, dominated policymaking in the post-World War Two era until the early 1970s, and spawned extensive state involvement in economic activity, particularly through the direct participation of government agencies in production and the widespread regulation of private economic activity. The influence of this line of thought on modern Western economic history was enormous and gave rise to a vast public sector in most advanced economies. Not only was government activity in public utilities, like electricity and water drastically expanded, but the state also sometimes participated directly in other sectors, such as banking and insurance. Moreover, under the additional influence of various ethical theories concerning 'social justice' and 'desirable' distributions of income and wealth in society, government regulation of private economic activity became extensive, especially in the sphere of labour regulation. The net result has been the growth of the 'welfare state', with public policies now affecting virtually all areas of social life.

2.4   SCEPTICISM REGARDING GOVERNMENT INTERVENTION

With the publication of Francis Bator's classic paper in the *Quarterly Journal of Economics* in 1958, the core theory of market failure had been fully articulated and many of its implications for government intervention explored. The acceptance of the market failure paradigm into mainstream economics greatly increased its impact in debates on appropriate public policy, and inevitably provided significant backing for arguments in favour of more government involvement in modern advanced market economies. Without wishing to exaggerate the effects of the theory of market failure on actual public policymaking, minimize the influence of many other determinants of government behaviour, or gloss over the difficulties encountered in intertemporal and international comparisons of government activity, Table 2.1 provides at least some idea of the growth of government

Table 2.1   General government outlays as percentage of GDP 1970–87

	Australia		UK		USA	
	1970	1987	1970	1987	1970	1987
Total Outlays in the Traditional Domain[a]	25.5	36.4	39.3	45.5	32.2	36.7
Public goods	6.6	6.7	8.9	8.9	11.1	9.7
Defence	3.1	2.3	4.8	4.9	7.5	6.6
General public services	3.4	4.4	4.1	4.0	3.6	3.1
The Welfare State						
Merit goods	8.3	12.1	12.8	12.1	8.7	6.0
Education	4.2	5.2	5.3	5.1	5.3	4.5
Health	3.2	5.3	4.0	5.1	2.8	0.9
Housing and other	0.9	1.6	3.5	1.9	0.6	0.6
Income Maintenance	3.8	7.3	7.3	13.2	6.3	7.9
Pensions	3.1	4.5	5.2	6.8	5.3	7.0
Sickness	0.1	0.2	0.9	0.3	0.1	0.2
Family allowances	0.6	1.0	0.7	1.8	0.5	0.4
Unemployment	0.0	1.0	0.5	1.8	0.4	0.3
Other	0.0	0.5	0.0	2.5	0.0	n.a.
The Mixed Economy						
Economic services	4.6	5.1	5.2	4.3	3.9	5.7
Capital transactions	2.4	1.1	2.8	1.0	1.2	1.8
Subsidies	0.9	1.2	1.1	1.3	0.4	0.7
Other	1.3	2.8	1.3	2.0	2.3	3.2
Public debt interest	2.5	4.0	4.0	4.5	2.3	5.0
Balancing Item[b]	−0.3	1.2	1.1	2.6	0.0	2.2
Net Lending	2.2	0.5	2.5	−2.8	−0.6	−3.7

Notes:
[a] Totals may not add owing to rounding.
[b] The 'Balancing Item' is required owing to inconsistencies in the data coverage of other categories.
n.a. – Not available.
Source: Adapted from Saunders (1993, p.30, Table 4.2).

expenditure in Australia, the United Kingdom and the United States over the period 1970 to 1987.

A perusal of Table 2.1 indicates, with some exceptions, a general pattern of greater government involvement in all three countries. Of course, since Table 2.1 provides information only on direct government expenditure, and excludes other forms of government activity, such as regulation, it drastically understates the real extent of government intervention. Nevertheless Table 2.1 is an unmistakable illustration of the massive increase in government activity in recent times.

An Idealized State

It should be clear from the discussion so far that arguments for government intervention flowing from the market failure paradigm rest on an idealized conception of the state. In essence, this conception of the state views government not only as omnipotent but also benevolent. Chang (1994, p.25) has summarized this theory of the state as follows:

> In many theories of state intervention it is (implicitly) assumed that the state knows everything and can do everything. Welfare economics is an extreme case of this tendency. In welfare economics it is assumed that the state has all the relevant information for social–welfare–maximising intervention and is able to achieve what it sets out to do.

The harmonious nature of this idealized state, as contrasted with the 'chaotic' market, has been succinctly captured by Mitchell and Simmons (1994, p.35):

> Politics are assumed to make things better. Political processes distribute wealth more equally with the result that the political and economic power of those who operate the economy is reduced. Political interference in the workplace protects labor from being victimized by management, and political actions afford consumers greater protection. This idealized democratic state is guided by an invisible hand that improves on the chaos of the market. It lifts people from the morally degenerating or at best amoral self interest of the market into more responsible and more socially beneficial activities. Government allows for the expression of competing values and becomes the tool for resolving conflicts between them. Competent, scientific managers protect citizens from themselves, from organized interests, and from big business.

Scepticism Regarding Market Failure

The public interest approach, based on the theory of market failure and its implicit conception of an idealized state, rests upon a number of heroic and untenable assumptions. Firstly, it presumes the policymakers can accurately determine the extent of market failure. Secondly, it presupposes that governments possess the ability to intervene efficiently. And thirdly, it accepts that policymakers frame public policy in an altruistic manner.

By the mid-1960s various economists, policy analysts, political scientists and other began to question the public interest approach, and its underlying theory of market failure and a benevolent and omnipotent state. In essence, four major areas of criticism emerged. Firstly, the assumption of the public interest school that the state could somehow accurately assess the extent of welfare losses attendant upon market failure, and design and implement appropriate counter policy measures, was subjected to scathing attack. Hayek (1973, 14) in *Law, Legislation and Liberty*, for instance, denounced these presumptions as a 'synoptic delusion' or '... the fiction that all the relevant facts are known to some one mind, and that is possible to construct form this knowledge the particulars of a desirable social order.' In general, it is argued that given the present limited understanding of economic processes, it is highly unlikely that the authorities can possess sufficient knowledge of welfare losses in existing markets to intervene rationally. Secondly, some critics questioned the ability of governments to intervene effectively in the public interest, and have identified a number of factors which inhibit the capacity of the state to be fully and efficiently responsive to the citizenry. Thirdly, commentators rejected the presumption of altruistic behaviour underlying the public interest approach in favour of a self-interested model of human behaviour along the lines of the *homo economicus* postulate of economic theory. Anthony Downs (1957, 136) put the argument thus:

> The complexities of this problem have diverted attention from the second difficulty raised by the view that government's function is to maximise social welfare. Even if social welfare could be defined and methods of maximising it could be agreed upon, what reason is there to believe that the men who run the government would be motivated to maximise it?

Finally, the development of the theory of the 'second best' by Lipsey and Lancaster (1956) sheds light on the desirability of intervention aimed at generating Pareto optimality even if policymakers knew the extent of market failure, intervened efficiently and framed policy in an altruistic manner. In essence, the theory of the second best demonstrates that if market failure is present in one sector of the economy, then a higher level of social welfare may be attained by deliberately violating Pareto efficiency conditions in other sectors, rather than by intervening to restore Pareto efficiency in the initial case of market failure.

This paradigm shift in perceptions on the nature of state intervention has had dramatic implications regarding both the desirability and efficiency of microeconomic policy. The earlier traditional view that the existence of market failure necessitated policy intervention aimed at creating allocative efficiency, and consequently the actions of policymakers could be explained as a benevolent attempt at generating the optimal conditions required for the maximization of social welfare, no longer enjoyed a consensus among policy analysts. The new, more sceptical, view emphasized the problems associated with government intervention and the self-interested motivation behind such intervention. The perceived inability of public policy to achieve socially optimal outcomes was given the generic name of government failure, and the costs associated with government failure were set against the purported benefits of intervention designed to ameliorate market failure.

2.5   THE NIRVANA FALLACY

A separate but perhaps even more destructive critique of the theory of market failure has attacked its methodological underpinnings as totally flawed. In essence, this line of argument holds that the market failure paradigm embodies a methodology which compares actual economic arrangements against some idealized theoretical norm (that is, allocative efficiency) thereby violating the fundamental concept of opportunity lost, which constrains economists to evaluate existing outcomes against the next best feasible alternative, and not against some abstract idealized hypothetical criterion.

Harold Demsetz (1969, p.1) has labelled this the 'nirvana problem' and contrasted it with a 'comparative institutions' approach which could avoid the nirvana problem:

> The view that now pervades much public policy economic implicitly presents the relevant choice as between an ideal norm and an existing 'imperfect' institutional arrangement. This nirvana approach differs considerably from a comparative institution approach in which the relevant choice is between alternative real institutional arrangements. In practice, those who adopt the nirvana viewpoint seek to discover discrepancies between the idea and the real and if discrepancies are found, they deduce that the real is inefficient. Users of the comparative institution approach attempt to assess which alternative real institutional arrangement seems best able to cope with the economic problem; practitioners

of this approach may use an ideal norm to provide standards from which divergences are assessed for all practical alternatives of interest and select as efficient that alternative which seems most likely to minimize the divergence. (emphasis added)

The fundamental problem with the market failure paradigm is that its thoughtless application leads to the nirvana problem (Demsetz, 1969, p.3):

Given the nirvana view of the problem, a deduced discrepancy between the ideal and the real is sufficient to call forth perfection by incantation, that is, by committing the grass is always greener fallacy.

Citing the historical examples of '... the grant of monopoly and tariff privileges by governments', Demsetz (1969, p.19) demonstrates how the evolution of economic theory in refining the concept of competition '... has led to serious errors' involving the nirvana problem. It is worth citing him at length on this issue (Demsetz, 1969, p.19):

The problem of efficiency and the possibilities of achieving efficiency through reform were associated historically with the grant of monopoly and tariff privileges by governments. In their historical settings, criticisms of inefficiency took on the characteristic of comparative institution and not the nirvana approach. Critics of governmental policies who asked for reform were seeking to substitute an institutional arrangement that was both real and fairly well understood. They were confident of the beneficial results and of the practicality of allowing market enterprise to allocate resources. And, although the operation of political forces had not been subjected to the same careful study, the critics did know what they expected if governmentally created protection from those market forces were removed.

A process of refining the analytical concept of competition then set in, culminating in the currently accepted necessary conditions for perfect competition. These conditions, of course, can be only approximated by real institutions. On top of these are placed additional condition on the nature of production, commodities, and preferences that are necessary if the equivalence of perfect competition and Pareto efficiency is to be established.

While the application of these conceptual refinements is an aid to solving some economic problems, especially in positive economics, their application to normative problems has led to serious errors. If an economy has no serious indivisibilities, if information is complete, etc., then the modern analysis can describe the characteristics of an efficient long-run equilibrium; this description is the main result of modern welfare analysis. But modern analysis has yet to describe efficiency in a world where indivisibilities are present and knowledge is costly to produce. To say that private enterprise is inefficient because indivisibilities and imperfect knowledge are part of life, or because people are susceptible to the human weaknesses subsumed in the term moral hazards, or because marketing commodity-options is not costless, or because persons are risk-averse, is to say little more than that the competitive equilibrium would be different if these were not the facts of life. But, if they are the facts of life, if, that is, they cannot be erased from life at zero cost, then truly efficient institutions will yield different long-run equilibrium conditions than those now used to describe ideal norm.

An alternative to the nirvana approach resides in adopting the comparative institutions approach and developing a general theory of organizational failure which subsumes both market and nonmarket institutional arrangements, and evaluates the performance of existing organizational structures in terms of feasible real-world options. This would attempt to put analytical flesh on Coase's (1964, p.195) dictum that 'until we realise we are choosing between social arrangements that are more or less all failures, we are not likely to make much headway.' The construction of a more useful theory of organizational performance would not only draw on recent developments within economics, and especially new institutional economics, but also on advances made in ancillary social disciplines, particularly in public policy analysis. Instead of the conventional view of institutional characteristics as constraints on policy design, a general theory of organizational failure would endogenize organizational structure and make it a policy variable, alongside the traditional policy instruments.

2.6 CONCLUDING REMARKS

Given these various criticisms which have been directed at the theory of market failure and concomitant attempts to apply this paradigm in policy settings, the question naturally arises as to what status we should now grant the market failure model.

Firstly, it is quite clear that the market failure paradigm held completely unrealistic expectations about the abilities and capacities of governments to deal with economic and social problems. This point of view is widely shared in the relevant literature. For example, Weisbrod (1978, p.30) has observed that '... reliance on government to correct both the inefficiencies and the inequities of private markets has been extensive. Until very recently this implicit confidence by economists in government was largely detached from any analysis of whether that confidence was justified.' Similarly Chang (1994, p.33) has challenged '... the naive belief about the state held by some welfare economists that, once we can somehow have a "benevolent state", it will solve all problems'.

Secondly, the asymmetry between the conventional market failure paradigm's dichotomy of imperfect markets and perfect governments is quite untenable in the realm of policy prescription and accordingly needs to be augmented by a positive theory of how real governments actually behave. A theory of government failure is thus necessary to act as a conceptual analogue of the extant market failure paradigm '... so that the comparison between markets and governments can be made more systematically, and the choices between them arrived at more intelligently' (Wolf, 1987, p.43). Fortunately, at least three separate genre of theories of government failure have been developed to fill this vacuum. We shall examine this literature in detail in Chapter 3.

Thirdly, Demsetz's (1969) nirvana fallacy critique of the methodological underpinning of the theory of market failure has undoubted validity. The basic approach adopted by this paradigm of determining whether real-world market outcomes diverge from an equality of social costs and social benefits, thereby exhibiting allocative inefficiency, and the attendant policy prescription for corrective government intervention, is indefensible once the imperfection associated with all government action is recognized. Buchanan (1983, p.16) has summarized the nature of the traditional market failure paradigm by observing that 'to the theoretical welfare economists, markets "failed" in the allocative process; "ideal" government was assumed to be the alternative.' By contrast, rational policy formulation should rest on a comparative institutions approach which obliges policymakers to compare actual feasible alternatives rather than actual arrangements with hypothetical alternatives.

Despite the devastating nature of this criticism of the theory of market failure, it seems clear that the efficiency criteria developed by the paradigm can still play a decisive role in the policy formulation process. Put simply, policymakers require economic efficiency criteria in their evaluation of alternative feasible real-world institutional alternatives. For example, suppose that an economic investigation of some industry reveals that actual market outcomes diverge from an allocatively efficient outcome by some given measured amount. Suppose further that two possible alternative forms of government intervention are available to policymakers.

By invoking the standard marginal social benefit equals marginal social cost criterion we can answer two questions essential for rational policy formulations. Firstly, we can determine which of the two feasible proposed forms of government intervention is the least allocatively inefficient. And secondly, by comparing the degree of allocative inefficiency associated with the least inefficient kind of government intervention with the extent of allocative inefficiency exhibited by the existing market outcome, we can ascertain whether to intervene or not. In sum, the economic efficiency yardsticks developed by the conventional market failure literature should be employed within the framework of the comparative institutions methodology to inform policymakers.

3 Government Failure and Government Intervention

3.1 INTRODUCTION

Although the development and extension of the theory of market failure represents an impressive intellectual achievement, it is clear from the discussion in Chapter 2 that this paradigm has too many flaws for it to accurately prescribe the appropriate degree of government intervention in a modern advanced market economy. In addition to manifestations of market failure, based on either efficiency or equity considerations, policymakers require more realistic models of both the intentions and abilities of governments to intervene effectively. The extensive and evolving literature on government failure has '... provided a valuable corrective to the naive belief about the state held by some welfare economists that, once we can somehow have a "benevolent" state, it will solve all problems' (Chang, 1994, p. 23).

Despite the fact that the contemporary literature on government failure postdates the market failure paradigm, economists and political philosophers have long understood that government intervention was less then perfect and could have very high costs. For example, in his 1762 *The Social Contract* (1968) Jean-Jacque Rousseau expressed concern about the apparently inherent tendency of governments to usurp the rights of the citizenry and argued that a constitutional system of the separation of powers was necessary to inhibit the encroachment of the state. Similarly, West (1990, p.128) has argued that in the *Wealth of Nations* and other texts, Adam Smith clearly recognized that 'the wealth of nations ... is substantially correlated with the wealth of wisdom in their political constitutions.' Given the longevity of apprehension surrounding the efficiency of government intervention, it is somewhat surprising that mainstream economics has ignored the potential costs associated with state intervention. Nevertheless, an extensive literature on government failure is now available and it forms the focus of this chapter.

The chapter itself is divided into four main sections. In section 2 we outline alternative conceptions of the state to the idealized model implicit in the market failure paradigm. Discussion of the literature on government failure falls into two parts. In section 3 we examine positive theories of government failure, consisting of the capture theory of regulation and public choice theory, whereas section 4 is devoted to a review of the normative theory of government failure. The chapter ends with a discussion of the appropriate role of government which is informed by both the market failure and government failure paradigms as well as some additional contemporary perceptions.

3.2 ALTERNATIVE THEORIES OF THE STATE

The conception of the ideal state embedded in the market failure paradigm, whose behaviour approximates the wisdom of Plato's Philosopher King, has been subjected to scathing attacks from numerous quarters, as we saw in Chapter 2. But if we reject this naive construction of the state, what alternative theories of government should we accept?

Several theories of the state have been embraced by economists and they range across the entire political spectrum. Various attempts have been made to classify these theories of the state. For instance, North (1979, p.250) has argued that it is possible to categorize all theories of the state into two broad groups: '...(1) a contract theory and (2) a predatory or exploitation theory'. Contractarian theories of the state examine the theoretical conditions under which rational individuals would enter into a 'social contract' with other individuals thereby forming a communal society. Often employing John Rawls' (1971) *A Theory of Justice* conceptual device of a 'veil of ignorance', where *ex ante* individuals do not know their economic and other attributes, contractarian theories emphasize the exchange relationships underlying social contracts. As Buchanan (1994, p.13) has observed 'in agreeing to be governed, explicitly or implicitly, the individual exchanges his or her own liberty with others who similarly give up liberties in exchange for the benefits offered by a regime characterised by behavioural limits.' Although obviously no historical examples of a pre-contractarian 'state of nature' exist, contractarian philosophers employ this methodology to develop an idealized model of the state against which real-world constitutional orders can be compared. Normative public choice theory, especially constitutional economics, draws heavily on this methodology (see, for example, Buchanan and Tullock (1962) and Nozick (1974)). Chang and Rowthorn (1995, pp.8–9) have outlined the significance of this work as follows:

> The new contractarians argued that any form of state beyond the old liberal minimalist state, which does no more than provide law and order (including, among other things, the protection of property rights) cannot be justified in the eyes of those who believe in the sanctity of individual

freedom. A major source of popularity of these writings lay in their emphasis on individual freedom and their articulation of modern discontents with the welfare state and its alleged restrictions on personal choice. The welfare state was no longer to be seen as a benign, if paternalistic, institution, but as a leviathan which must be restrained to preserve our liberties and the vitality of civil society.

By contrast, exploitation or predatory theories of the state downplay any gains which may flow from contracting and focus instead on the battle for wealth transfers made possible by the existence of a centralized authority. With respect to this kind of theory, North (1979, p.251) has noted that 'this view considers the state to be the agency of a group or class; its function, to extract income from the rest of the constituents in the interest of that group or class. The predatory state would specify a set of property rights that maximised the revenue of the group in power, regardless of its impact on the wealth of society as a whole.' Adherents to this view of the state reject the notion that government intervention may be explained as an attempt at securing the optimal conditions required for the maximization of social welfare, in favour of the presumption that public policy seeks to reallocate resources towards the politically dominant group regardless of the impact on social welfare. Predatory or exploitation theories of the state embrace a host of widely divergent economic philosophies ranging from Marxism through to many scholars in the positive theoretical tradition of public choice theory.

Similarly, Chang (1994, p.18) has proposed a tripartite classification of theories of the state made up of the '...autonomous-state approach, the interest-group approach and the self-seeking bureaucrats approach'. The autonomous state approach views the state as a separate and independent force in society. A variant of this approach, characteristic of neoclassical political economy and aligned with North's (1979) 'predatory' category, postulates that the state acts as a revenue-maximizing monopolist without regard for general social wellbeing. The second interest group approach views the state as simply a medium through which economic interest groups and other social movements contest the nature of public policy and the resultant allocation of fiscal rewards amongst each other. Perhaps the best-known economic theory adopting this conception of the state is the so-called 'regulatory-capture' theory of the Chicago School. Finally, the self-seeking bureaucrats approach directly attacks the 'benevolent state' conception of the market failure paradigm by assuming that government employees act behaviourally in terms of the *homo economicus* assumption. In other words, bureaucrats seek to maximize their own utility rather than general social welfare. As we shall see, this theory of the state underlies both the legislative failure and bureaucratic failure dimensions of government failure in positive public choice theory.

3.3   POSITIVE THEORIES OF GOVERNMENT FAILURE

Capture Theory of Regulation

Perhaps the earliest formal approach to the notion of government failure is known as the economic theory of regulation or the 'capture' theory of regulation. The capture theory of regulation, developed by Stigler (1971) and extended by Peltzman (1976), took the original market failure argument in favour of the regulation of 'natural' monopolies, like electricity and water utilities, as its starting point. In terms of the market failure paradigm, a government regulatory agency must ensure that prices are set which do not take advantage of the monopolists position and allow consumers to enjoy more consumer surplus. However, Stigler (1971) argued that since this form of regulation is a bureaucratic process, producers of the regulated industry have strong incentives to place pressure on regulators to increase prices thus increasing their profits. Stigler (1971) proposed that the strength of producer interest groups would determine how successful they would be in applying pressure on regulators to increase their incomes, and subsequent empirical work tended to support this view (see, for example, Hann and Bird, 1990). The essence of Stigler's argument is that 'regulation is acquired by the industry and is designed and operated primarily for its benefit' (Stigler, 1975, p.114). Peltzman (1976) extended Stigler's (1971) model and integrated both producers and consumers. Peltzman argued that regulation is supplied by politicians seeking to maximize votes they accrue from responding to interest groups representing consumers and producers. Accordingly, regulated prices, subsidies, entry restrictions, and other issues will be set such that the loss of votes from consumer groups will be exactly offset by the gain from producer groups in the form of political campaign contributions and the like.

The capture theory of regulation thus focuses on the determination of monopoly profits and their distribution through the regulatory system. Although it is premised on a process of interaction between interest groups and regulators, this process is not systematically modelled. Moreover, the normative or welfare consequences of this view of regulation are not explored.

Public Choice Theory

The most significant approach to the phenomenon of government failure is public choice theory. In essence, public choice theory applies the standard behavioural postulate of *homo economicus* to non-market or political processes underlying policy formulation and implementation, and has developed a positive critique of government intervention flowing from this methodology. As the stylized fictive description of human motivation in economics, the *homo economicus* postulate holds that people are egoistic rational maximizers of their own welfare and forms the behavioural model of the so-called methodological individualism characteristic of economic science. In his classic text *Public Choice II*, Dennis Mueller (1989, p.1) delineated public choice theory as follows: 'Public choice can be defined as the economic study of nonmarket decision making, or simply the application of economics to political science. The subject matter of public choice is the same as that of political science: the theory of the state, voting rules, voter behaviour, party politics, the bureaucracy, and so on.' In stark contrast to the market failure paradigm of conventional welfare economics, public choice theorists denounce the 'benevolent despot' conception of government implicit in that approach, and instead have developed models of decision making in representative democracies based on the assumption '... that people should be treated as rational utility-maximisers in all of their behavioural capacities' (Buchanan, 1978, p.17). In other words, voters, politicians, bureaucrats and members of special interest groups are presumed to use the resources and opportunities available to them to pursue their own objectives. Buchanan (1975) has argued that the scope of public choice theory consists of three broad strands: namely, the economics of the pre-constitutional stage of society, the economics of constitution making, and the economics of post-constitutional politics.

The application of the *homo economicus* assumption to the perceived behaviour of governments has given rise to various typologies of government failure. For instance, one of the earliest taxonomic systems was established by O'Dowd (1978). O'Dowd (p.360) argued that all forms of government failure fell into a generic tripartite classification: namely 'inherent impossibilities', 'political failures', and 'bureaucratic failures'. These three forms of government failure were described as follows:

> The first type covers the cases where a government attempts to do something which simply cannot be done; the second, where although what is attempted is theoretically possible, the political constraints under which the government operates make it impossible in practice

that they should follow the necessary policies with the necessary degree of consistency and persistence to achieve their stated aim. The third type covers the cases where although the political heads of the government are capable of both forming and persisting with the genuine intention of carrying out a policy, the administrative machinery at their disposal is fundamentally incapable of implementing it in accordance with their intentions.

Similarly, a more recent and closely related taxonomy has been articulated by Dollery and Wallis (1997). They argue that it is possible to identify three main forms of government failure. Firstly, legislative failure refers to the '... allocative inefficiency (which) arises from the excessive provision of public goods as politicians pursue strategies designed to maximise their chances of re-election rather than policies which would further the common good' (Dollery and Wallis, 1997, p.360). Secondly, '... even if socially beneficial policies were enacted, bureaucratic failure will ensure that these policies are not efficiently implemented ... [because] public servants lack sufficient incentives to carry out policies efficiently' (ibid.). The third form of government failure resides in rent-seeking since government intervention virtually always creates wealth transfers and 'people thus devote scarce resources which could have been employed in wealth creation towards redistributing existing wealth in their favour' (ibid.).

But perhaps the most comprehensive taxonomy of government failure has been developed by Weisbrod. Weisbrod (1978) has advanced a four-fold typology of government failure. 'Legislative failure' has much the same meaning as that ascribed to it by Dollery and Wallis (1997). Secondly, 'administrative failure' derives from the fact that the '... administration of any law inevitably requires discretion, and the combination of information and incentives acts to affect the manner in which the discretion if exercised' (Weisbrod, 1978, p.36). Thirdly, 'judicial failure' occurs when the legal system fails to deliver judicially optimal outcomes. And finally, 'enforcement failure' is defined as the sub-optimal '... enforcement and non-enforcement of judicial, legislative, or administrative directives [which] can thus vitiate the effectiveness of actions of these other stages' (ibid., p.39).

The application of the *homo economicus* postulate to contemporary representative democracies yields a relatively simple model of political behaviour. If we assume the body politic is compromised of four main groups, namely citizens or voters, elected officials or politicians, public servants or bureaucratics, and interest groups or lobbying individuals, then on the basis of the *homo economicus* assumption we can eschew complex, conflicting and multi-faceted human motivations in favour of straight forward self-interest. Accordingly, public choice theorists have been able to assign clear maximinds to each of these four groups. Citizens as voters are assumed to be rational utility maximizing individuals who seek material and other benefits from the political system. Politicians are primarily motivated by re-election considerations and are thus presumed to be vote maximizers. Bureaucrats are viewed as motivated by job security and employment perquisites and are thus assumed to be bureau budget maximizers. Finally, interest groups are perceived as wealth and income maximizers who seek to turn public organization and public funds to private advantage. Mitchell and Simmons (1994, p.42) have developed a useful illustration of this model of representative democracy. This model of politics illustrated in Figure 3.1 essentially reduces the complexities of political life in contemporary industrialized societies to a political mechanism for allocating scarce resources that parallels the market mechanism. Indeed, people are assumed to behave as *homo economicus* in both the economic and political spheres of their existences. Buchanan (1994, p.83) has put this argument as follows:

> If we adhere strictly to the individualistic benchmark, there can be no fundamental distinction between economics and politics, or more generally, between the economy and the polity. The state, as any other collective organization, is created by individuals, and the state acts on behalf of individuals. Politics, in this individualistic framework, becomes a

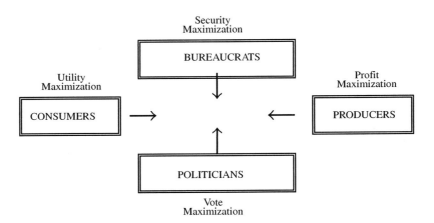

Figure 3.1   Public choice model of politics

complex exchange process, in which individuals seek to accomplish purposes collectively that they cannot accomplish noncollectively or privately in any tolerable efficient manner. The catallactic perspective on simple exchange of economic goods merges into the contractarian perspective on politics and political order.

Legislative Failure

It is now possible to appreciate the genesis of the various taxonomies of government failure. For example, in the typology of government failure advanced by Dollery and Wallis (1997), voter maximizing politicians intent on election or re-election generate legislative failure by seeking to appease special interest groups and others by 'porkbarrelling' thereby inducing a bias towards the excessive provision of public goods and the attendant secular growth of government. In the classic analysis of Anthony Downs (1957), for instance, the phenomenon of 'logrolling' leads to higher levels of government expenditure despite a lack of majority support amongst an electorate. The argument runs as follows: politicians are elected on the basis of a 'package' of policies, and do not have to please the majority of voters on every policy. Voters are 'rationally ignorant' of the full consequences of the policies of politicians since, because they cannot influence the outcome of elections (except minusculely through the exercise of their single vote), they do not possess sufficient incentives to invest the time and effort involved in assessing in detail the policy proposals of different politicians. This leads to logrolling of votes which favours special interest legislation. For example, assume a politician stands on a package of three unpopular individual policies A, B and C. In a rural farming constituency containing a regional centre with a university and a substantial population of retirees, let policy A represent increased farm subsidies, policy B lower university fees, and policy C higher age pensions. On the basis of the *homo economicus* postulate, we can anticipate that each of these three special interest groups will have intense preferences for that programme offering direct benefits to its constituent members. Accordingly, suppose the pattern of electoral support is as illustrated in Table 3.1. Thus a politician proposing unpopular policies A, B and C can defeat a politician who opposes them by logrolling the votes of interest groups, because these interest groups have intense preferences against the diluted preferences of the majority. Logrolling accordingly implies a preponderance of special interest legislation and an oversupply of public goods.

Table 3.1   Electoral support for policies

Policy	Favoured by	Opposed by
A	20%	80%
B	20%	80%
C	20%	80%

Bureaucratic Failure

Attempts by economists to model the behaviour of public bureaucracies date back at least as far as von Mises (1945) and a substantial descriptive model was presented by Downs (1967). But the first rigorous economic model of bureaucracy was developed by Niskanen (1968, 1971, 1975, 1991), whose work provoked much subsequent modelling activity (see, for example, Bendor 1990), including notable efforts by Migue and Belanger (1974), Tullock (1974), Orzechowski (1977), Romer and Rosenthal (1979), and Breton and Wintrobe (1982). Niskanen's budget-maximizing model nevertheless still represents the mainstream position of American public choice theorists (Mueller, 1990, pp.250–8) and its institutional assumptions are primarily those of the US political system. This has led one prominent European public choice theorist to bemoan the continued absence of a convincing economic theory of bureaucracy outside the American constitutional framework (Schneider, 1991). Dunleavy's (1985, 1989a, 1989b, 1991, 1992) work partly meets this criticism, extending the Niskanen model by replacing its budget maximization hypothesis and creating a theoretical framework more suitable for the analysis of bureaucracies in parliamentary systems.

In his classic analysis, William Niskanen (1971) argued that bureaucrats sought to maximize the size of their budgets, since larger budgets implied increased salaries, power and prestige. Bureaucrats can increase the size of their budgets by oversupplying output, or by inefficiently supplying output, or both. Bureaucrats are said to bear an agent/principal relationship to politicians who in turn bear an agent/political relationship to voters. Bureaucrats benefit directly from large governmental budgets and thus have intense preferences for high levels of expenditure. By contrast, taxpayers typically only benefit indirectly from government expenditure, and have preferences for low taxation levels. The objectives of agents and principals thus diverge. But because bureaucrats have greater per capita incentives to increase expenditure than the corresponding incentives of taxpayers to decrease taxes, public sector expenditure will be higher than desired.

Chang and Rowthorn (1995, p.9) have outlined the general significance of the arguments underlying bureaucratic failure as follows:

> These models saw the root of many problems of the contemporary capitalist countries – for example, the over-extension of the bureaucracy, the waste of resources in government administration, the inefficiency of the public enterprises – in the inability of the principals (the public) to monitor the self-seeking behaviour of their agents in public affairs (the bureaucrats). These models were usually presented as neutral efficiency arguments, but have had much deeper political impacts. By arguing that the same assumption of self-centred behaviour should be applied both to the private sector agents and the public sector agents, they not only questioned the public's trust in the benign paternalism of the welfare state but also undermined the self-confidence of government officials and their commitment to a public service ethos.

Both the legislative failure and bureaucratic manifestations of government failure could be viewed as symptomatic of the more pervasive phenomenon of agency failure. In essence, agency failure arises because agents lack the incentives to act in their principal's interest. If we conceive of the public sector in a representative democracy as being constituted by an interlocking series of principal–agent relationships, then the importance of agency failure becomes apparent. For example, Moe (1984, p.765) observes that 'the whole of politics can be seen as a chain of principal–agent relationships, from citizen to politician to bureaucratic superior to bureaucratic subordinate and on down the hierarchy of government to the lowest-level bureaucrats who actually deliver services directly to citizens.' This view leads to an approach to public sector reform which seeks to reduce the scope for agency failure in these relationships. It has been argued that this view, particularly as it applies to public bureaux, neglects crucial institutional features of contemporary public sectors. For example, it ignores significant differences between 'technocrats' in 'control agencies' and 'bureaucrats' in 'spending departments' (Williamson, 1994). We take up this theme in Chapter 5.

Rent Seeking

A third dimension of government failure resides in the ways in which citizens as wealth maximizers seek to use government intervention to create economic rents for themselves. The genesis of the modern theory of rent

seeking may be traced to the theoretical framework provided by Gordon
Tullock (1967) in a celebrated analysis of the welfare losses caused by theft.
Further impetus came from Krueger (1974) who coined the term rent seeking to describe the generic range of behaviour exemplified by her investigation into competition for premium fetching import licences. The resultant
burgeoning literature has provided fascinating insights into the interplay
between state intervention and maximizing economic agents which includes
attempts at interpreting economic history (Delorme, Kamerchen and
Mbaku, 1986; Ekelund and Tollison, 1982; North, 1979; North and
Thomas, 1973; and Olson, 1982) within the context of the analytical apparatus provided by the theory of rent seeking. In orthodox economic theory
the concept of economic rent has traditionally been defined in terms of
opportunity cost. Thus rent is simply that part of the reward accruing to the
owner of a resource over and above the payment the resource would receive
in any alternative employment. In standard textbook usage, rent refers to
that portion of revenue in excess of opportunity cost. Given the customary
assumption of maximizing behaviour on the part of economic agents, and
an absence of constraints on resource mobility, in the stylized world of
neoclassical theory competitive forces will ensure the dissipation of rent in
a manner which produces socially desirable outcomes. Under these circumstances, maximizing behaviour by resource owners aimed at securing rent
is no different from any other form of wealth maximizing behaviour.
Indeed, it merely serves to reinforce '... the original contributions of the
classical economists themselves, whose great discovery was that individuals
acting in pursuit of their own interests may unintentionally generate results
that serve the overall "social interest" ...' (Buchanan, 1986, p.24). The existence of positive rent in a competitive market will attract resources in
the same way as the existence of potential profits, and consequently result
in the erosion of such rent through a socially desirable reallocation of
resources. However, once we adjust the social mechanisms in which this
process occurs, the consequence of maximizing behaviour motivated by
the possibility of economic rent may be quite different viewed from the
perspective of society at large. Buchanan (1980, p.4) has neatly summarized
the nature of rent seeking in this alternative setting:

> The term rent-seeking is designed to describe behaviour in institutional
> settings where individual efforts to maximise value generate social
> waste rather than social surplus. Again I should like to emphasise that at
> the level of the individual decision makers, the behaviour, as such, is
> not different from that of profit seeking in market interactions. The
> unintended consequences of individual value maximization shift from

those that may be classified as 'good' to those that seem clearly to be 'bad' not because individuals become different moral beings and modify their actions accordingly, but because institutional structure changes. The setting within which individual choices are made is transformed. As institutions have moved away from ordered markets toward the near chaos of direct political allocation rent-seeking has emerged as a significant social phenomenon.

The theory of rent seeking is thus appropriate for the analysis of the origins of, and competition for artificially created rent, and not for short-lived rents (or quasi-rents) which characterize dynamic market processes. The existence of contrived rent implies the possibility of wealth transfers between individuals and groups in society, and rent-seeking behaviour encompasses attempts by economic actors at creating and competing for these wealth transfers. Rent seeking consequently refers to '... the expenditure of scarce resources to capture an artificially created transfer' (Tollison, 1982: p.579). Given the massive extension of state intervention in modern times, and its ability to affect the redistribution of property rights and hence generate wealth transfers, the primary source and focus of rent-seeking activity has, not surprisingly, been government-protected monopoly power.

Once we allow for the advent of competing interest groups and assume that the state is responsive to those groups who emerge dominant (that is, the predatory conception of the state), additional forms of rent-seeking behaviour manifest themselves. In most societies the state agency concerned with a particular area of economic endeavour is legislatively empowered to vest responsibility for various activities in the hands of representatives of organized interest groups. A salient example often cited in this regard is professional occupational licensure (Blair and Rubin, 1980). More specifically, monopoly power over the granting of property rights may be deliberately conferred on producer bodies themselves. Given the immense advantages concomitant with legislative transfers of property rights which usually imply the possibility of wealth transfers, it is not surprising that rent-seeking behaviour arises aimed at securing such property rights. Consequently, in addition to rent seeking aimed at capturing the benefits generated by existing state intervention, in a society where severe constitutional limitations on state involvement are absent, rent seeking by interest groups (and individuals) will occur with the object of attaining intervention and its attendant advantages. It is thus possible to identify at least two forms of rent-seeking behaviour. Firstly, rent seeking directed at securing initial state intervention which will induce contrived rent through the artificial limitation of market processes thus allowing for wealth transfers to occur. And secondly, rent seeking aimed at capturing the resultant rent and maintaining a position of capture.

Criticisms of Public Choice Theory

The public choice approach to the analysis of political processes has been subjected to vociferous attack on a number of points (see, for example, Self (1993) and Stretton and Orchard (1994)). Self (ibid., p.48) has pinpointed several main 'targets' of 'outsider's criticism':

> The truth and testability of the theories; the assumption of rational egoist motivation; the hostility to ideas of public interest; the fitness of market models of political activity; and the nature and concealment of the theorists' values.

By way of contrast, Stretton and Orchard (ibid., pp.253–6) have identified three basic ways in which the public choice model is 'flawed': these are 'no understanding of the public interest'; a 'confusion of political liberty with market freedom'; and a 'confusion between wants and needs'.

Perhaps a more discerning review of the critique of public choice theory has been provided by Boston, Martin, Pallot and Walsh (1996). In the first place, Boston *et al.* highlight criticism of the *homo economicus* postulate on grounds of behavioural implausibility as especially telling. They summarize this line of argument as follows (ibid., p.30):

> In short, human beings are not merely economic beings, but also political, cultural, and moral beings who inhabit an economic system that is profoundly influenced by, and in a sense dependent upon, the attitudes, habits, beliefs, aspirations, ideals, and ethical standards of its members. Any theory that downplays or ignores these broader contextual factors, social relations, and normative commitments is at best incomplete, and at worst misleading and damaging.

And secondly, Boston *et al.* (ibid., pp.30–2) identify 'limited predictive power' as a powerful criticism of public choice theory. Indeed, a salient contemporary example of the predictive shortcomings of public choice theory is its conspicuous failure to anticipate radical policy reform of the kind experienced in New Zealand – an issue that we will examine in more detail in Chapter 5.

From their analysis of the critique of the public choice model, Boston *et al.* (ibid., p.32) draw the following broad implications:

> One clear inference, however, is the need for theories that take into account a wider range of considerations, particularly the importance of ideas and values, in explaining human behaviour and policy choices. Further, once the assumption that politicians, bureaucrats, and voters are wholly or exclusively self-interested is abandoned, the problem of provider capture need no longer occupy centre stage (though, of course, it should not be ignored). Thus, rather than focusing primarily on how to immunise the political system against the dangers posed by vested interests, more attention should be given to ensuring that the decision-making arrangements are open, democratic, and fair (i.e. that they provide an opportunity for all interests to be adequately represented). This has important implications for constitutional arrangements, the machinery of government, and the role of pressure groups in the policy-making process.

Some of these criticisms will be revisited and amplified in later discussions on the role of leadership in the political economy of policy reform. In particular, Chapter 6 will focus on the limitations of economic discourse generally, and public choice theory in particular, which arise *inter alia* from their reluctance to examine the expressive dimension of human behaviour.

In at least two respects extant public choice theory does not provide policymakers with a conceptual analogue of the market failure paradigm to inform public policy decisions. Firstly, the public choice approach is a positive, and not a normative, theory of government processes, and thus cannot provide an idealized or optimal vision of policy intervention against which actual government behaviour can be compared, in the same way as welfare economics furnishes the theory of market failure with a yardstick to evaluate real-world markets. And secondly, public choice theory is premised on the behavioural postulate of *homo economicus* and follows methodological individualism, which may not always capture the full intricacies of politicized policy environments.

3.4 NORMATIVE THEORIES OF GOVERNMENT FAILURE

However, several recent attempts have been made to construct a normative theory of government failure. Although Wolf's (1979a, 1979b, 1983,

1987, 1989) taxonomy of nonmarket failure is perhaps the most comprehensive of these new theories, criticism of his typology has led to the development of alternative theories of government failure by both Le Grand (1991) and Vining and Weimer (1991).

Wolf's Theory of Nonmarket Failure

In a series of pathbreaking publications Wolf has consciously sought to construct a theoretical framework to serve as a conceptual analogue to the established theory of market failure. The purpose of his model is '... to redress the asymmetry in the standard economic treatment of the short-comings to markets and governments by developing and applying a theory of "nonmarket" – that is, government failure – so that the comparison between markets and governments can be made more systematically, and choice between them arrived at more intelligently' (1987, p.43). The theory of nonmarket failure itself mirrors the orthodox methodology followed in the theory of market failure by seeking to attribute various kinds of non-market failure to peculiarities in underlying 'demand' and 'supply' conditions. Wolf (1979, p.117–18) stresses such methodological parallels, and argues that 'just as some types of incentive encourage market failure, so too incentives influencing particular non-market organizations may lead to behaviour and outcomes that diverge from ones that are socially preferable, according to the same criteria of preferability as those for markets efficiency and distributional equity'. Moreover, in response to the question of why certain patterns of nonmarket failure manifest themselves, he hypothesizes that 'the answer lies in the distinctive supply and demand characteristics that differentiate nonmarket outputs from market outputs' (1979, p.118).

   Wolf (1989, pp.51–5) identifies four basic attributes of nonmarket supply. Firstly, he argues that 'nonmarket outputs are often hard to define in principle, ill-defined in practice, and extremely difficult to measure as to quantity or to evaluate as quality'. Accordingly, inputs generally become a proxy measure for output. Secondly, Wolf postulates that nonmarket outputs are usually produced by a single public agency often operating as a legally constituted monopoly. The resultant lack of competition makes any meaningful estimates of economic efficiency difficult, and consequently serves to obscure allocative and productive efficiencies. Thirdly, Wolf argues that 'technology of producing nonmarket outputs is frequently unknown, or if known, is associated with considerable uncertainty and ambiguity', and consequently may exacerbate economic inefficiencies. Finally, Wolf proposes nonmarket production activity is usually characterized by the lack of any 'bottom-line' evaluation mechanism equivalent to profit or loss for appraising success. Moreover, there is often no specified procedure for terminating unsuccessful production.

Wolf (ibid., pp.39–50) identifies five basic 'conditions' of nonmarket demand. In the first instance Wolf (1987, p.55) postulates that '...an increased public awareness of market shortcomings' has led to a reduced tolerance of them, and consequently heightened public desire for state intervention. A second characteristic attributed to the demand for nonmarket activity resides in 'political organization and enfranchisement' (Wolf, 1988, p.40), and the resultant increases in the effectiveness of special interest groups in the political process. Thirdly, maximizing politicians and bureaucrats are rewarded for propagating interventionist 'solutions' to perceived social 'problems' without reference to the costs of implementation. Fourthly, the demand for nonmarket activity is further enhanced by the 'high time-discount of political actors' (Wolf, 1989, p.40) due to relatively short electoral periods of office experienced by politicians in most representative democracies. An important outcome of these constitutional arrangements is a higher rate of time-discounting amongst politicians as compared with society at large, and a resultant emphasis on current rather than future costs and benefits. The final 'condition' of nonmarket demand identified by Wolf (ibid., p.41) is '...the decoupling between those who receive the benefits, and those who pay the costs, of government programmes'. Wolf argues that decoupling occurs in two different forms. On the one hand, 'microdecoupling' arises when the benefits of collective action accrue to a particular group, whereas the costs of such action are dispersed amongst all groups. On the other hand, 'macrodecoupling' occurs where the benefits of collective action are shared by all groups, but the costs of this action are concentrated on some specific group.

These various peculiarities in the nature of nonmarket demand and supply form the foundation of Wolf's theory of government failure and the resultant taxonomy of nonmarket failure. Moreover, the structure of arguments intrinsic to this theory deliberately replicates the logic of the theory of market failure. Wolf (1979a, p.115) puts the matter thus:

The supply and demand characteristics of the nonmarket sector are fundamental to the theory of nonmarket failure. They provide a basis for formulating a typology of nonmarket failure analogous to that which already exists for market failure. In both cases, the 'failures' – whether market or nonmarket – are evaluated against the same criteria of success: allocative efficiency and distributional equity judged according to some explicit social or ethical norm.

Inclusive of distributional inequities, Wolf has developed a fourfold taxonomy of nonmarket failure. Firstly, and evidently by far the most important form of nonmarket failure (Wolf, 1979b, p.132) resides in 'internalities and private goals'. These refer to intraorganizational allocation and evaluation procedures which determine distributional outcomes for agencies and agency personnel alike, and accordingly constitutes part of their respective utility functions. Although both market and nonmarket firms must perforce employ an 'internal version of the price system' for intrafirm resource allocation, market pressures ensure that the 'internal standards' of market organizations are strongly linked to the 'external price system', whereas nonmarket organizations may have internalities largely unrelated to optimal performance. This may mean that the actual behaviour of some public firm may diverge from its intended or ideal role. Thus, just as the problem of externalities in market failure arises from a predominance of private costs in private sector decisionmaking, so the problem of internalities in nonmarket failure stems from the ascendancy of private motives in public sector decisionmaking. Examples of internalities are easy to find within the public bureau milieu of the budget-maximizing bureaucrat, and include the 'more is better' approach and the 'more complex is better' yardstick – both instances of Wolf's (1989) contention that 'Cadillac quality' is encouraged in public agencies. Secondly, 'redundant and rising costs' represent another kind of nonmarket failure. In essence, Wolf argues that while market processes impose a relationship between production costs and output prices, this relationship is generally absent in nonmarket activity since revenues derive from nonmarket sources, like government tax income. Consequently, 'where the revenues that sustain an activity are unrelated to the costs of producing it, more resources may be used than necessary to produce a given output, or more of the nonmarket activity may be provided than is warranted by the original market-failure reason for undertaking it in the first place' (ibid., p.63). As an example, Wolf (ibid.) cites the case of government agencies trying to provide 'dignified' employment for disabled people by attempting to train them to unrealistically high levels.

The third type of nonmarket failure in the Wolfian taxonomy is termed 'derived externalities'. Derived externalities are the unintended and unanticipated side effects of government intervention designed to ameliorate perceived instances of market failure. Just as externalities generated in market relationships represent costs and benefits not considered by economic agents, so derived externalities in the nonmarket sphere '... are side effects that are not realised by the agency responsible for creating them, and hence do not affect the agency's calculations or behaviour'

(Wolf, 1989, p.77). In common with market externalities, derived externalities may be both positive and negative. A good contemporary example of negative derived externalities can be found in child allowances paid to single mothers. The intended outcome of these payments is the prevention of child poverty in single parent families, but an unanticipated result is the increase in the number of children born to single mothers in their quest for higher welfare payments from governments.

In his classification of market failure Wolf includes 'distributional equity' to the conventional categories of externalities and public goods, increasing returns to scale, and market imperfections, despite acknowledging the fact that most economists view market failures exclusively in terms of efficiency (ibid., p.28). Accordingly, in order to maintain the symmetry of his typology of nonmarket failure with the orthodox theory of market failure, Wolf incorporates adverse distributional consequences as his final category of nonmarket failure. Whilst hypothesizing that '... there is an identifiable process by which inequities can result from nonmarket activities ...' similar to inequalities flowing from market outcomes, Wolf (ibid., p.84) nevertheless argues that nonmarket inequities characteristically occur in terms of power and privilege, whereas distributional market failures typically appear in income and wealth differences. Instances of distributional inequities include 'corrupt practices', like '... bribery to obtain contracts with foreign governments for sales abroad of weapons or other controlled imports, and import licenses or preferential exchange rates conferred on the relatives, friends, or associates of officials and politicians who exercise discretionary authority' (ibid.).

Le Grand's Theory of Government Failure

Le Grand (1991) argued that whilst Wolf's attempt at creating a theory of government failure conceptually analogous to the conventional theory of market failure is undoubtedly an innovative step, various problems in the construction of this theory rendered it less influential than may otherwise have been expected. Accordingly, Le Grand (ibid., p.424) has sought '... to construct an alternative formulation of the theory of market failure that is, I hope, clearer, analytically more precise and more comprehensive.' In essence, Le Grand's 'alternative' theory of government failure amounts to the development of a tripartite classification of government intervention in a market economy, which is subject to evaluation in terms of two measures of economic efficiency and an undefined equity criterion. Le Grand (ibid., p.431) argues that government can involve itself in an area of social and economic activity in any, or all, of three ways: *provision, taxation or subsidy* and *regulation* (original emphasis), and then examines various examples of these forms of state intervention using allocative efficiency, X-inefficiency, and egalitarianism in economic outcomes. Any perceived limitations of this approach are met with the qualification that 'I have only been able to give an outline of a more consistent theory of government failure here' (ibid., p.442).

Government provision, where government '... can provide a commodity itself through owning and operating the relevant agencies and employing the relevant personnel' (ibid., p.431) is argued to be economically inefficient in either of two generic cases. Firstly, where governments enjoy a monopoly in the provision of goods and services, both allocative inefficiency and X-inefficiency can be anticipated in excess of that which would obtain under private provision. And secondly, where government provision occurs in competitive circumstances, but competition derives from organizations which do not seek to maximize profits. In this latter case one can once again anticipate allocative inefficiency and X-inefficiency. No *a priori* expectations are held on the equity consequences of government provision relative to private provision. However, Le Grand (ibid., p.440) does argue that the replacement of a public monopoly by a private monopoly '... might have an inegalitarian impact on that distribution, because (a) the latter would have more incentive to exploit its position to maximise profits and (b) any profits would accrue to its shareholders instead of to all taxpayers.'

Under government taxation or subsidy, government '... can *tax* the commodity, thus raising its price above the level that would have been attained in a competitive market, or it can *subsidise* the commodity, thus lowering its price below the market level' (ibid., p.431) (original emphasis). In both instances prices will diverge from true production costs, or marginal social costs, and consequently the price mechanism will not induce allocative efficiency. Alternative allocative procedures must thus be adopted. Majoritarian voting possesses the twin advantages of enabling all of a given population an equal say in deciding on the optimal level of provision of some good, but also has numerous disadvantages, including no measure of preference intensities, high organizational costs, and problems associated with the median voter theorem? However, taxes and subsidies will certainly modify the incentives confronting consumers and producers, reallocate resources, and impose deadweight welfare losses. Overall, the empirical evidence on the economic efficiency of this form of government intervention is mixed. Moreover, the equity status of government taxation or subsidy is also far from clearcut. Thus, whilst '... it is possible that a combination of tax finance and subsidised service ... is more egalitarian than if neither the taxes concerned nor the subsidies existed ... there is no guarantee that they will promote equity either' (ibid., p.441).

Finally, governments '... can *regulate* the production and distribution of the commodity, prescribing the structure of the markets or the quantity, quality or price of the commodity concerned' (ibid., p.431). Le Grand argues that although in principle state regulation can result in optimal quantity, quality, price, and market structure outcomes, in practice at least two factors inhibit the efficiency of regulatory programmes. Firstly, it is often difficult, or even impossible, to acquire the information necessary for successful regulatory regimes to operate. And secondly, the pheno- menon of regulatory capture means producer groups can control the process of regulation, and influence it in their own direction. Accordingly, government regulation will usually generate both allocative inefficiency and X-inefficiency, and by stifling long-run incentives may also imbue dynamic inefficiency (ibid., 1991). In equity terms, Le Grand notes that while regulation can redistribute income towards poorer individuals and groups, perverse regressive distributional consequences are equally likely.

Vining and Weimer's Theory of Government Production Failure

Vining and Weimer (1991, p.1) argued that 'absent a convincing normative theory of government production, the debates over the appropriate bound- aries of government and the desirability of privatization must be resolved without a firm conceptual grounding.' Moreover, they note that whilst 'Charles Wolf has made an important start by attempting to draw parallels between market failures and the manifestations of government supply failures' (ibid.), Wolf's taxonomy of nonmarket failure has at least two significant shortcomings. Firstly, since Wolf's approach is neither explic- itly normative nor positive, its role as an analytical tool in the evaluation of public policy is limited. And secondly, Vining and Weimer (ibid., p.2) observe that 'although Wolf draws loose parallels with market failures, he does not take advantage of many of the well-developed implications that can be directly applied to diagnosing problems of government supply.' Accordingly, in order to remedy these perceived deficiencies in the exist- ing theory of government failure, Vining and Weimer (p.1) '... seek to provide a useful framework for understanding the efficiency consequences of alternative patterns of government supply by developing a normative perspective on when the government should produce a good or service itself and a positive perspective on government supply in general.' This analytical apparatus can also be viewed as '... a framework for diagnosing hierarchical, or organizational, failure' (ibid., p.3). The theory itself draws heavily on recent developments in the literature on industrial organization, and especially the theory of contestable markets. A market may be described as perfectly contestable if no barriers to entry or exit exist (Baumol, Panzar and Willig, 1982). Consequently, contestability can act as a surrogate for competition in markets dominated by one or a few firms. In other words, 'perfect contestability permits competition *for* the market to substitute effectively for competition *in* the market' (Vining and Weimer, 1991, p.6) (original emphasis). Conventionally, contestability is held to be largely dependent on the extent of asset specificity and the attendant problem of sunk costs. Specific assets are assets whose value is much greater in a particular use or relationship than in the next best alternative, whereas sunk costs refer to costs that cannot be recovered.

However, in the realm of government production, Vining and Weimer (1991) argue that it is possible to identify further aspects of contestability. Firstly, they postulate the existence of *contestability of supply* which corresponds most closely with conventional notions of contestable markets, but nevertheless incorporates some of the unique characteristics of public sector supply. Contestability of supply in this context refers to actual or potential competition faced by a public agency in the market for its output. Given difficulties in monitoring arising from the nature of government supply, 'trust that the organisation producing the good will not engage in "opportunism"... by not complying with contract terms or by exploiting bargaining power when contract terms do not cover contingencies that arise...' (ibid., p.6) becomes an important element in contestability of supply. Examples of public goods where 'trust' is essential abound, and this explains continued public production with the best known example being the armed forces. The underlying argument has been generalized by Vining and Weimer (1991, pp.6–7) as follows:

> ... [W]hen the risk of opportunism, determined by the cost of non-compliance and the opportunity for non-compliance in contracting, is high, trust is an important specific asset to the production of the good. Thus, the supply of the good is unlikely to be contestable ... Consequently, government production is an appropriate organizational arrangement when the risk of opportunism is high.

A second attribute of the contestability of government production of public goods resides in *contestability of ownership* which refers to '... the credibility of the threat of transfer of ownership of the organisation' (ibid., p.6). Although transfer of ownership of some bureau may occur between agencies or departments within the broad public sector, privatization is obviously important in this context.

From the perspective of positive economics the efficiency characteristics of these two forms of contestability are relatively straightforward; where both supply and ownership are highly contestable, powerful incentives exist which promote allocative and X-efficiency, and prices should closely reflect marginal cost. The normative conclusion is that under these circumstances contracting will be the most socially efficient mode of provision. Moreover, the converse conclusion may be drawn where contestability is low. Under these latter conditions, government production will be more socially efficient provided the *ex ante* rules limiting managerial discretion are effective in keeping rent capture below levels that would obtain under contracting.

Criticisms of the Theory

Various responses to the emerging body of literature on normative economic theories of government or nonmarket failure are possible. One way of organizing derivative comment is to consider generic criticism separately from specific critiques of particular theories. In the following discussion we consider only general criticisms.

Policy analysts are now usually aware that all public policy instruments are significantly less than perfect. Accordingly, since policy analysis often involves selecting the most appropriate policy instrument from a range of market and nonmarket alternatives, analysts require a comprehensive theory which facilitates comparison of the relative efficiency of different instruments. In other words, effective policy analysis requires a general theory of organizational failure, rather than conceptually distinct theories of market failure and nonmarket failure. This has been recognized by Williamson (1989, p.92) who has argued that '...all forms of organization, not just markets, need be assessed comparatively...'. There is thus a need for common criteria which apply equally to market and government organizations. Put differently, '... whether 'x' is called a comparative efficiency of the market or a comparative inefficiency of the nonmarket is arbitrary if all that matters is that market and nonmarket differ in this respect' (ibid., p.93).

Two of the three normative economic theories of government failure do at least approach this ideal, although they remain problematic in many respects. Le Grand (1991) employs two measures of economic efficiency and an equity criterion to evaluate various forms of government intervention, and since in principle these yardsticks can also be applied to market outcomes, a comparative framework for policy analysis can emerge.

Similarly, Vining and Weimer (1991) develop two new criteria, contestability of supply and contestability of ownership, which can supplement existing normative standards for adjudging the performance of nonmarket and market institutions alike. Even Wolf's (1979a, 1979b, 1983, 1987, 1989) theory of nonmarket failure, whilst explicitly concerned with creating a conceptual analogue to the existing theory of market failure, employs distributional equity for evaluating both markets and governments.

However, given the current state of the art in the normative evaluation of alternative social states, a completely unified or general theory of comparative organizational behaviour is unlikely to appear in the near future. In part, the problem revolves around the concept of allocative efficiency, which is not only a standard welfare criterion in the theory of market failure, but is also used by Wolf, Le Grand, and Vining and Weimer. Allocative efficiency refers to a distribution of productive resources amongst alternative uses which yields an optimal mix of output. In markets characterized by perfect competition, the optimal output combination arises through consumers responding to prices which reflect the true costs of production, or marginal social costs. Allocative efficiency thus involves an interaction between the productive capacity of society and the consumption desires of society. Put differently, both the demand and supply blades of the Marshallian scissors are necessary to determine the allocatively efficient level of output. But government production is often concerned with supplying public goods, and the non-exclusive nature of these goods means that no direct method of revealing consumption preferences and thus demand curves is available. This implies that it is not possible to determine allocative efficiency under these circumstances. Because consumers pay directly in market transactions no equivalent problem exists. Consequently, although allocative efficiency is applicable in the theory of market failure, it does not have any operational counterpart in a general theory of government failure.

Finally, as we have seen in Chapter 2, some theorists have argued that the entire enterprise aimed at constructing a normative theory of government failure along the lines of the traditional theory of market failure is misplaced. In essence, this line of argument holds that the Paretian welfare underpinnings of the market failure paradigm are flawed, and accordingly attempts to simulate this model in the context of government behaviour simply compound these problems. Peacock (1981, p.41) argues that efforts in this direction simply encourage confusion between '... the actual incidence of "collective failure" with the incidence which would obtain were government to follow the strict dictates of welfare economics'.

3.5   THE APPROPRIATE ROLE OF GOVERNMENT

A consequence of the government failure literature has been to ignite a vigorous search for ways of reducing the extent and magnitude of government – a central theme of this book. Various approaches have been proposed, most of which focus on either matching the role of the state to its capabilities or enhancing the capacity of the state. Both schools share a growing awareness that although governments cannot create wealth *per se* they nevertheless can play a key role in the process of economic development. Indeed, it is now common to refer to the 'enabling state' as a crucial ingredient in achieving higher rates of economic growth (*World Bank Development Report*, 1997). At the very least the state must provide various fundamentally important functions, including the creation and maintenance of law and order, the provision of basic social services and physical infrastructure, and the establishment of a stable and coherent policy environment. But apart from these minimalist functions, the state can enhance economic activity in other ways too. Chhibber (1997, p.17) has put the argument thus:

> Although the importance of these fundamentals for development has long been widely accepted, new insights are emerging as to the appropriate mix of market and government activities in achieving them. We now see that markets and governments are complementary: the state is essential for putting in place the appropriate institutional foundations for markets.

It need hardly be added that for the state to play an effective catalytic role in the process of economic development, it must possess some minimal level of administrative capacity. Levy (1997, p.21) argues that for the state to intervene constructively it must exhibit two basic characteristics: Firstly, government officials and agencies must have the ability to manage technical complexity; and second, checks and balances must be in force in the country to restrain agencies, officials, and politicians from departing from their stated commitments and lapsing into arbitrary and unpredictable enforcement.

Matching the Role of the State to Capacity

A useful way of conceptualizing the problem of matching the role of the state to its capabilities is provided in Figure 3.2, which illustrates the potential functions government can fulfil, depending on the efficiency and effectiveness of state institutions. Figure 3.2 outlines three basic levels at which the state can intervene, depending on its institutional capacity. Minimal functions, like the provision of law and order and disaster relief, must be provided by all states, even those with very low state capacity. The alternative is the total disintegration of the nation state, with all its attendant misery. Chhibber (ibid.) has forcefully underscored this point:

It is true that state-sponsored development has failed. But the agonies of collapsed states such as Liberia and Somalia demonstrate all too clearly

	Addressing market failure	Improving equity		
Minimal functions	Providing pure public goods: Defense Law and order Property rights Macroeconomic management Public health	Protecting the poor: Antipoverty programs Disaster relief		
Intermediate functions	Addressing externalities: Basic education Environmental protection	Regulating monopoly: Utility regulation Antitrust policy	Overcoming imperfect information: Insurace (health, life, pensions) Financial regulation Consumer protection	Providing social insurance: Redistributive pensions Family allowances Unemployment insurance
Activist functions	Coordinating private activity: Fostering markets Cluster initiatives	Redistribution: Asset redistribution		

Figure 3.2   The role of the state
Source: *World Bank Development Report* (1997, Table 1.1, p.27).

the consequences of statelessness. Good government is not a luxury but a vital necessity, without which there can be no development, economic or social.

Intermediate functions, such as public education and the provision of social welfare services, must also be provided by governments, However, in contrast to its minimal function role, the methods used to provide intermediate functions can vary depending on the level of state capacity. That is, in the case of these intermediate functions, government provision can be separated from government production. The *World Bank Development Report* (1997, p. 27) has described the role of government in the provision of intermediate functions as follows:

> Here, too, the government cannot choose whether, but only how best to intervene, and government can work in partnership with markets and civil society to ensure that these public goods are provided.

Finally, activist functions, like intervention to stimulate new markets and generate increased co-ordination between existing markets, should only be undertaken by countries with a highly sophisticated state capacity and even then only with great care.

Enhancing the Capacity of the State

Although the government failure literature has primarily served to focus attention on the costs attached to government intervention, it has also aroused interest in the ancillary question of whether it is possible to correct, or at least reduce government failures. Various options have been explored. For example, Chang (1994) has argued that it is possible to mitigate the information problem facing governments and reduce the amount and type of rent-seeking activity taking place. The information problem can be addressed in two ways. Firstly, Chang (ibid., p.36) contends that the information processing ability of the state can be improved by '... freeing the top-decision maker from routinised decisions will enhance the overall ability of the state to process information.' And secondly, redesigned organization structures can also ameliorate the problem of informational asymmetrics and associated agency costs in government bureaucracies, and Chang (ibid.) cites the apparent tradition of information-sharing between Japanese corporate business and the Japanese state agencies.

Chang (ibid.) also argues that the rent-seeking dimension of government failure depends on the institutional characteristics of the society in question.

In particular, Chang (ibid., p.38) maintains that '... since rent-seeking involves state-created rents, the vulnerability of the state becomes a crucial issue, since if the state is invulnerable to outside influence, there will be no rent-seeking however big the rent may be.' Thus, in countries where power resides in the bureaucracy, like Gaullist France, Japan and South Korea, Chang (ibid.) asserts that bureaucrats are immune to rent-seeking advances from interest groups. Somewhat more plausibly, Chang (ibid., p.39) argues that state 'invulnerability' may be increased and rent seeking thereby decreased when government '... has voluntarily abdicated its power to make decisions' through '... picking the winner ... by methods such as a genuine lottery, equal sharing, rotation ...' and so on.

Perhaps a more promising approach to remedying government failure has been suggested by the 1997 *World Development Report*, which emphasizes three 'essential building blocks' for an 'effective public sector'. Firstly, the institutions involved in the policymaking process must possess various important characteristics. Thus 'although the precise institutional arrangements vary, effective public sectors the world over have generally been characterized by strong central capacity for macroeconomic and strategic policy formulation; by mechanisms to delegate, discipline, and debate policies among government agencies; and by institutionalized links to stakeholders outside the government, providing transparency and accountability and encouraging feedback.' (ibid., p.81).

Secondly, well-formulated policy will only succeed if they are implemented through efficient and effective delivery systems. The 1997 *World Development Report* emphasizes the significance of New Public Management (NPM) reforms of the recent past, including using market mechanism for the delivery of contestable services, internal competition in the public sector, and performance-based public agencies. Finally, the importance of 'motivated and capable staff' is stressed. Factors such as 'merit-based recruitment and promotion', 'adequate compensation', and 'building *esprit de corps*' are believed to be crucial in this regard. The efficiency of NPM as a method of reducing government failure will be taken up in Chapter 4 and alternatives to NPM in the subsequent chapters.

A further consequence of the government failure literature has been a general reassessment of the theory of the state. As we have seen, a broad consensus now exists that, contrary to the market failure paradigm, the state is not benevolent, omnipotent, and omniscient. This realization has led some writers to attempt to redefine the nature of the state by developing a synthesis of the various new concepts of the role of the state. For instance, Chang and Rowthorn (1995, p.34) have argued that 'three critical elements' exist which a 'satisfactory theory of state intervention' should embody:

> The first is the need to bring politics back into the theory. The second is the role of the state as the creator and manipulator (both in good and bad senses) of institutions. The third is the role of the state as an entrepreneur, a notion which has been talked about a lot but with little theoretical treatment.

In their attempt at creating a preliminary model of the state along these lines, Chang and Rowthorn (1995, p.46) suggest that '... a modern economy requires a state which can effectively perform the roles of the ultimate entrepreneur and the conflict manager'. In its entrepreneurial role, the state is envisaged as providing a strategic 'vision' of the future and pursuing this vision by co-ordinating externalities and private firms through institution building. By contrast, in its conflict management role, the state must oversee the redistribution of economic benefits inevitably attendant upon economic growth in order to arrest the growth of interest groups inimical to economic development.

Similarly, Chang (1994, p.44) has proposed a 'new institutionalist theory of the state' which focuses on the role of the state in lowering transactions costs by co-ordinating economic activity. This co-ordination function has three main dimensions: namely, changing the institutional structure of society, promoting a national 'value system' which facilitates the exchange of information and bargaining, and providing a 'focal point', like an indicative plan, to enhance the co-ordination of economic activity and reduce transaction costs. Chang (ibid., p.54) has summarized his conception of the state as follows:

> We emphasised that the state may resolve the coordination problem at a lower cost than the market (and other economic institutions) and thus reduce transaction costs, which are the costs of coordination, in the economy. Institution of an effective property-rights system, macroeconomic stabilization, organising society into large groups, promoting national ideologies, and coordinating complementary investment decision are examples of such a role. This type of intervention is particularly attractive because it is relatively cheap compared with other types, which may indeed incur large transaction costs (for example central planning).

In essence, these attempts at reconceptualizing the role of the state appear to focus on redefining '... the boundary drawn along the conventional market failure-government failure axis' (Chang and Rowthorn, 1995, p.43). But emphasis still falls on markets and governments as alternative institutional mechanisms for solving social and economic problems to the exclusion of other social agencies. For most of the remainder of this book we attempt to show that, in addition to markets and institutions, other social forces, like leadership, can plan decisive roles in the resolution of societal problems. In common with Boston *et al.* (1996, p.31), who note that '... organizations have three separate mechanisms available to them as they seek to achieve their goals and maintain control: markets, hierarchies, and culture (or clans)', we believe that factors such as culture and ethics should be explicitly introduced into any useful theory of the appropriate role of the state.

4 New Institutional Economics, New Public Management and Government Failure

4.1 INTRODUCTION

Although the growing literature on government failure has undermined the authority of the once dominant market failure paradigm from its throne in policy analysis, and obliged both theorists and practitioners alike to rethink the appropriate role of government in advanced market economics, uncertainty still surrounds the implications of this literature for public sector reform. After all, as we saw in Chapter 3, an emerging consensus is developing around the concept of the 'enabling state' as a means of describing socially desirable forms of government intervention. Moreover, this consensus represents something of a compromise between the interventionist bias of the market failure paradigm and the radical proposals for limited government offered by the public choice variant of the government failure literature. But both the theory of market failure and its government failure counterpart focused heavily on the desirability or otherwise of government intervention in market or exchange processes rather than on the public sector *per se*. With relatively few exceptions, like the economic theory of bureaucracy (Niskanen, 1972) and its derivative notion of bureaucratic failure, until very recently economists have ignored public sector organizations. If the core assumptions of economic analysis consist of rational maximizing behaviour, stable preferences and comparable equilibria, and if neoclassical economics adds peripheral concepts like perfect information and costless market exchange (Eggertsson, 1990), then this reticence about examining hierarchical relationships characteristic of public bureaux would appear warranted. However, with the development of New Institutional Economics (NIE) and its emphasis on introducing institutional realism into economic analysis, especially agency theory and transaction costs economics, economists now possess powerful tools for the analysis of organizational behaviour and design. In this chapter we take up the question of NIE and its explanatory abilities in a public sector context.

A second consequence of the debate over the appropriate role of government has been an emphasis on reducing the extent and magnitude of government failure. To a significant degree this question has revolved around decreasing the size of the public sector through privatization and other means: that is, 'matching the role of the state to its capacity' in the language of the 1997 *World Bank Development Report*. But core functions which must remain within the public sector call for different solutions to the problem of government failure. The predominant response to this need to 'enhance the capacity of the state' has been managerial. Indeed, a new public administration management philosophy known as 'New Public Management' (NPM) has been developed as a means of reducing government failure. In this chapter we will use the term 'generic managerialism' (GM) to refer to the particular stream of management theory that has been applied to public sector organizations. We use the term NPM to refer to the amalgam of NIE and GM from which a policy paradigm has been constructed that provides the principles or 'broadly similar set of administrative doctrines' (Hood, 1991, p.1) that have been employed to reform the structure of the public sector in many countries since the early 1980s.

The chapter itself is divided into five main sections. In section 2 we outline the essence of NIE and focus on its two chief strands, agency theory and transaction costs economics. In section 3 we examine the applicability of NIE to the analysis of problems in a public sector context. The nature of GM is investigated in section 4, and especially the compatibility of its NIE and managerialist elements. Section 5 considers the extent to which the public sector reforms associated with NPM can be seen as solutions to the problems of government failure. The chapter ends with a brief discussion of the policy implications of the aforegoing discussion.

4.2   NEW INSTITUTIONAL ECONOMICS

In common with the major earlier institutionalist tradition associated with Thorstein Veblen, Wesley Mitchell, John R. Commons and Clarence Ayres, New Institutional Economics (NIE) represents a loose collection of ideas aimed at bringing institutional characteristics back to the core of economic analysis (Rutherford, 1996). However, unlike the older tradition, NIE scholars have few problems with *a priori* deductive theorizing. For example, Furubotn and Richter (1992, p.1) have observed that:

> The change in analytic approach adopted by the new institutionalists has not resulted from any deliberate attempt to set up a new and distinct

type of doctrine in conflict with conventional theory. Rather, the tendency to introduce greater institutional detail into economic models has come about gradually over time because of the recognition that standard neoclassical analysis is overly abstract and incapable of dealing effectively with many current problems of interest to theorists and policymakers.

Given its somewhat disparate nature, NIE is difficult to define with any degree of precision. Frant (1991, pp.112–13) has identified three 'precursors' of NIE. Firstly, Coase's (1937) focus on the importance of transactions and the related problems of whether to employ markets or hierarchies to handle transactions, which emphasized the costs attached to using the price mechanism. Secondly, the literature on the economics of property rights deriving from Coase's (1960) famous paper on how the assignation of property rights influences outcomes in the presence of externalities, which led to the so-called 'Coase theorem'. And thirdly, Alchian and Demsetz' (1972) seminal attempt to apply the property rights paradigm to organizations engaged in productive activity, with the problems inherent in 'team production', like 'shirking' and 'monitoring'.

Disagreement exists on the major dimensions of NIE. For instance, Rutherford (1996, pp.2–3) adopts a fairly broad view of the main elements of NIE by including the economics of property rights (Alchian and Demsetz, 1973), law and economics (Posner, 1977), rent seeking and distributional coalitions (Olson, 1982), agency theory (Jensen and Meckling, 1976), transaction costs economics (Williamson, 1975), game theory in institutional situations (Shubik, 1975), and the new economic history of Douglas North (1981). Matthews (1986) has developed a fourfold taxonomy of NIE in which institutions are viewed as property rights, as kinds of contracts, as conventions, and as governance structures. By contrast, Boston *et al.* (1996) constrain their policy-orientated view of NIE to only two strands, namely agency theory and transaction cost economics. We follow this narrow taxonomy below.

Although NIE does not contest the methodology of contemporary neoclassical economics, it does make several crucial changes to it. Firstly, following Simon (1975), NIE recognizes that in the real world, individuals possess an inherently limited capacity to process information and accordingly are 'boundedly rational' in the sense that their calculations include only immediate and readily assimilated information. Bounded rationality necessarily implies that the complexities of actual economic exchange cannot be fully captured by hierarchical contracts or market mechanisms. This leads to a second difference between NIE and conventional economic analysis. Since bounded rationality prevents the construction of complete contracts between agents and principals, scope exists for opportunistic behaviour by economic agents, who can conceal their preferences and actions from contractual partners (Williamson, 1975). Indeed, it is precisely because of real-world phenomena, like bounded rationality and incomplete contracts, that economic activities have to be conducted in an environment characterized by asymmetric information and costly transactions, and it is these features which lend crucial importance to institutions.

Perhaps even more significant than these methodological issues are the differences between NIE and orthodox neoclassical analysis on the question of what should constitute the appropriate measure(s) to gauge economic efficiency. In common with the conventional approach, normative problems are usually framed in individualistic terms and focus on the efficiency of alternative conceivable institutional arrangements. But many theorists working in the NIE tradition have expressed strong reservations about using the Pareto efficiency criterion to justify government intervention. For instance, as we have seen in Chapter 2, Demsetz' (1969) 'nirvana fallacy' argument holds that by comparing real-world arrangements against the ideal of allocative efficiency rather than feasible institutional alternatives, policymakers have become far too inclined to prescribe government intervention. Similarly, De Alessi (1983) has argued that many of the supposed inefficiencies identified in practical institutional situations by neoclassical economics are actually due to the existence of transaction costs.

Arguments along these lines have led many in the NIE tradition to favour a comparative institutions approach to the question of economic efficiency. The essence of this approach has been summarized by Furubotn and Richter (1992, p.12) as follows:

Granting that the conventional efficiency standard is unsatisfactory, there is reason to seek a different criterion and move toward a concept of economic efficiency that takes fuller account of those real-life constraints that actually limit individual choices. This approach is precisely the one that many new institutionalist writers have adopted. These theorists point out that, in the real world, alternative systems of property rights exist and transaction costs are inevitably greater than zero. Hence, the 'generalisation' of neoclassical doctrine is advocated. The objective is, of course, to include in any general equilibrium model all of the constraints that decision makers must face in seeking to maximise utility.

The efficiency criterion required by this approach has been specified by De Alessi (1983, p.69) in the following terms:

> Efficiency is being defined as constrained maximisation. Efficiency conditions are seen as the properties of a determinate (equilibrium) solution implied by a given theoretical construct. On this view, a system's solutions are always efficient if they meet the constraints that characterise it.

Often notions of efficiency employed in the comparative institutions approach focus on either productive or dynamic efficiency rather than on allocative efficiency. For example, North (1981) emphasizes the relative efficiency of institutions with reference to their impact on 'social output' or 'economic growth' and the ways in which they minimize transaction costs through time. This kind of argument does not indicate how 'economic efficiency' defined in this way enhances individual utility or social welfare and accordingly is not completely satisfactory.

In general, it seems clear that theorists in the NIE tradition advocate a concept of efficiency that embodies organizational costs, like transactions costs, which can be used to evaluate various feasible reorganizations of economic activity that could yield social gains net of the costs of reorganization. (See, for example, Coase (1960), Demsetz (1969), Dahlman (1979), and Bromley (1989)). This intellectual project is not without its critics (Samuels (1972); Schmid (1987)), and may be simply tautological. This argument has been summarized by Papandreou (1994, pp.273–4) as follows:

> The traditional notion of optimality in welfare economics has been criticised for comparing real-world outcomes with unattainable outcomes of a transaction-costless world. The alternative notion of 'attainable' optimality implicit in models with endogenous transaction costs, suffers in that by offering a causal explanation of economic interaction it precludes other feasible alternatives with which to compare the outcome of the model. By disallowing comparisons of the 'real-world' microeconomic model with microeconomic models that have different organisational costs, the set of feasible outcomes collapses to the outcome of the 'real-world' model. Accordingly, the outcome that exists is the only possible one.

Transaction Costs

Despite the fact that Coase (1937, p.390) originally specified transaction costs as the '... cost of using the price mechanism' more than sixty years ago, a satisfactory definition of this concept remains problematic. As Allen (1991, p.2) has observed, 'the literature on transactions costs is replete with papers which use the term and provide examples, but which never pause to define the phrase.'

In general terms, a transaction can be defined as an agreed exchange or transfer of goods and services across technologically separable boundaries. The costs involved in such an agreement and which facilitate such a transfer are collectively known as transaction costs (Williamson, 1985). In other words, transaction costs are the costs of facilitating economic exchange or, in the language of Kenneth Arrow (1969, p.48), the costs incurred in 'running the economic system'. Transaction costs are contrasted with transformation costs (sometimes also called production costs) which are the costs involved in transforming inputs into outputs.

Theorists have adopted two generic ways of specifying transaction costs. Firstly, it has been common to adopt somewhat narrow definitions of transaction costs closely bound up with the notion of property rights. For example, Eggertsson (1991, p.14) delineated transaction costs as 'the costs that arise when individuals exchange property rights to economic assets and enforce their exclusive rights'. Similarly, Barzel (1982) and McManus (1975) emphasize the costs of enforcement and negotiation of property rights. A second and more contemporary view of the nature of transaction costs focuses on the costs of creating and maintaining the institutions characteristic of modern market economics. Furubotn and Richter (1992, p.8) have described this approach as '... most easily understood as embracing all those costs that are connected with (i) the creation or change of an institution or organisation, and (ii) the use of the institution or organisation'. In the present context we follow this latter approach.

The theory of transaction costs arose from Coase's (1937) question of why it is that two institutions, the market and the firm, perform the same basic functions and yet continue to coexist. He argued that these two alternative methods of co-ordinating economic activities exist because there are transaction costs associated with using the price mechanism. Accordingly, rational economic agents will seek to minimize transaction costs and will use either markets or hierarchies, whichever is cheapest. Thus, for example, whether a firm decides to own or lease a particular machine will depend on the transaction costs involved.

The modern theory of transaction costs has developed this line of thought and emphasizes the importance of the institutions underpinning exchange relationships, namely markets, contracts and firms in private sector settings. Transaction costs theory thus seeks to characterize the properties of transactions in order to determine which institution is optimal in any specific case. Williamson (1979) has argued that the critical features of transactions are their uncertainty, the frequency with which they recur, and the extent to which parties to these transactions are obliged to make investments in transaction-specific assets. For example, once parties in an initial competitive market commit themselves to a specialized transaction (involving, say, substantial investments in specific assets, or high 'asset specificity'), then this leads an ongoing 'small number' bargaining situation between the two parties, often termed bilateral bargaining. Williamson (1985, p.47) has hypothesized that these kinds of arrangements encourage opportunistic behaviour or 'self-interest seeking with guile', and he has called them 'idiosyncratic' transactions, since the benefits of the transaction are dependent on the absence of opportunistic behaviour in its execution. Obviously specialized institutional arrangements will be required to govern idiosyncratic transactions.

Similarly, pervasive uncertainty, or the absence of perfect information, will also have a decisive effect on whether markets, contracts or firms will be chosen to govern transactions. In general, Williamson (1979) has argued that high levels of uncertainty will inhibit the use of long-term contracts in these cases. Analogous arguments also exist with respect to transactional frequency. For instance, in the absence of asset specificity, infrequent transactions will not usually require contracts and will simply be undertaken through the market mechanism. Figure 4.1 developed by Williamson (1979) provides a useful scheme for linking transactional characteristics and governance structures. For example, whereas for moderate to high levels of asset specificity, infrequent transactions will lead to 'trilateral governance' (or third-party binding arbitration agreements), frequent transactions will either result in bilateral contracting between the buyer and seller, or in buyers purchasing the relevant productive capacity and integrating it into their firms.

Frequency		Asset Specificity		
		NONSPECIALIZED	MIXED	IDIOSYNCRATIC
Frequency	OCCASIONAL	Market governance	Trilateral governance	
	RECURRENT		Bilateral governance	Ownership integration

Figure 4.1   Governance structure and the characteristics of transactions
Source: Williamson (1979, p.253).

In common with other areas of NIE, transaction costs economics has been subjected to severe criticism. The first and most damaging line of attack is based on the proposition that it is not obvious that economic agents should wish to minimize total transaction costs rather than simply the transaction costs borne directly by themselves. Put differently, transaction costs minimization may take the form of a contest over 'cost shifting' rather than a search for the optimal institutional arrangements. Secondly, although an attractive idea in principle, the disaggregation of total costs into transformation costs and transaction costs may not always be feasible in practice (Dollery and Leong, 1998). As Lane (1995, p.229) has inquired: 'could one measure the reduction in transaction costs by moving from a system of individual contracts to a hierarchy like a firm or bureau?'. The transaction costs theory has also been criticized for the narrowness of its *homo economicus* behavioural assumption, which is asserted to disregard cultural, social and other dimensions of human conduct.

For these and other reasons, transaction cost theory can at best offer only a partial explanation for real-world differences in economic organization. Whilst it does advance our understanding of the benefits and costs of alternative governance structures, it should nevertheless be applied with care and in tandem with other NIE models, like agency theory.

Agency Theory

The literature on agency theory is centrally concerned with the ways in which one economic agent (the principal) can design and implement a contractual compensation system to motivate another economic agent (the agent) to act in the principal's pecuniary interests. Accordingly, agency theory is chiefly focused on the problem of economic incentives. By contrast, conventional neoclassical economics, with its reductionist construct of the organization as simply a production function converting inputs into outputs in the most productively efficient manner, assumed away principal–agent problems and the associated question of incentives. In the orthodox tradition, principals were perfectly informed on the nature of the tasks agents were hired to performs and their subsequent actions could be costlessly monitored. Agency theory can thus be viewed as the extension of the neoclassical theory of the firm to embrace 'the problems posed by limited information and goal conflict within organisations' (Levinthal, 1988, p.154). In other words, just as transaction costs theory adds realism to the theory of markets by including the costs attached to exchange relationships, so too agency theory adds realism to the conventional 'black box' conception of organizations.

A principal–agent relationship comes into being whenever a principal delegates authority to an agent whose behaviour has an impact on the principal's welfare. Numerous principal–agent relationships exist across virtually the entire spectrum of human endeavour. For example, principal–agent relationships include voters and their elected representatives, patients and physicians, employers and employees, shareholders and corporate managers, and so forth. The essence of all these principal–agent relationships involve a trade-off for the principal. By delegating authority to an agent, the principal economises on scarce resources by adopting an informed and able agent, but simultaneously takes on the risk that since the interests of the principal and agent will never be identical, the agent may fail to maximize the wealth of the principal. For instance, despite being paid a proportionate commission, real estate agents may wish to sell a property quickly at a lower price than could otherwise be obtained for the owner of the property. Since the interests of principals and agents are likely to diverge in most real-world relationships, agency theory focuses on the costs attached to such relationships and the efforts that both principals and agents will take to economize on these costs. In their seminal contribution, Jensen and Meckling (1976) identified three categories of agency costs. Firstly, monitoring costs arise from the resources principals invest in monitoring the behaviour of agents and creating incentives for desirable behaviour. Secondly, bonding costs will derive from resources invested by agents to guarantee successful outcomes to their principals. And thirdly, residual loss costs consist in the losses to their wellbeing suffered by principals due to a divergence between their interests and those of their agents. According to Jensen and Meckling (1976), total agency costs are thus comprised of the aggregate of monitoring costs, bonding costs and residual loss costs.

The extent of total agency costs are postulated as dependent on the characteristics of particular principal–agent relationships. For example, in a typical agency relationship agents almost always possess more information about both the task assigned and the relative efficacy of their own performance. Agents often take advantage of this asymmetry of information by engaging in shirking or opportunistic behaviour inimicable to the interests of principals, and clearly the greater the extent of this behaviour the higher will be the level of total agency costs.

Although in its initial stages agency theory was applied exclusively to the firm, and especially the modern corporation with its characteristic separation of ownership from control quintessentially representative of a principal–agent relationship, it was soon used more widely once its explanatory powers were recognized. Jensen and Meckling (ibid., p.309) themselves recognized the generality of agency theory:

> The problem of inducing an 'agent' to behave as if he [or she] were maximizing the 'principal's' welfare is quite general. It exists in all organizations and in all co-operative efforts – at every level of management in firms, in universities, in mutual companies, in co-operatives, in governmental authorities and bureaus, in unions, and in relationships normally classified as agency relationships such as are common in the performing arts and the market for real estate.

Two specific aspects of the agency problem have received widespread attention the literature. Firstly, the phenomenon of adverse selection occurs due to informational asymmetries in principal–agent relationships. For example, because unhealthy people are more inclined to purchase health insurance they will be over-represented in the pool of insured people. In turn, this will force the price of insurance to rise inducing many low-risk healthy individuals to forego health insurance. Secondly, the problem of moral hazard arises when a party to a contractual relationship can affect the outcome of this arrangement to their own advantage. For instance, if a person is fully insured and cannot be accurately monitored by an insurance company, then their behaviour may change after the insurance has been purchased to induce larger payments. Adverse selection occurs due to information asymmetries in principal–agent relationships. For example, older people typically experience more difficulties in obtaining health insurance.

Given the problems inherent in principal–agent relationships, like adverse selection and moral hazard, a good deal of agency theory has focused resolving these problems by specifying the optimal form of contracting (Rees, 1985a; 1985b). Substantial progress has been made in a variety of economic relationships, including labour, land, credit, and product markets, and more recently in the public sector.

Agency theory is not without its critics (see, for instance, Davis and Gardner (1995)). In common with other areas of NIE, including transaction costs economics, agency theory has been criticized for the restrictive and descriptively unrealistic nature of its *homo economicus* behavioural postulate, which is postulated as neglecting the complexities of human relationships. More specifically, agency theory has been attacked for overlooking issues of authority and power in principal–agent relationships, and in particular for emphasizing the role of opportunistic behaviour by agents while ignoring opportunism by principals. It has also been argued that agency theory places a heavy reliance on single principal–agent models which ignore questions of competing principals or of uncertainty surrounding the identity of principals. Moreover, it has been observed that the policy implications which flow from agency theory are unclear, especially in public sector contexts.

4.3   NEW INSTITUTIONAL ECONOMICS AND THE PUBLIC SECTOR

As we have seen, the development of the major strands of NIE took place in an attempt to add greater institutional realism to abstract neoclassical economics in its efforts aimed at explaining and predicting the behaviour of utility maximizing individuals and profit maximizing firms in market relationships. The question thus arises as to whether the major elements of NIE can shed any light on behaviour in nonmarket or public sector contexts. Looked at from a different angle, this question reduces to the degree of similarity between the private and public sectors. Can NIE have the same descriptive and predictive powers in a nonmarket setting that it enjoys in a market milieu?

The distinction between the public and private sectors in the mixed economies of advanced representative democracies is extremely difficult to pinpoint with any degree of precision and appears ultimately to depend on value judgements about the characteristics of the 'good society'. (See, for example, Perry and Rainey, 1988; Bozemann, 1987; Sinclair, 1989.) Boston (1995, p.84) has summarized some of the complexities involved as follows:

> The issue as to what are the proper or legitimate functions of the state raises important philosophical questions over which there is never likely to be complete agreement. On the one hand, libertarians maintain that the functions of the state should be limited to the protection of life and property. This includes the provision of defence forces and a police force, together with the collection of taxes necessary to fund such services, but little else. On the other hand, those who reject libertarianism – including conservatives, liberals, social democrats and socialists – maintain that the state has responsibilities which extend well beyond matters of external and internal security and the protection of property rights. Equally vital are the administration of justice, environmental protection, the regulation of commerce, and the provision of income support and various social services.

Quite apart from disputes over the appropriate functional roles of government, it is virtually impossible to define the meaning of the term 'public sector' in any coherent manner. Jan-Erik Lane (1995, p.15) has conceptualized these definitional difficulties as follows:

> The basic problem here is what could be called the 'demarcation problem'; it involves deliberations about what the concepts 'public' and 'private' refer to as well as about the criteria that may guide the choice of what is to be public, private or some public–private mixture, and how such decisions may be implemented. The demarcation between the public and the private involves semantic questions, issues involved in derivation of an optimum or feasible solution to the problem of what is to be private or public and matters concerning the practicality of implementing any such solution.

It is sometimes argued that this 'demarcation problem' between the public and private is misplaced and what really matters is the mode of social organization. For example, von Mises (1962, p.31) has argued that 'there are two methods for the conduct of affairs within the frame of human society ... one is bureaucratic management, the other is profit management.' This classification largely coincides with Boulding's (1978) distinction between the 'threat system' and the 'exchange system' we considered in Chapter 2 and perhaps even roughly overlaps Wolf's (1989) dichotomy between 'markets' and 'governments'. But a demarcation drawn along the lines of markets versus hierarchies by no means captures the full complexities of the public sector. Several other polar dimensions of public sector and private sector activity need to be considered, not least '... exchange and authority, competition and hierarchy, laissez-faire and planning, market economy and command economy, capitalism and socialism, and freedom versus authority' (Lane, 1995, p.19). In other words, there is no single method of making a satisfactory private–public distinction since issues like authority, bureaucracy, competition, ownership, regulation, public allocation, and so on, are all relevant.

However, Wolf (1989, p.127) has argued that 'one general and neglected' dimension of the distinction between public and private sector activity resides in '... the differing processes by which performance is monitored in the market and nonmarket domains'. In the public sector 'responsibility for monitoring nonmarket output usually is lodged in another public body: a cognizant legislative committee in the federal, state, or municipal legislature ... [and] the principal monitors are not consumers of output' (ibid., 1989, pp.127–8). The inevitable result is that '... control over the costs and quality of nonmarket output is thus oblique and indirect, several steps removed from the production process, and therefore attenuated' (ibid., p.128).

This contrasts sharply with 'typical' private sector activity where '… control over performance is ultimately exercised by consumer behaviour and by competing producers whose competition often occurs across product lines as well as within them' (ibid., p.129). Accordingly, although both public and private sector organizations generate output using a combination of markets and hierarchies, fundamental differences in the management of production exist. Notwithstanding our earlier qualifications surrounding the 'demarcation problem', if we accept the generality of this argument across the multitude of public and private organizations, then this may well circumscribe and qualify the applicability of NIE to the public sector.

If we adopt a few plausible assumptions regarding the nature of public and private organizations deriving from Wolf's (1989) observations as 'stylized facts', then this may shed some light on the potential applicability of NIE for policy formulation and implementation in the public sector. Firstly, it seems reasonable to postulate that public agencies are more reliant on hierarchical organizational structures with multiple levels of principal–agent relationships than their private sector counterparts, given the typical 'conditions of nonmarket supply' specified by Wolf (1989) and outlined in Chapter 3 (especially the purported 'difficulty in defining and measuring output' and 'single-source production as well as the fact that often their output is not traded'). Accordingly, the insights provided by agency theory are likely to be particularly useful in the analysis of public agencies. However, because the monitoring process is usually 'indirect' and not motivated by considerations of profit maximization due to Wolf's (1989, p.54) 'absence of bottomline and termination mechanism[s]', principals have fewer incentives to closely monitor the behaviour of agents, with the result that shirking and opportunistic behaviour are likely to be relatively high, boosting total transaction costs.

Secondly, and by way of contrast, private firms are comparatively more dependent on market relationships than hierarchical structures in their productive activities with fewer principal–agent relationships than equivalently sized public agencies. But because of stronger pecuniary incentives for principals to monitor the performance of agents, deriving from their profit maximization maximand, per capita total agency costs are likely to be lower *ceteris paribus*.

Thirdly, if we conceive of the production and interchange of intermediate outputs within different parts of some organization as a kind of intra-organizational market, then hierarchical organizational structures can be viewed as a substitute for market relationships, along the lines of Coase (1937) and Weimer and Vining (1996, p.96) have put this argument as follows:

> This perspective makes the distinction between markets and hierarchies less significant. Markets embody some hierarchy, typically a centrally enforced system of property rights but also perhaps various regulations by government agencies. Within hierarchical organizations, considerable discretion is often delegated to people whose behavior can be understood as the pursuit of self-interest subject to various administrative constraints. Indeed, the boundaries of hierarchical organizations become blurred when the organizations contract with nonmembers for the provision of services.

Once it is realized that these stylized facts can be placed in somewhat more complex private–public interactions, then the importance of NIE becomes even more apparent. Figure 4.2 provides an illustration of these complexities.

A perusal of Figure 4.2 highlights the various public and private production and provision options. We have discussed the generic public provision and production and private provision and production models in relation to the potential explanatory power of NIE. Once public funding and private production (lower left quadrant) and private funding and public production (upper right quadrant) are considered, then principal–agent relationships and attendant transaction costs can be expected to change. For example, activities taking place in the upper right hand quadrant will presumably more closely approximate private production and provision rather than public production and provision. Similarly, activity occurring in the lower left hand quadrant would probably be characterized by relatively indirect monitoring by public principals and a comparatively high

	Public provision	Private provision
Public production	Non-commercial and non-contracted, 'core' public functions	Commercial functions undertaken by public organizations
Private production	State-funded goods and services provided by private organizations	Commercial functions undertaken by private organizations

Figure 4.2   Public and private production and provision options
Source: Adapted from Boston (1995, Figure 4.1, p.82).

degree of reliance on market relationships rather than hierarchies by private agents.

Despite the reservations expressed by Moe (1984) and others about the careless application of NIE to the public sector, and notwithstanding the complex nature of the public sector, it would thus appear that NIE has much to offer. Indeed, the deployment of rational choice models using the *homo economicus* assumption to questions in public economics has a long tradition, and includes game theory, social choice theory, and public choice theory, as Ordeshook (1986) has demonstrated. NIE appears to be especially helpful in the analysis of public–private interactions, like privatization and competitive tendering, since agency theory and transaction costs economics go to the core of these interactions. Frant (1991, p.121) has argued that the application of NIE is essential and its neglect in the past has led to misdirected empirical research:

> Many public utilities are not government bureaus but independent public corporations or authorities. Such organizations have governance structures – and, in a certain sense, property-rights structures – quite different from those of bureaus. One might suspect, then, that their efficiency properties would be quite different. Yet researchers studying public utilities have not distinguished between these two types of organizations. (Admittedly, the task would be time-consuming because most data sources do not make the distinction). Would the generally negative findings of researchers looking for superior efficiency from private sector utilities be different if the comparison group were bureaus rather than all public agencies? We do not know.

Vining and Weimer (1996) have sought to answer the somewhat broader question of what neoclassical economics augmented by NIE have to offer in the analysis of the public sector. They conclude that the market failure paradigm assists in the diagnosis of organizational problems whereas the agency theory and transaction costs strands of NIE can assist in the practical design of appropriate organizational structures. Their arguments are summarized in Figure 4.3.

From the foregoing discussion it seems abundantly clear that NIE represents a powerful conceptual tool in the positive analysis of public sector institutions and their dealings with private market participants. But this does not mean that normative policy prescriptions flowing from NIE are entirely unproblemmatic.

An evaluation of the views of leading NIE protagonists seems to indicate a distinct bias towards market solutions to social problems and a pervasive belief in the inherent superiority of markets over governments.

Economic Approach	Central Notion	Area of Application
Neoclasssical Welfare Economics	Market failures occur when violations of the assumptions of the competitive framework lead to equilibria that are not Pareto efficient.	Administrative rules and incentives to increase efficiency of intra-organizational markets: solving organizational public good, common property resource, and natural monopoly problems.
NIE: Agency Theory	Contracts structure the relationship between prinicipals and agents to minimize agency cost, which is the sum of the costs of structuring, monitoring, and bonding contracts and the loss from residual discretion.	Organizational design: creating incentives for the production and revelation of information and improve the efficiency of intra- and inter-organizational transactions.
NIE: Transaction Cost Theory	Institutional arrangements economize on transaction cost: the sum of precontract bargaining and postcontract compliance (opportunism) costs.	Organizational design: creating hostages, bonds, and other mechanisms for generating credible commitment and discouraging opportunism.

Figure 4.3   Economics and public sector analysis
Source: Adapted from Vining and Weimer (1996, Table 1, p.112).

Rutherford (1995, p.162) has observed that a striking feature of NIE is its '…more positive view of markets, and of non-governmental processes more generally, and its more negative view of government. Not only are economic markets usually seen as giving rise to efficient outcomes, but this idea of competition leading to efficient results is also frequently extended to social institutions, conventions, and norms.' Accordingly, care should be taken in the adoption of NIE policy prescriptions. For example, NIE typically favours market competition over regulation of firms to avoid 'regulatory capture' and to harness the efficiency-inducing market incentives. Similarly, NIE is usually much more forgiving of horizontal and vertical integration than anti-monopoly laws, presumably because transaction cost analysis provides efficiency, rather than monopolistic, arguments for integration. This dogmatic perception of the superiority of markets appears unfortunate, and should be eschewed in favour of a case-by-case pragmatism. Rutherford (1996, p.172) has summed up this argument as follows:

> ... [M]any writers within the NIE have argued for the efficiency of market and spontaneous processes very broadly, utilizing only weak arguments by analogy. A closer analysis of invisible-hand, common law, and even competitive market processes reveals that there are no guarantees that the inefficient will be eliminated in favour of the efficient or socially beneficial. This may occur, but whether or not it does will depend on the specifics of the case.

4.4 GENERIC MANAGERIALISM

Notwithstanding its controversial and ill-defined character, 'generic managerialism' (GM), sometimes also referred to as corporate management, managerialism, or new managerialism (Boston, 1991, pp.8–9), can be viewed as the second great wave of radical reform in the administration of the modern state (Barzelay, 1992). The first revolution in public administration, said to have occurred initially in Britain in the nineteenth century and termed 'Progressive-Era' Public Administration (PPA) (Hood, 1994, p.125), sought to '... professionalise the public service in the sense of ensuring that selection and promotion were on merit rather than patronage, rule rather than discretion governed how public bureaucratic process and decisions operated, and public service was oriented by norms of impersonality, correct procedure and consistency' (Yeatman, 1997, p.175). It is has been argued that like this first revolution which reflected new private sector methods of organizing the mass production of standardized output, so too GM mirrors the post-Fordist emphasis on customized products and organizational flexibility (Barzelay, 1992). Hood (1994, p.126) has argued that exponents of PPA stressed two basic features of organizational design: the public sector should be starkly distinguished from the private sector in terms of its operations, and rules of procedure should be developed to limit discretionary behaviour by bureaucrats and politicians. By contrast, GM can be seen as diluting these two ingredients of PPA. Hood (ibid., p.129) has argued that GM:

> ... [S]trikes directly at the heart of the two basic doctrines of PPA described above. One of its themes is the doctrine of lessening or removing organizational differences between the public and private

sector, to reduce avoidable public sector inefficiency. The doctrine is that methods of doing business in public organizations need to be shifted away from heavy emphasis on general rules of procedure and be focused more on getting results.

Peters (1996b) has located GM among four 'models' for 'reforming' government. These are the market, participatory, flexible and deregulated models. Peters (1996b) proposes that the market model has three broad 'intellectual roots' which are a belief in the superior efficiency of markets, an awareness of the failings of bureaucracies (stemming from the literature on government failure in general and bureaucratic failure in particular), and an emphasis on GM. Peters (1996b, p.28) argues that GM is ...' founded upon the assumption that management is management, no matter where it takes place', and accordingly notions that public sector management is a specialized area of expertise are facetious.

Approaching the question from a somewhat different angle, Yeatman maintains that GM represents an attempt to augment and modify the PPA tradition to enable it to meet a changing external environment. More specifically, Yeatman (1997, p.177) has argued that GM is designed to allow public sector management to accommodate three 'related contemporary dynamics'. These include 'increased social and cultural complexity', 'increased uncertainty' and unpredictability, and heightened expectations of government service provision on the part of the citizenry. A more pragmatic perspective has been offered by Ingraham (1996, p.377) who argues that reform characterized by the GM paradigm can be ascribed largely to problems '... associated with overregulation and with the bureaucratic pathologies civil service systems create'. Chief among these are 'excessive and constraining rules and regulations', 'oversized overly expensive agencies', 'isolation from elected officials', 'isolation from citizens', and 'fragmentation'. Osborn and Gaebler (1992) in their populist *Reinventing Government* argued that public administration systems in advanced Western democracies were excessively hierarchical and bound by multiple stultifying layers of bureaucratic regulation no longer appropriate in an era of choice and flexibility. Adopting a rather wider perspective, Hood (1991) has argued that the rise of GM over the recent past should not be seen as an isolated phenomenon but rather seen as part of at least four other megatrends, notably attempts to constrain the growth of government in Western democracies, a shift away from public production towards corporatization and privatization, the extensive use of information technology in the public sector, and the internationalization of public administration into a generic management philosophy.

Similarly, Wright (1994) has argued that although variations in the nature, pace, timing, and style of public sector reform in Western Europe clearly exist between different countries, broadly convergent pressures have led to fairly homogeneous reform programmes. These pressures include 'internationalization' of economies, the 'increasing regulatory creep of Brussels', 'technological change', 'generalized disgruntlement at the performance of the public sector', and 'the so-called managerial revolution'. Bekke, Perry and Toonen (1996, p.323) have adopted an analoguous line of argument by proposing that 'lack of congruence between civil service systems and their constitutional environments produces the strongest forces for change; lesser pressures for change are produced by a lack of congruence at the collective choice and operational levels' which helps to explain the 'recent universality of changes in civil service systems'.

A useful way of differentiating GM from PPA has been developed by Hood (1991; 1994) by focusing on the core issues of 'public service distinctiveness' and 'rules versus discretion'. The outcome of this process is illustrated in Figure 4.4. Figure 4.4 also helps us to define the chief ingredients of GM. For example, NPM moves away from the procedurally based management framework of PPA by emphasizing the importance of 'hands-on' professional management and the 'freedom to manage', the introduction of performance appraisal with explicit performance standards, and a greater use of output controls with their stress on results rather than procedures. Implicit in these strategies is a specific view on the nature of management which is held to be generic, portable and capable of reacting decisively to environmental change in a positive manner.

Similarly, Figure 4.4 underscores the strong inter-relationships between economics and GM. Notions of competition, contestable markets, and market-driven resource allocation are taken directly from standard textbook expositions of neoclassical economics whereas concepts like incentive structures, the producer–purchaser split, and competitive tendering derive straight from new institutional economics, particularly agency theory and transaction costs economics. Indeed, Hood (1991, pp.5–6) has argued that it is possible to derive a core set of doctrines to guide administrative reform from a 'marriage of two different streams of ideas – economics, and especially new institutional economics and public choice theory, and 'managerialism', with its emphasis on 'professional management', which is 'portable', 'paramount', 'discretionary', 'central', and 'indispensable'. Hood uses the term 'New Public Management' (NPM) to refer to this amalgam. We will use the term NPM in a similar sense to describe a 'policy paradigm' that is derived from a stream of economic and management theories. The role policy advisers play in constructing such

	No.	Doctrine	Assumed link to performance	Replaces	Operational significance
	1	'Unbundle' the public service into corporatized units organized by product	Make units 'manageable'; focus blame; create anti-waste lobby by splitting provision and production	Belief that public service needs to be uniform and inclusive to be accountable without underlaps and overlaps	Erosion of single service employment; arm's-length dealings; devolved budgets
Public service distinctiveness	2	More contract-based competitive provision, with internal markets and term contracts	Rivalry will cut costs and push up standards; contracts will make performance standards explicit	Flexibility, independence and lower transaction costs require loosely specified employment contracts and open-ended provision	Distinction of primary and secondary public service labour force
	3	Stress on private-sector styles of management practice	Need to apply 'proven' private sector management tools in the public sector	Stress on public service 'ethic'; fixed pay and hiring rules' model employer stance; centralized staffing structure, jobs for life	Move from double imbalance PS pay, career service, unmonetized rewards, 'due process' employee entitlements
	4	Put more emphasis on visible 'hands-on' top management	Accountability requires clear assignment of responsibility, not diffusion of power	Paramount stress on policy skills and rules, not active management	More 'freedom to manage' by discretionary power
Rules vs discretion	5	Make performance standards and measures explicit, formal and measurable	Accountability means clearly stated aims; efficiency needs 'hard look' at goals	Qualitative and implicit standards and norms	Erosion of self-management by professionals
	6	Greater emphasis on output controls	Need for greater stress on results	Stress on procedure and control by 'collibration' (opposed maximizers)	Resources and pay based on performance; blurring of funds for pay and for activity

Figure 4.4   Progressive-Era Public Administration and New Public Management compared
Source: Hood (1994, p. 130, Table 7.1).

paradigms and in screening ambiguities and blurring fine distinctions in the theories they draw from will be discussed further in Chapters 5 and 8.

An alternative way of distilling the essence of NPM is to observe public service systems where it has been implemented. Perhaps the most comprehensive example of NPM in practice can be found in contemporary New Zealand. Boston (1995, p.x–xi) has highlighted three salient features of NPM, at least in its New Zealand manifestation. Firstly, it places a heavy emphasis on privatization, competitive tendering, and the contracting out of publicly funded services, with the result that '... private sector organisations are now delivering a wide range of public services, some of which were previously the exclusive domain of government departments' (ibid., p.x). Secondly, Boston argues that NIE forms a crucial platform for NPM, especially agency theory and its focus on minimizing agency costs. Thus, institutional design influenced by the NPM paradigm typically eschews accountability to multiple principals in the belief that a single agent–principal hierarchical relationship reduces agency costs. Thirdly, and closely related to agency theory, the New Zealand variant of NPM has a '... strong emphasis on contractual relationships and the language of contract' (ibid., p.xi). In accordance with both agency theory and transaction costs economics, this facilitates the selection of the appropriate modes of production and service delivery from the whole range of market and hierarchical institutional possibilities and allows this choice to be dependent on the nature of the service in question. Boston (ibid.) has summarized this approach as follows:

> One of the key manifestations of this 'contractualism' or 'new contractualism', as it is variously called, has been the introduction of a wide range of contractualist instruments (eg. purchase agreements, performance agreements, ownership agreements, and so on). For instance, in addition to their contracts of employment, departmental heads now have performance agreements with their portfolio ministers. Indeed, performance agreements have become an increasingly common instrument of control and accountability at all levels in public organizations. Similarly, formal contracts of various kinds are now used to govern the relationships between public organizations (eg. between funders and purchasers, purchasers and providers, funders and regulators, and so on). While some of these contracts are legally binding, others are more in the nature of mutual undertakings. Regardless of their legal status, however, the aim of these contracts is to specify as precisely as possible the requirements of the principal and to ensure the agents can be held to account for their performance.

The application of agency theory and its attendant contractualism to public sector activity serves to underline an important dimension of NPM: namely, the clear distinction it draws between the role of the state in policy formulation, implementation and regulation, and the manner in which services are delivered and purchased. In essence, separation of the provision and production of public services distinguishes between the purchaser and provider of government services, or the purchaser–provider split. This serves to demonstrate how agency theory can enhance efficiency when it is used in tandem with the orthodox economic theory of competitive markets. For example, a local authority can contract with private companies to provide, say, refuse collection services. Competitive tendering will invoke cost reducing market forces in the tendering process and carefully written contractual agreements will allow the local authority to monitor performance to ensure satisfactory outcomes. With fixed price contracts, the provider faces powerful incentives to minimize production costs whereas the purchaser must ensure maximum compliance with the terms of the contract. Whiest we have been emphasizing the theoretical antecedents of policy instruments like competitive tendering, it is worth noting that intuitive, pragmatic and other considerations also play a role as Bailey (1995, p.143) has emphasized:

> There is, indeed, an element of pragmatism in seeking to make existing resources go further by improving efficiency. More generally, achieving better value for money requires improved economy efficiency and effectiveness in the provision of public and private sector outputs – the '3 Es'. Economic theory suggests that the most effective ways of promoting the '3 Es' is to stimulate competition, reward enterprise and effort, and give the customer (or service client) more economic power.

Not all commentators are convinced by arguments proclaiming a harmonious congruence between NPM and NIE. For example, in Yeatman's account of the origins of NPM outlined earlier, we saw that she stressed the 'three contemporary dynamics of complexity, uncertainty and democratisation' (1997, p.182). Her version of NPM, which she calls the 'post-bureaucratic model', emphasizes three characteristics of the modern cultural milieu. Firstly, uncertainty and ongoing change mean that managers have to develop a 'tolerance of ambiguity' and are required to 'use their judgement'. Secondly, 'if public managers are to exercise judgement in becoming more proactive, creative, customer-responsive and quality-oriented, then they have to be empowered to develop these capacities and trusted to use them. This means a significant loosening of control within the system and a greater reliance on information giving and receiving through various forms of accountability' (ibid.). Moreover, trust bares an intimate relationship to risk and can be viewed as '...risk management under conditions where risk is a central feature of the system' (ibid., p.183). And thirdly, in order for 'mutual adjustment' between service provider and client to succeed, the capacity for 'judgement and trust' must also be extended to the customer. These features of the post-bureaucratic model are thus non-dualistic and involve mutual dependency in both policy formulation and implementation. On this basis, Yeatman (ibid., p.184) argues that 'it bears emphasis that this model cannot and will not legitimise the current ways of reinventing the old dualism of policy and administration: for example, the dualism of funding and provision; the dualism of steering and rowing or the dualism of principal and agent'.

By contrast, the economic strands of the NPM paradigm, or what Yeatman (ibid.) refers to as the 'economic rationalist model', explicitly embody a dualistic approach with its language of contractualism and principal–agent relationships. Moreover, its rational choice model of human decisionmaking cannot cope with complexity, uncertainty and democratization. It follows that '... to the extent that the post-bureaucratic and economic rationalist models are confused together as they are, the tendency for the economic rationalist model to reinvent and re-emphasise a policy–administration dualism causes the new paradigm to lose visibility and to be poorly understood' (ibid., p.187).

This purported tension between NPM and NIE has been spelt out in some detail by Yeatman. Indeed, she has drawn up a comprehensive table which serves to illustrate what she terms 'contrasting approaches' to NPM under the titles 'post-bureaucratic model' and 'economic rationalist model (public choice and agency theory)' (ibid., p.185). This is reproduced in the form of Figure 4.5.

Aside from whether or not one accepts the sharp dichotomization between Yeatman's two versions of NPM, the contrast she draws does highlight the fact that Hood's (1991, p.516) 'marriage of two different streams of ideas' may not entirely be a match made in heaven! Regardless of the validity of Yeatmans' duality argument, it is hard to deny the 'managerialism' strand of NPM's emphasis on effectiveness does not entirely coincide with the NIE strand's focus on efficiency. However, Yeatman (1997) is clearly wrong on some matters of detail. For instance, her stress in Figure 4.5 on 'economically efficient allocative decision-making' appears confused as to the meaning of economic efficiency and neglects productive efficiency, undoubtedly more important in a public sector environment since allocative decisions are typically taken at the political level and thus represent a *fait accompli* in policy formulation and implementation.

To some extent, Yeatman's distinction between her post-bureaucratic model and an NIE-orientated NPM model represents a conflict of values

Post-bureaucratic model
Orientation to: management for change under conditions of complexity and uncertainty system orientation: open emphasis on: linking efficiency to effectiveness (outcomes focus) accountability to customers mutual adjustment between service provider and customer policy as an emergent strategy – thus, feedback loops between policy conception and implementation → importance of interactive relationship between 'policy' and 'administration' (no dualism) knowing how rather than knowing what: problem-solving in relation to irreducible differences of perspective and change relational mode: consultation who determines policy? (who is the policy-making subject?): the relevant policy community ethical orientation: interactive accountability, trust and risk

Economic rationalist model (public choice and agency theory)
Orientation to: economic efficiency and utility maximisation system orientation: economically efficient allocative decision-making which is rationally (scientifically) informed as far as conditions permit policy as rational choice – thus, decisionistic and intellectualistic policy is decided then it is carried out → policy administration dualism (separation of conception and implementation) knowing what: the basis of rational choice (scientism) relational mode: (within) direction; (without) contract who determines policy? (who is the policy-making subject?): a unitarian decision maker (the government, the CEO; the principal in the principal-agent relationship) ethical orientation: rationally grounded responsibility and control

Figure 4.5 Tensions between the 'post-bureaucratic' and 'economic rationalist' models of NPM
Source: Yeatman (1997, p.185, Figure 2).

rather than a clash over substance. This argument is perhaps best illustrated with reference to Hood's (1991, p.10) 'cluster of administrative values'. Following Harmon and Mayer (1986) and Strange (1988), Hood (1991) and Hood and Jackson (1991) developed a tripartite classification of administrative values: that is, 'sigma-type' values highlight 'economy' and 'parsimony'; 'theta-type' values stress 'honesty' and 'fairness'; and 'lambda-type' values emphasize 'security' and 'resilience'. Figure 4.6 summarizes the content of these three different clusters of values.

Hood (1991, p.12) argues that sigma-type values 'match resources to defined tasks', and examples include 'just-in-time' inventory controls and 'payment-by-results' remuneration systems. By contrast, theta-type values are founded on notions of 'honesty', 'fairness', and 'equity' and are given concrete expression in institutions such as anti-corruption commissions and methods of including public opinion and implementation. On the other hand, lambda-type values stress 'reliability', 'robustness', and 'adaptivity' and reflect traditional public administration's concerns with continuity and security.

Whilst clearly sigma, theta, and lambda values can overlap, like the intersecting circles of Venn diagrams, it seems certain that not all values subsumed under these three headings can coexist simultaneously.

	Sigma-type values KEEP IT LEAN AND PURPOSEFUL	*Theta-type values* KEEP IT HONEST AND FAIR	*Lambda-type values* KEEP IT ROBUST AND RESILIENT
STANDARD OF SUCCESS	*Frugality* (matching of resources to tasks for given goals)	*Rectitude* (achievement of fairness mutuality, the proper discharge of duties)	*Resilience* (achievement of reliability, adaptivity, robustness)
STANDARD OF FAILURE	*Waste* (muddle, confusion, inefficiency)	*Malversation* (unfairness, bias, abuse of office)	*Catastrophe* (risk, breakdown, collapse)
CURRENCY OF SUCCESS AND FAILURE	*Money and time* (resource costs of producers and consumers)	*Trust and entitlements* (consent, legitimacy, due process, political entitlements)	*Security and survival* (confidence, life and limb)
CONTROL EMPHASIS	*Output*	*Process*	*Input/Process*
SLACK	*Low*	*Medium*	*High*
GOALS	*Fixed/Single*	*Incompatible* 'Double bind'	*Emergent/Multiple*
INFORMATION	Costed, segmented (commercial assets)	Structured	Rich exchange, collective asset
COUPLING	*Tight*	*Medium*	*Loose*

Figure 4.6 Hood's three sets of core values in public management
Source: Hood (1991, p.11, Table 2).

For example, '... a central concern with *honesty* and the avoidance of policy distortion in public administration may have different design implications from a central concern with *frugality*, and a central concern with *resilience* may also have different design implication' (ibid., p.15) (original emphasis). A close parallel can be drawn with Yeatman's (1997) post-bureaucratic model's emphasis on 'democratization', and related notions of 'reciprocity' between clients and service providers (which mirror theta-type values), and her 'economic rationalist' model of NPM (which represents sigma-type values). This problem of a relationship between normative values and policy instruments echoes our earlier discussion in this chapter of the constellation of market-orientated values associated with NIE.

Criticisms

NPM and its derivative management techniques have faced vigorous criticism from the onset. Just as it is difficult to define NPM with any degree of precision, so too critiques of the doctrine(s) reflect its ethereal character. Perhaps the most damaging line of attack has been to question the generality or universality of NPM. Various arguments have been advanced in the context. For example, Alford (1993) and others have claimed that while many of the functions of management in the public and private sectors are similar, the context within which management occurs is very different. Accordingly, NPM's emphasis on the generic and portable nature of management is misplaced since the public sector is *sui generis*. Similarly, Hood (1991, p.9) has summarized the normative case against NPM as follows: 'Contrary to NPM's claim to be a public management for all seasons, these critics argue that different administrative values have different implications for fundamental aspects of administrative design – implications which go beyond altering the "settings" of the systems'.

A second line of attack has emphasized the damage the application of NPM has done to traditional bureaucratic structures. Nethercote (1989) has argued that NPM's changes to budgetary procedures have seriously weakened essential competencies in the civil service. In a similar vein, Hood and Jackson (1992) have pointed to a reduced capacity for governments to deal with disasters and catastrophes as a consequence of NPM – inspired reforms.

In much the same way as Yeatman (1997), some critics have underscored the internal incoherence of NPM and inconsistencies between its various ingredients. For example, Hood (1990) has argued that the managerialist emphasis on centralized control and 'top-down' policy implementation is incompatible with the NIE stress on the importance of decentralization and devolution of power in bureaucratic hierarchies.

A somewhat different critique of NPM has stressed its advantages to management as a distinct interest group within bureaucratic structures. Hood (1991, p.9) has described this genre of argument in the following terms: 'The claim is that NPM is a self-serving movement designed to promote the career interest of an elite group of "new managerialists" (top managers and officials in central controlling departments, management consultants and business schools) rather than the mass of public service customers or low-level staff.' Furthermore, Chapter 8 will examine another way of categorizing the criticisms of NPM. It will use Hirschman's (1991) tripartite taxonomy of reactionary rhetoric – the jeopardy, perversity, and futility theses – to indicate both the pattern and direction of argumentation that has emerged in the debate over the implementation of NPM.

4.5   NEW PUBLIC MANAGEMENT AND GOVERNMENT FAILURE

Attempts at public sector reform stemming from a belief in the pervasiveness of government failure which involve NPM at least to some degree are legion. As Peters (1996a, p.21) has observed that:

> [W]hether administrative change is being considered in the most afflu-ent country of Western Europe or the poorest country of Africa the operative assumption appears to be that the best or even the only way to obtain better results from public-sector organizations is to adopt some sort of a market-based mechanism to replace the traditional bureaucracy.

In the developed world, which possesses abundant administrative capacity, reforms have typically been directed towards reducing the size and increasing the efficiency of core national public sectors. For instance, in Britain there has been a vigorous programme of privatization while the civil service has been radically restructured through the 'Next Steps' ini-tiative with many services, formerly provided by public agencies at the central and local government level, being contracted out to private sector suppliers. Similarly, in Australia the Commonwealth Public Service has experienced substantial changes over the period from 1983 to 1993. In Canada, a comprehensive series of changes designed to improve public sector performance has been pursued under the *Public Service 2000* programme. In the United States, the quest for a government that 'works better and costs less' has been assigned a high priority by the Clinton

administration with a new system of performance assessment being introduced throughout the federal government largely as a result of the work of
a National Performance Review taskforce, chaired by Vice-President
Gore. In Italy, a 'global strategy' of reform was launched, which had much
in common with the 'Fewer Civil Servants but a Better Civil Service'
programme in Holland, the French 'Committee on Evaluation', the Greek
'Modernization Programme' and the Irish 'fundamental structure reforms',
to name but a few of the European public sector reform policies (Wright,
1994). But perhaps the most far-reaching and comprehensive programme
of governmental reforms has been pursued in New Zealand. This reform
programme has been marked by the 'conceptual rigour and theoretical
conherence' of the model of public management which emerged from it,
and the series of reforms implemented between the mid-1980s and early
1990s were not just *ad hoc* responses to perceived problems but formed
part of 'a carefully crafted, integrated and mutually reinforcing reform
agenda' (Boston *et al.*, 1996, p.3). The similarities in the public sector
reform programmes followed in these countries, with their typical mix of
commercialization, corporatization, privatization, deregulation of public
sector management, devolution of management responsibility, performance monitoring and contracting-out, clearly all draw on NPM, although
controversy surrounds the extent to which NPM influenced policymakers.
For example, Hood (1996, p.270) has argued that while many commentators '... speak of a global revolution in the adoption of NPM ... even from
casual observation, it is clear that some countries have laid more emphasis
on these ideas than others and that NPM styles have varied even within the
same "family groups" of countries'.

Despite national differences in the nature of public sector reform
programmes, a number of common themes can be recognized (see, for
instance, Halligan, 1996; Nutley and Osborne, 1994; Perry, 1996; Ranson
and Stewart, 1994). Wright has argued that it is possible to identify seven
'interconnected levels' in reform initiatives. First, there appears to be a
'reduction in the size, resources and scope and direct leverage of the
national public sector' (1994, p.110). Second, attempts have been made to
improve the 'monitoring capacity' of civil service systems by budgetary,
planning and evaluation reforms. Third, efforts have been made to enhance
the management of the public sector using standard NPM techniques like
regulation, fragmentation, competition, 'hands-on' management, performance measurement, output orientation, privatization, parsimony, and
'customerization'. Fourth, reform programmes systematically dismantled
the 'traditional statutory framework for civil servants' based on factors
like permanence and tenure. Fifth, attempts to achieve a 'democratization'

of the public sector through greater public consultation have been made. Six, efforts have been made to render the public sector more 'user-friendly' by means of greater accountability, responsiveness and visibility. Seven, emphasis has fallen on restructuring and reorganizing the public sector in an effort to streamline its activities. Finally, reformers have sought to 'transform the culture' of civil services by inducing an 'entrepreneurial' focus and conceiving of service recipients as 'customers'.

Advocates of NPM have been able to legitimate these reforms as a response to the problems of government failure. Perhaps the best way to appreciate this line of argument is to employ Wolf's (1989) 'attributes of nonmarket supply' as a convenient illustrative heuristic device. As we saw in Chapter 3, Wolf (1989, pp.51–5) identified four basic characteristics of nonmarket supply. Firstly, he argued that 'nonmarket outputs are often hard to define in principle, ill-defined in practice, and extremely difficult to measure as to quantity or to evaluate as to quality' (ibid., p.51). Inputs are thus used as a proxy measure for output. Secondly, Wolf maintained that nonmarket outputs are typically provided by a single monopolistic public agency. The resultant lack of competition makes any meaningful estimates of economic efficiency difficult. Thirdly, Wolf (ibid., p.52) observed that the 'technology of producing nonmarket outputs is frequently unknown or, if known, is associated with considerable uncertainty and ambiguity', and accordingly may worsen economic inefficiencies. Finally, Wolf argued that nonmarket productive activity often lacks any 'bottom-line' evaluation mechanism equivalent to profit or loss for appraising success. Moreover, there is usually no specified procedure for terminating unsuccessful production analogous to bankruptcies in the private sector.

NPM can be viewed as a means of removing, or at least mitigating, the effects of each of these attributes of nonmarket supply identified by Wolf (1989). In the first place, the difficulties associated with defining, evaluating and monitoring the output of public agencies can be reduced as a result of the organizational restructuring pursued under NPM. NPM has sought to break up large-scale bureaucratic structures into manageable units dealing with one another on an 'arms-length' basis with each focused on achieving clearly defined single objectives and producing specified 'outputs'. Over the course of restructuring, attention has focused on separating commercial from non-commercial functions, policy advice from policy implementation, and the provision from the centralized purchasing of public services. The underlying rationale holds that the closer public agencies approach 'the ideal of single-objective, trackable and manageable units' (Hood, 1991, p.12), the easier it is to match resources to defined tasks and to shift from controlling the input to monitoring the output of these organizations. The restructuring of the public sector has made it possible to assign the responsibility for managing these units to named persons. Disaggregation has thus become compatible with the development of managerial responsibility. It has also been accompanied by the development of output-based accounting systems which make intensive use of information technology. This has made it feasible to use quantifiable output indicators and targets to monitor the performance of public agencies and to hold their managers accountable for this performance. At the same time, reformers have sought to give public sector managers greater 'freedom to manage'. They have typically been given greater discretion over the hiring and remuneration of staff subject to the constraint of a 'one-line' budgetary allocation. They have been actively encouraged to apply private sector management techniques, such as the use of short-term labour contracts, the formulation of mission statements and corporate plans, the development of new management information systems, and the greater use of public relations techniques. The logic of the shift from *ex ante* input controls to *ex post* output monitoring has probably been carried furthest in New Zealand where, under the State Sector Act of 1988 and the Public Finance Act of 1989, the chief executives (CEs) of government departments are employed on five-year contracts with performance-linked remuneration packages and a requirement to negotiate annual performance agreements with their portfolio ministers. These agreements specify the output of the government department concerned. The performance of the CE in managing the delivery of this output by their department is independently monitored by the State Services Commission.

Organizational restructuring in the public sector has made it possible to mitigate the noncontestability of government supply which Wolf (1989) identified as the second attribute of nonmarket production. Thus, even in the case of those public services which cannot be contracted out, it has been possible to create an internal or quasi-market for these services within the public sector. One way of doing this has been through the separation of the purchasing and provision of public services. Accordingly, the health sector reforms introduced in New Zealand in 1992, which closely mirrored those implemented under the Thatcher government in the UK, involved the establishment of 'regional health authorities' (RHAs) to purchase the health services provided both by state-owned 'crown health enterprises' (CHEs) and other private health organizations. This set up a framework whereby a number of CHEs could compete not only with each other but also with other private bodies to provide clearly specified outputs to the relevant RHA. The introduction of competition into the health sector was specifically designed to provide the managers of health enterprises with incentives to cut costs and improve the efficiency and competitiveness of their organizations.

The shift toward a system of output monitoring in the public sector would also help mitigate the problems associated with the uncertain or ambiguous technology which Wolf (1989) identified as the third attribute of nonmarket supply. Again reference can be made to the New Zealand case where considerable emphasis has been placed on the distinction between 'inputs', 'outputs' and 'outcomes'. Thus, while the CEs of government departments have the freedom and responsibility to look for greater efficiencies in combining inputs to produce clearly defined outputs, the responsibility for using these outputs to generate socially desired 'outcomes' rests with their portfolio ministers. These ministers therefore have an incentive to develop the policymaking capacity of their advisory staff so that they have a clearer understanding of the relationships between agency outputs and social outcomes.

Finally, NPM has sought to address the problems associated with the lack of bottom line and termination mechanisms by establishing a framework within which the supply of management to the public sector can be made more contestable. This reflects the influence on NPM of the 'managerialist' notion of 'professional management expertise as portable, paramount over technical expertise, requiring high discretionary power to achieve results ("free to manage"), and central and indispensable to better organizational performance' (Hood, 1991, p.6). If organizational performance is linked to management expertise, and if the latter is viewed as a generic, portable skill, then it follows that no specific asset will be lost if the manager of a poorly performing agency is replaced. The shift to fixed-term contracts among CEs in New Zealand can be seen as an attempt to make the management of public agencies more contestable.

4.6   CONCLUDING REMARKS

The NPM paradigm, representing as it does a somewhat uneasy combination of neoclassical economics, NIE and managerialism, can thus be seen as a policy instrument specifically designed to deal with the kinds of government failure identified in the literature reviewed in Chapter 3. The essence of the NPM approach to public sector reform has been summarized by Peters (1996b, p.25) as follows:

It tends to consider public sector agencies as facing the same managerial and service delivery tasks as would organizations in the private sector, and it sees those agencies as being amenable to the same techniques for performing those tasks. It assumes that if the rule-based authority structure usually associated with bureaucracy is removed or deemphasized, then the creative and administrative talent of individuals working within the public sector will flower. Although usually associated with the political right, some devotees of this approach consider that its successful implementation would result in a more effective and efficient public sector, whether delivering defense or social services.

Although public sector reform programmes embody these elements to a greater and lesser degree among the OECD countries, a common feature of many of these reform initiatives is the radical nature of the prescriptions they advocate. The fact that many of these radical reforms have actually been implemented represents a puzzling aspect of public sector reform, given the obvious difficulties inherent in the application of sweeping changes to the basic institutional structures of representative democracies, especially in the light of the previous glacial rate of transformation of civil service systems in earlier periods. This puzzle will be taken up in Chapter 5.

5 The Political Economy of Paradigmatic Policy Change

5.1 INTRODUCTION

Chapters 2 and 3 traced developments within those streams of economic theory which are centrally concerned with ascertaining an appropriate role for government in a mixed market economy. Chapter 2 examined how welfare economics can provide a rationale for an incremental interventionism by governments seeking to correct various sources of market failure. It also considered the grounds for a growing scepticism about the capacity of governments to effectively perform this role. This scepticism has been reinforced by both positive and normative theories of government failure of the type examined in Chapter 3. Chapter 4 then considered the contribution those literatures that have made to the 'New Public Management' (NPM) and focused on the extent to which the public sector reforms associated with this approach can be viewed as solutions to problems of government failure.

The policy scepticism inherent in theories of government failure would be expected to influence not only the *type* of reforms proposed but the *way* in which these reform are implemented. More specifically, a sceptical theoretical perspective would be anticipated to lead to a more cautious, conservative approach to the formulation, implementation and evaluation of actual reforms in practice. This was certainly expected by many of the leading writers on government failure. They appear to take the view that the old certainties about the effectiveness of governments and markets in resolving social problems are likely to give way to a less rigid and more pragmatic approach to policymaking in which 'the actual choice is some compromise between imperfect markets and imperfect governments' (Wolf, 1989, p.11). According to this view, both the formulation of reform proposals and the evaluation of extant reforms are likely to be more cautious and careful when they are based on a balanced evaluation of both market and government failure.

It is thus somewhat surprising to find that the shift from a market failure to a government failure paradigm has in many countries produced radical and discontinuous changes in economic policy. This is vividly illustrated by the public sector reforms introduced in New Zealand. The New Zealand Treasury's post-election briefing paper to the Labour government in 1987 (cryptically entitled 'Government Management') provided the blueprint for subsequent public sector reforms legislated for in the State Sector Act of 1988 and Public Finance Act of 1989. This briefing paper explicitly advocated a comparative institutions approach to determining the appropriate level of government intervention in the economy. It also fully endorsed a more sceptical perspective on government intervention and the theories of government failure which have tended to shape this perspective. Yet far from producing a more conservative approach to policy-making, this document set the stage for a public sector reform process that has impressed supporters and critics alike, in both New Zealand and abroad, with its bold radicalism.

Allen Schick, an American scholar of public policy who was commissioned by the New Zealand Treasury and State Services Commission in 1996 to write a report on these public management reforms, has been immensely impressed by the bold, innovative and radical way in which they were formulated and implemented. In his view the reforms were not just 'enormous, ambitious, and, in large part, unprecedented anywhere in the world' but 'half a dozen years later' they have wrought a 'transformation of the State sector from centralised control of money, personnel and other resources to devolved arrangements that give managers control of inputs, provide them with incentives to be productive, and hold them accountable for results' which Schick (1996, p.2) describes as 'extraordinary'. What strikes Schick (ibid.) is that this revolution in public management has been achieved 'without going through the protracted pilot testing and cautious implementation that have slowed innovation in other countries'.

These public sector reforms were advanced in parallel with the (by now very familiar) processes of 'liberalization' and 'stabilization'. 'Liberalization' is usually taken to mean the whole range of microeconomic reforms designed to open and free up goods, financial and labour markets. 'Stabilization' can be taken to refer to macroeconomic policies which seek to reduce public debt in relation to GDP and control inflation. Like 'privatization'; or the sale of state-owned enterprises; these reform processes – sometimes referred to as the Washington consensus – essentially limit the scope for government failure in forms such as rent seeking, agency capture, bureaucratic empire-building and short-term political interference in the setting of monetary and fiscal policy. They complement the process of 'commercialization', or 'the application of business principles to the public sector (or a particular public sector activity)' (Easton, 1997, pp.25–6) – which aims to reduce government failure in the residual areas of government activity. A comprehensive reform programme (CRP) which encompasses liberalization, stabilization, privatization and commercialization (LSPC) can thus be viewed as a concerted attack on pervasive problems of government failure.

In New Zealand these reform processes were advanced through a series of 'policy blitzkreigs' that were launched during the period from 1984 to 1991 and spanned the tenure of a 'centre-left' Labour government (from 1984 to 1990) and a centre-right National government (after 1990). They were launched in the areas of financial deregulation, tariff liberalization and removal of agricultural subsidies in 1984, tax and state-owned enterprise reform in 1986, the management of government departments in 1988 and of the public health sector in 1991, and in the targeting of social welfare assistance and labour market deregulation in 1991. In each case, 'the lightning strike involved a policy goal radically different from the existing configuration, to be attained in a short period, following a surprise announcement and a very rapid implementation' (Easton 1994, p.215).

In some countries, especially in Latin America and Eastern Europe, the approach to implementing CRPs has been even more radical. In particular, governments elected during the economic chaos which follows a hyper-inflationary debt crisis or the time 'extraordinary politics' (Balcerowicz, 1994) which marks the transition from authoritarian to democratic rule, have taken advantage of the window of opportunity created by these conditions to push reform processes through to their logical destination in one 'big bang'.

The task of explaining the radicalism of the reform processes which have been directed toward limiting and reducing the problems of government failure has thus emerged as a significant puzzle for both economists and political scientists. In a recent survey of the political economy of policy reform, Rodrik (1996, p.10) has suggested that the main issue confronting the contributors to this literature relates to the following question:

Why are so many governments reforming now, after decades of adherence to policies of the opposite kind? This question poses a particularly important challenge to political economists: an understanding of these countries experiences now requires a theory that explains why seemingly dysfunctional policies had been mutually undertaken and then maintained for so long, but also why these policies were suddenly abandoned en masse during the 1980's often by the same politicians who had been among their most ardent supporters.

This issue clearly relates to the 'punctuated equilibrium' pattern the reform processes have been observed to follow in many countries. Gersick (1991) has observed that this pattern tends to typify the process of a paradigm shift in a range of different environments. In the context of policy-making, a punctuated equilibrium pattern would be observed when long periods of stability involving incremental adaptations to policy alternate with brief periods of 'qualitative, metamororphic change' or revolutionary upheaval. According to Hall (1993) a shift in policy paradigms will be reflected in a 'third order' change in the hierarchy of policy goals and the overarching terms of policy discourse. This order of policy change can be distinguished from a 'second order' change in policy instruments and a 'first order' adjustment in the settings of these instruments.

Quite clearly, then, the model of political economy of paradigmatic policy change which is advanced in this chapter will first have to explain the prolonged stability of reigning policy paradigms before examining the process of transition from one policy paradigm to another. This process will be illustrated with reference to the shift from an interventionist policy paradigm that focused on problems of market failure to one which seeks to advance LSPC processes in response to pervasive problems of government failure. Before this can be done, though, it is necessary to consider the distinctive role which expert policy advisers, operating within the boundaries of the state, can play in policy processes.

This chapter itself is divided into five main areas. Section 2 examines the role of policy advisers in policy formulation and implementation. Section 3 focuses on the political and other risks an incumbent government must face when they embrace policy reforms and the associated phenomenon of policy stability through time. The relationship between bureaucratic 'control agencies' and paradigmatic policy changes is dealt with in section 4, whereas section 5 discusses the role of 'leadership networks' in radical reform programmes. The chapter ends with some brief concluding remarks in section 6.

5.2   POLICY ADVISERS AND THE POLICY PROCESS

Although in a representative democracy, unelected policy advisers cannot make final policy decisions, they are often in a position to exercise considerable influence over the policy process. This seems to be particularly true of senior advisers working within central control agencies, like the Treasury and the Department of Finance in the Australian political milieu.

A striking case of this is provided by the New Zealand Treasury. The influential position of officials in this institution appears to arise not only because its official function of being the controller of the government's finances places it at the 'centre of the administration' so that 'its financial decisions and recommendations pervade every aspect of government activity' (Polaschek, 1958, p.252). It also exists because the Treasury is formally required to comment on all departmental submissions to the Cabinet which have economic implications. Since virtually every proposal presented to the Cabinet has some economic implications, this rule has allowed the Treasury to have the 'first word' in many Cabinet-level debates. This, in turn, has meant that the onus of making a particularly strong case is placed on any minister or department which presents a proposal without Treasury endorsement. Moreover, while the Cabinet receives advice from other sources on economic issues, only the Treasury has a comprehensive reporting role and maintains an interest in policy matters across the whole spectrum of government activity. The New Zealand Treasury thus differs from its counterparts in many other countries, including the United States, the United Kingdom and Australia in that its advice is not routinely contested by equally powerful bureaucratic rivals. Extensive reference to this institution will be made in this chapter since it provides an unambiguous example of a control agency that is able to influence the direction of policy development through its policy advice.

By and large, theories of government failure neglect the significant differences that can often be observed between 'technocrats' (defined by Williamson (1994, p.1) as 'those who advocate the organization and management of a country's industrial resources by technical experts for the good of the whole community') in control agencies and 'bureaucrats' in spending departments. The former often seem to be more motivated to contain spending across departments than to engage in empire-building budget expansion within departments. This may be because they are typically subject to at least part of the blame for budgetary 'blowouts' and for the failure of governments to sustain prudent fiscal policies. Moreover, the relationship between policy advisers within these control agencies and elected officials appears to be a special type of generic agent–principal relationships.

The Fiduciary Relationship Between Politicians and their Advisers

Martin (1991) has suggested that the fiduciary relationship between governing politicians and their policy advisers can be likened most closely to that between a barrister and client. While information assymetries characterize this relationship, in the sense that policy advisers often have more experience and expertise than their political principals, they are typically constrained from engaging in any short term, opportunistic exploitation of these assymetries by their need to retain the trust of these principals.

The relationship is thus essentially fiduciary. Technocrats can no longer function as advisers to elected politicians if these politicians withdraw their trust from them.

The trust which politicians place in their senior advisers will be based on more than their presumed loyalty. It will primarily be based on an expectation that the advisers can be relied upon to act in an appropriate way and that they will fulfil their professional obligations to provided free, frank and expert advice to whatever government holds office. March and Olsen have suggested that the behaviour of the expert policy advisers who represent an institution such as the Treasury will come closer to that expected of *homo sociolus* than *homo economicus*. Their behaviour is more likely to be governed by a 'logic of appropriateness associated with obligatory action' than by a 'logic of consequentiality associated with anticipatory choice' (1989, p.23). This is because an institution like the Treasury is highly dependent on the trust placed in it by the recipients of its services and this trust is based on a confidence that it will act according to a shared understanding of what is appropriate.

This understanding will operate at a number of levels. At the deepest level, it is an understanding of the appropriate role of the state in a mixed economy and therefore of the appropriate direction for any new policy initiative. In the case of the Treasury this understanding provides the framework within which it can come to an apprecaition of what functions it is appropriate to perform within the system of government and what role is appropriate for it to play within the policy process. This understanding will, of course, come from a shared 'paradigm'; that is, the common epistemological vision and value consensus of a knowledge-based community (Kuhn, 1962).

The Market Failure Paradigm and the Treasury's Reactive Control Role

Like similar institutions, particularly in English-speaking nations, the New Zealand Treasury appears to have operated within a market failure paradigm right up until the early 1980s. As Chapter 2 argued, the intellectual authority for this paradigm derives from its roots in conventional welfare economics. It should be pointed out, though, that the policy advisers who choose to work within a particular paradigm often play a significant 'brokering' role in distilling from it principles to guide the formulation of policy proposals and rules to guide their evaluation. This means that they typically screen out some of the subtleties, reservations and ambiguities that characterize the theories they draw upon. They do this to 'package' their advice in a way that satisfies the taste for certainty of politicians who 'being under pressure to act decisively and dramatically, will naturally be impatient with any manifestation of the philosophic doubts which plague economists and will risk making strong assumptions about the efficacy of the policy instruments which have been assigned to their control' (Peacock, 1979, p.231). Accordingly, despite the acknowledgement in normative economics prior to the 1970s of some of the second best and government failure problems associated with incremental interventionism, the dominant economic policy paradigm which institutions like the Treasury constructed from it, ensured that the focus of the policy process was firmly on problems of market failure.

The appropriate advisory role for a control agency such as the Treasury within a policy process that was primarily focused on the generation of solutions to problems of market failure came to be one of reactive control rather than of proactive leadership. Solutions to various problems of market failure would be generated outside the Treasury by various other participants in the policy process while the appropriate role for this institution was to ensure that the consequences of implementing these proposals were adequately considered. It should be clear, then, how it would be considered appropriate that the Treasury should provide a report on all proposals with economic implications. By performing this function, the Treasury could provide an institutional check against the propensity of activist elected representatives, with a short time horizon, to generate solutions to problems without adequate consideration of the costs of implementing them (Wolf, 1979a). In fulfilling this obligation Treasury officials acquired the reputation of being the 'abominable no-men' (Easton, 1997, p.99). However, someone, somewhere in the system, needed to be able to say 'no' and so it seemed entirely appropriate that as 'watchdogs of the public purse', the Treasury officials should undertake this responsibility.

These officials needed to be governed by a cluster of rules and to understand which rules were appropriate to particular situations so that they could act in a mutually consistent way in fulfilling their control functions. To the extent that they could be seen to be following rules which defined appropriate actions in particular situations, they would reinforce and strengthen the trust placed in them, and the institution they represented, by other participants in the policy process.

The Rules of Policy Evaluation

During the 1970s the rules which Treasury officials applied, wherever they could, to screen policy proposals generated outside this institution were derived from the techniques of cost–benefit analysis (Easton, 1997). These rules not only specified a consistent methodology for calculating cost and benefit streams, but also required that a real discount rate of ten per cent be applied in all cases. The application of this technique was nevertheless limited by quantification difficulties which could vary from proposal to proposal. Treasury officials still needed to follow additional rules to ensure that they exercised their judgement in an appropriate way. These rules appear to have been bounded by familiar 'Whitehall' style norms which oblige 'public servants' to provide 'free and frank advice' in the 'public interest' through a balanced assessment of the values, obligations and interests affected by the situation. Martin (1991, pp.382–3) provided the following summation of what the determination of the public interest in a particular situation involves:

> The public interest is a useful shorthand for a set of important process considerations. These can be reflected in a checklist of things to be taken into account in relation to any policy issue, viz:
> – regard for the law,
> – regard for the principles of natural justice,
> – consideration of the long as well as the short term,
> – acknowledgement of previous commitments,
> – avoidance of both the substance and appearance of personal or agency interest.

Within the boundaries supplied by these norms, Treasury officials still had to draw on what Easton (1997, p.86) calls the 'collective memory' of the institution which is 'physically embodied in its files and archives, in the learned studies which it commissions or encourages, and in the individual memories of the officials (which are in turn reinforced by maintaining informal contacts with retired officials, with think-tanks, and with people with expertise outside the ministry'. This collective memory would develop through an incrementalist process of precedent accretion. Even where situations arise for which no precedent has been established, there is nonetheless likely to have been some history of discussion about the issues relevant to these situations which can be drawn on to develop new precedents.

Through its understanding of the appropriateness of its own control functions, through the rules and traditional norms which governed the behaviour of its officials, and through the collective memory which they could draw on in exercising their judgements, the Treasury had thus established a stable and trusted identity in the policy community. The advice given by its officials could be trusted by policymakers since it emerged from a framework of rules which provided an adequate assurance that it was not only competent in its application of reputable techniques such as cost–benefit analysis, but also reliable in its provision of the information about costs, consequences and likely trade-offs between conflicting goals and values that is needed to make balanced policy decisions.

A Traditional Bias Toward Incrementalism

There is likely to be a significant risk for those expert policy advisers who operate within the boundaries of the state to shift outside the framework of a dominant policy paradigm. While they may engage, at least to some degree, in policy learning, this is mainly likely to induce them to recommend first and second order policy changes. They will be more averse to recommending third order (or paradigmatic) policy changes since these could transform their own role in a way which could potentially jeopardise the relationships of trust they have established with other participants in the policy process. However, it is not just policy advisers who may be averse to the risk of paradigm-shifting policy change. The significant risk factors incumbent governments must take into account before they engage in radical economic policy reform must also be considered.

5.3   THE POLITICAL RISKS TO PARADIGMATIC POLICY CHANGE

It is somewhat ironic that while public choice theory helped shape the government failure paradigm which provided the rationale for LSPC reform processes, it certainly did not predict that these radical and comprehensive reform programmes would be undertaken. This blemish on the predictive record of public choice theory has been seized on by some of its critics. For example, Boston (1991, p.14) has observed that:

> The policies of liberalization and deregulation pursued by OECD countries during the 1980s run counter to the predictions of public choice models (which assume that it is in the electoral interests of politicians to promote tight regulations). Nor does a public choice perspective readily explain New Zealand's bureaucratic revolution (i.e. it is doubtful whether the reforms were solely or even primarily the product of self-interested politicians, advised by self-interested bureaucrats, seeking to please a self-interested electorate by self-interested means). (p.14)

However, public choice theory may be drawn on to assist in explaining the long period of paradigm stability which typically preceded these reforms in terms of the high political risk that is often associated with paradigmatic policy change. The models of representative democracy formulated by Anthony Downs (1957) may be particularly insightful in this regard.

The Downsian Consensus

For example, Downs (1957) argued that if voter preferences on every issue are normally distributed across the ideological spectrum, then in a two-party electoral competition, party policy positions will converge. This is because both parties can maximize their votes by advocating policies which appeal to 'median voters'. This model appeared to help explain the consensual politics which many countries experienced from 1945 to the late 1970s. However, it did not account for the breakdown in consensual politics which occurred in countries like the UK and the US after this period.

This anomaly could be resolved if it is argued that the centrist position around which voter preferences can be normally distributed will itself be established with reference to a dominant policy paradigm. Governing parties will be reluctant to adopt radical policy changes since this could open up an ideological gap between themselves and the opposition party so that at least half of the 'moderate' voters who occupy this middle ground could vote for the opposition parties at the next election. Radical policy changes will therefore only be pursued if they are derived from a new policy paradigm which is expected to define a new centrist position around which a new consensus can be formed.

The Coalition of Minorities

Downs (1957) also proposed that if minority groups of voters have intense preferences in respect of single issues, then political parties may employ logrolling tactics by supporting sufficient single issues in their platforms to enable them to be elected by a 'coalition of minorities'. The phenomenon of logrolling is described in detail in Chapter 3. A special case of this phenomenon has been discussed in the debate on the political economy of policy reform. Some writers ascribe delays in the implementation of comprehensive reform programmes (CRPs) to the 'political gridlock' formed by 'veto groups' which stand to lose from the reforms.

The presumption made in these arguments is that a CRP constitutes 'good economics' in the sense that, in present value terms, the social benefits of reform exceed its social costs. The reforms can therefore be viewed as being analogous to 'an investment that should ultimately benefit the majority by enough to make them happy that they made it, but that in the short run will – like all investments – involve sacrifices' (Williamson, 1994, p.560). However, since the benefits of these reforms usually accrue over the long term while the costs are mainly incurred in the short run, the failure of governments to implement these reforms may be attributed to the myopic behavior of the main participants in the policy process. Along these lines Rodrik (1996, p.10) has observed that:

> Good economics does often turn out to be good politics, but only eventually. Policies that work do become popular, but the time lag can be long enough for the relationship not to be exploitable by would-be reformers. Conversely, bad economics can be popular, if only temporarily.

However, Rodrik (ibid., p.25) also does concede that to presume myopia is to depart in an *ad hoc* fashion from the standard neoclassical assumption that political agents are 'rational and forward-looking, with expectations that are consistent with the underlying properties of the model'.

This presumption of rationality does not have to be dispensed with if the political risks of comprehensive policy reform are related to the way its benefits and costs are distributed across groups. Thus, if the costs of a CRP are typically concentrated upon identifiable groups while the benefits are more diffusely distributed, then parties opposing the reform may be able to form an election-winning coalition of minorities from groups representing the identifiable losers.

Moreover, in his book *The Logic of Collective Action*, Mancur Olson (1965) suggested that groups representing sectional interests in government subsidies or regulations would acquire a political influence out of proportion to their potential membership. This is because their relatively small size and/or geographic concentration would allow their members to interact in a way that could overcome the free-rider problems that prevented collective action being undertaken on behalf of economy-wide interests such as those of taxpayers and consumers. Would-be reformers are thus likely to encounter strong resistance from sectional interest groups, particularly if they have been able to sustain a stable membership and develop a long term relationship with government agencies and (in some countries like the United States) the relevant legislative committees, creating 'iron triangles' committed to the growth of sectional interest budgets or regulation.

These 'iron triangles' can effectively resist the implementation of a CRP by building alliances through 'vote-trading' with other sectional groups which have an interest in blocking the removal of the subsidies or regulations which benefit them. Logrolling between these sectional interest groups can establish an election-winning 'coalition of minorities' which can block the initial advance of CRP even if it can be shown to benefit the majority of the population. Dunleavy (1991, p.42) has made the argument as follows:

> Unlike other forms of alliance-building, minimum winning coalitions should be stable ... Alliances between groups become more stable as they bargain over successive rounds of decisions. The longer a liberal democracy lasts undisturbed, the more the interest group universe settles into a fixed pattern of mobilisations and alliances'.

Ex Ante Uncertainty About the Identity of Winners and Losers

The political position of coalitions of identifiable losers from CRPs is likely to be strenghthened by the likelihood that, outside of these groups, there should be significant numbers of other voters who experience *ex ante* uncertainty about whether they will be net winners or losers from the reforms. In a series of papers, Rodrik and his collaborators (Rodrik, 1995, 1996; Fernandez and Rodrik, 1991) have demonstrated the possibility that a democratic majority in favour of reforms that are expected to benefit the majority may never form. The crucial assumption made in Rodrik's model is that *ex ante* uncertainty exists among some members of society as to the potential distribution of the benefits and costs of a CRP, *ex post*. This uncertainty does not have to be universal. It is only necessary for some (median voter) individuals, who are risk neutral, to feel uncertain as to whether they will be winners or losers in an *ex post* sense.

Given this assumption, it is easy to construct examples to show that a CRP will fail to secure an electoral majority if a relatively small cluster of individuals are uncertain about whether they will be in the group of 'winners' once the package is introduced. For example, suppose in a democratic economy with 100 voters, a CRP will increase the incomes of 51 voters by $10 each and decrease the incomes of the remaining 49 voters by $5 each so that the net social gain is $265. However, if 49 voters are unsure about their *ex post* position then, since only two of this latter group can join the winners, the net expected per capita benefits of reform for these uncertain voters will be $20(2 \times 10) - $245(49 \times 5)/51 = [$4.41]$, so that they will vote against the reform and block its introduction.

The problem of *ex ante* uncertainty described by Rodrik is likely to surround worker expectations about the consequences for them personally of the organizational restructuring and downsizing which seems to inevitably follow the greater exposure of more sheltered sectors of an economy to international competition. While they may anticipate that a CRP may produce a more dynamic economy which creates more jobs than it destroys, they will be nonetheless uncertain about the security of their own jobs and their capacity to move to new jobs. They may thus side with a coalition of minorities which stands opposed to the reforms.

Significant political risks are likely to attend radical reform. These include the potential vote loss associated with moving away from a centrist ideological position, the opposition of well-organized minorities and the support these coalitions may enjoy from voters who are simply uncertain about whether they will benefit or lose from the reforms. When these risks are added to the institutional risks facing technocrats who define their role in a policy process and the rules to govern their behaviour in terms of a dominant policy paradigm, then it is unsurprising that many countries experience long periods of paradigm stability in which policy changes are largely incremental in nature. What are the conditions, then, under which policymakers shift from one policy paradigm to another and seek to radically reconstruct policy according to principles derived from the new paradigm?

5.4   CONTROL AGENCIES AND PARADIGMATIC POLICY CHANGE

The shift from Keynesian demand management and import-substituting industrialization to a policy paradigm from which the LSPC principles can be derived exemplifies what Hall (1993) terms 'third order policy change'. Hall has suggested that this type of shift will be a process that goes through a number of distinct stages. These are shown in Table 5.1.

During the first stage, the authority of the reigning policy paradigm is gradually eroded by the accumulation of 'anomalies' and the resort by policymakers to 'ad hoc experimentation' that stretches its coherence. The most striking anomaly with a paradigm that came to be associated with piecemeal, incremental interventions to correct instances of 'market failure' was that it neglected the potential for government failure created by these interventions. The growth of governments beyond their financial and regulatory capacity and the resulting problems of pervasive price distortions, inflation, fiscal stress and, in some cases, debt crisis has been attributed, at least in part, to this anomaly. Moreover, the coherence of an interventionist paradigm can clearly be stretched in cases where new

Table 5.1   The stages of paradigm shift

Stages	Characteristics
1. Erosion of authority	Anomalies accumulate and efforts are made to stretch the reigning paradigm to account for them.
2. Fragmentation of authority	Puzzlement and confusion prevails as a number of incommensurable paradigms are proposed as alternatives to the existing paradigm.
3. Institutionalization of a new paradigm	The advocates of a new paradigm secure positions of authority and alter existing organization and decision-making arrangments in order to institutionalize the new paradigm.

forms of state intervention are introduced to correct the problems and distortions associated with existing interventions. The 'theory of second best' (Lipsey and Lancaster, 1956) highlighted the problems with piecemeal interventionism by analyzing the conditions under which a piecemeal correction of an instance of market failure may move an economy, in which such imperfections occur in more than one sector, even further away from a constrained global optimum.

The breakdown and erosion of authority of the old paradigm is likely to eventually lead to a second stage of 'fragmentation' during which policy participants engage in an active search for alternatives. As Gersick (1991) has pointed out, emotional discomfort, uncertainty and puzzlement are likely to be experienced by many of these agents during this phase. Moreover, as Hall (1993) has argued the sense of 'puzzlement at the top' is likely to exacerbated by the incommensurability of the different paradigms that are pushed forward for consideration. He writes that

> Paradigms are by definition never fully commensurable in scientific or technical terms. Because each paradigm contains its own account of how the world facing policymakers operates and each account is different, it is often impossible for the advocates of different paradigms to agree on a common body of data against which a technical judgment in favor of one paradigm over another might be made (p.280).

Those policymakers who are genuinely puzzled may thus be predisposed, at these times, to look for leadership from radical reformers who advocate the reconstruction of public policy on the basis of a new paradigm provided that this paradigm is both coherent and authoritative.

The policy paradigm that is associated with the advancement of LSPC principles would seem to exhibit both these characteristics. Its coherence derives from the way it seeks to limit and reduce government failure through a radical reform programme which advances these principles. Its authority is buttressed by the strong advocacy of these processes by institutions such as the IMF, the World Bank and the OECD. The implicit threat that reforms which advance these processes could be required as a condition for receiving aid from these institutions only serves to reinforce this authority. The policy leadership that is required to reshape economic policy according to this new paradigm must, however, be derived from domestic sources. Their collective task will be completed during the third stage when a new dominant paradigm is institutionalized so that it is embodied in the rules and operating routines of the control agencies and forms the locus around which a new policy consensus can be forged.

Treasury Leadership in the UK and New Zealand

The New Zealand experience is once again instructive in this regard since it indicates the typical sources from which this leadership may be forthcoming. Many commentators on the 'New Zealand experiment' have highlighted the Treasury as being a particularly significant source of leadership for this reform programme. In this regard the New Zealand experience differs from that of the United Kingdom.

Hall (ibid., p.285) argues that with the breakdown of a Keynesian policy paradigm in Britain in the mid-1970s the 'locus of authority' over macroeconomic issues began to shift way from its Treasury which 'hitherto ... had enjoyed a virtual monopoly over such matters'. The shift from Keynesianism to monetarism was led by a faction within the Conservative party whose cause was championed by a section of the British media. They were able to assume leadership of the Conservative party and when the Thatcher government took office in 1979, they were then able to institutionalize the monetrist paradigm. Margaret Thatcher, herself, played a key role in this regard (ibid., p.287):

> She packed the influential economic committees of the cabinet with its supporters, appointed an outside monetarist to be chief economic advisor at the Treasury, and in conjunction with a few advisers, virtually dictated the outlines of macroeconomic policy for several years. The locus of authority over policymaking in the period shifted dramatically towards the prime minister. Over time, an aggressive policy of promoting civil servants who were highly pliable or sympathetic to monetarist views

implanted the new paradigm even more firmly…. It was not civil servants or policy experts engaged by the government, but politicians and the media, who played the pre-eminent role in this process of policy change. The vast majority of government economists were virtually as Keynesian in 1979 as they had been in 1970. The monetarist assault was led by influential journalists, such as William Rees-Mogg and Samuel Brittan, and key politicians like Margaret Thatcher and Sir Keith Joseph, who persuaded others of the advantages of their cause and virtually forced the Whitehall machine to alter its mode of macreconomic policymaking…

A group of senior officials in the New Zealand Treasury appeared to have absorbed lessons from the British experience and sought in early 1980s to pre-empt a shift in the locus of authority away from their institution by playing a leading role in the formulation of a new LSPC paradigm. This new policy line was set out in a series of briefing papers to incoming governments after 1984 which provided the blueprint for the subsequent LSPC reform process.

The Reinvention of the New Zealand Treasury

In directing the attention of the policy community toward problems of government failure, the senior officials who wrote these papers were effectively defining a new role for the Treasury in the policy process. They essentially redefined its advisory role in a way which involved it exercising, to a greater degree than before, its agenda-setting capacity. It now became evident to observers, such as Boston (1989, p.133), that the Treasury's power and influence had come to rest, above all, on its capacity to 'set the broad philosophical or theoretical framework within which most policy options – certainly in the economic and social policy arenas – are formulated and determined. By doing so the Treasury is able to define the central question for analysis, exclude certain issues from consideration, and reject policy solutions which do not conform to the accepted wisdom.' Moreover, the Treasury did not just set the agenda for reform – it also generated the bulk of the reform proposals. It appears to have reinvented itself as a credible and legitimate source of policy leadership. Easton (1997, p.99) has put it as follows:

The role of Treasury changed. Suddenly the abominable no-men were saying yes. Instead of opposing proposals for change, they were advocating them.

The 'old' Treasury might have been partly blamed in the economic crisis of the 1980s, but the 'new' Treasury could not be so implicated since it was demonstrably contributing to the policy leadership required to design and launch a comprehensive reform programme to turn around the New Zealand economy.

As the New Zealand Treasury forged a new identity based on its new understanding of its appropriate role in the policy process, it largely dispensed with rules which were designed to ensure that its advisory staff could be trusted to make a balanced consideration of the consequences of policy proposals. They were freed to devise bold and innovative reform proposals provided that these were directed toward the advancement of the parallel LSPC reform processes. The control function of Treasury changed from one of evaluating the consequences of policy proposals to one of ensuring their consistency with the principles it had established and coherence with the reform processes it had set in motion. A circularity was thus established between the design and evaluation of reforms which protected them from subsequent reversal since even the emergence of adverse consequences could not justify the reversal of a reform which could be shown to be coherent with the overall reform direction.

The New Zealand Treasury was empowered to perform this new control function by a 1985 overhaul of the machinery through which Cabinet received policy advice. This saw a Cabinet Policy Committee being established with the task of ensuring the clarity and coherence of all policy. Since this structure was serviced by the Treasury, it could perform a 'gatekeeper function' (Kelsey, 1995), ensuring that in most situations its own policy line would be ascendant, since as Boston (1992, p.194) has observed 'any policy analysts ... who reject the prevailing Treasury orthodoxy are at a major disadvantage. For in order to have their views taken seriously they must first demonstrate the validity and coherence of their own analytical framework, and this is no mean feat, particularly if it has to be done in the face of determined Treasury opposition.

The senior officials who led these changes must have realized that the reinvention of the Treasury as a source of policy leadership, its framing of an agenda for policy reform, and its insistence that reform proceed according to the principles it had specified *ex ante* would be controversial: it would split the policy community and disturb the stable equilibrium of political trust that allowed the 'old Treasury' to perform its traditional functions within this community. The Treasury clearly needed to operate within a network within which other members could endorse its new role and undertake the political or mangagement tasks required to implement the LSPC reform process. The nature of this network will now be considered.

5.5   COLLECTIVE POLICY LEADERSHIP IN NEW ZEALAND

The opportunity for the New Zealand Treasury to exert, to the greatest possible degree, the leverage it potentially had over the policy process would only arise when it enjoyed a mutually empowering relationship of trust with its finance minister and they both could depend on the support in cabinet of their Prime Minister. This situation of maximum opportunity appears to have prevailed in New Zealand during the first four years of David Lange's Labour administration, which held office between 1984 and 1990, and during the first two year's of Jim Bolger's National Party Government which has been in power since. During both periods the premiers were prepared to give free rein over economic policy to their respective finance ministers (that is, Roger Douglas in Lange's Labour Government and Ruth Richardson in Bolger's National Government) who shared the same commitment to advance a LSPC reform process as their Treasury advisers. By so doing they could claim credit for the provision by their governments of coherent, decisive leadership at a time of economic crisis.

Both Lange and Bolger rationalized their support of the radical reforms launched by their finance ministers in terms of the post-election crises that confronted their governments. In the case of the Lange government, the pretext for reform was provided by a currency crisis. During the 1984 election campaign the New Zealand dollar was subject to a speculative attack in foreign exchange markets. The Treasury and the Reserve Bank advised the then incumbent Prime Minister, Robert Muldoon, to devalue the currency. He refused, and the attacks on the dollar increased to crisis levels until devaluation was finally undertaken in the first post-election policy announcement of the new Labour government. The next logical steps seemed to be the deregulation of financial markets and the floating of the exchange rate. The window of opportunity was thus opened for the Treasury and Douglas to propose a comprehensive programme of liberalization and stabilization as a coherent strategy to deal with New Zealand's underlying structural problems.

In the case of the Bolger Government, the pretext for the programme of fiscal austerity and labour deregulation launched at the end of 1990 was provided by a post-election blowout in forecasted budget deficits and the need for the new government to bail-out the partly state-owned Bank of New Zealand. The 'crisis hypothesis' of policy reform which holds that public perception of a crisis is needed to create the conditions under which it is politically possible to undertake extensive policy reforms (Williamson, 1994) would certainly appear to be relevant to the situation prevailing after the 1984 and 1990 elections in New Zealand. The political skills the reformist factions in both governments exercised to take advantage of this 'window of opportunity' merit further consideration.

The 'Troika' and the 'Blitzkreig'

During the first term of the Labour Government (1984–7) Douglas formed a particularly effective 'Troika' with his ministerial associates David Caygill and Richard Prebble, and encountered little resistance in their drive to push through legislation based on the Treasury's policy proposals. The pattern of policymaking within the Cabinet of the Fourth Labour government has been described by Easton (1997, p.75) as follows:

> The policy process went like this. The Troika, having come to some policy decision based on Treasury advice, would persuade (Prime Minister) Lange and (his deputy) Palmer of its correctness. The tight five would then take a proposal to a Cabinet committee. The recommendations would then go to Cabinet, and then on to caucus. At each step in this decision tier, there was already a majority in agreement. This most obviously applied at the caucus level. The Cabinet ... usually supported the ... decision under the principle of collective responsibility. Allowing for a few other functionaries (whips, chairpersons of committees, the caucus secretary), and a few reliable loyalists, the Cabinet (which might have been split when it made its decision) had a natural majority in the caucus. (Often the caucus would not even be consulted, because the Cabinet knew it could rely on retrospective acquiescence.) The same process of majoritarian loyalism gave the government its majority in Parliament .... This was a formidable degree of leverage by a few politicians over the entire country.

Armed with the set of reform proposals which had been worked out in advance by their Treasury advisors, Douglas and Richardson advanced the reform process through a series of policy 'blitzkreigs'. This reliance on speed and stealth was designed to reduce the capacity of vested interests to mobilize resistance to structural reforms and gain the support of groups who would be uncertain *ex ante* about whether they would be winners or losers in the redistribution of income which would follow the reforms.

Although the sequencing of reforms in New Zealand has been evaluated as sub-optimal in terms of its economic outcomes, it did succeed in generating a political momentum for reform since 'a series of disequilibria were established which justified the addition of further deregulatory moves to the government's agenda' (Evans *et. al.*, 1996, p.1871). Douglas, in particular, appears to have been concerned with sequencing the reforms so that no stable coalition could be formed to oppose them. His first move to deregulate the financial sector generated little resistance since most of groups affected supported the reforms. By moving next to withdraw farm subsidies, he generated support from farmers for tariff reductions which, in turn, caused farmers and manufacturers to pressure government to reduce its spending so that real interest and exchange rates could fall. By the time Richardson had assumed office, political pressure for further reform had created a window of opportunity for the new National Government to deregulate the labour market and reduce welfare benefits.

The Treasury's leverage over policy could not be expected to remain at the peaks attained during the periods when Douglas and Richardson dominated Cabinet debate over economic policy direction. It was inevitable that under both Labour and National governments the Cabinet would eventually have to respond to pragmatic concerns that reform was proceeding too far and too fast in one direction. Other members of the reformist network which was forming around the new Treasury thus needed to be mobilized to take up its advocacy tasks when it was encountering resistance at Cabinet level.

The Business Roundtable and the 'New Executive'

Since setting up an office in Wellington in 1986 under the direction of former Treasury official, Roger Kerr, the Business Roundtable, a self-selected lobby group which includes in its membership (which is by invitation only) the chief executives of some of New Zealand's largest companies, has performed this function. It has persistently advocated the advancement of the LSPC reform process so that new ground could be broken in applying the principles laid down by Treasury. Easton has put this as follows:

> The Roundtable (did not) lead the commercialisation revolution. Their public commitment occurred well after the strategy was under way, although without their involvement it probably would not have gone as far.... If Treasury had its public advocacy blocked, the Roundtable would often take the case up. Instances included the competition policy reform, student fees, social welfare, health and labour market reform. When many of the Treasury's policy initiatives were stalled in the late 1980s, following the resignation of Roger Douglas, it was the Roundtable which took over. This was most evident in its leadership of

the policy development which resulted in the Employment Contracts Act (1997, p.116).

This raises the question of why New Zealand's business elite were prepared to identify themselves with the policy position of the Business Roundtable. They would have realized that there would be winners and losers in the LSPC reform process advocated by this institution and have been uncertain, *ex ante*, about 'where the chips would fall' for the sector or industry whose interests they were representing.

'Friends' of the Roundtable, such as Roger Douglas (1993, p.57) have claimed that these narrow, sectional considerations did not influence its policy 'position statements', being unstinting in their praise for the way it 'put self interest and privilege aside in the national interest', issuing 'reasoned, research discussion papers in the full glare of public debate'. Easton (1997, p.115), however, remains sceptical. He points out that 'the Business Roundtable ignored any matter where a purist New Right position would infringe their immediate interests. Thus they did not comment on tariff policy, research and development policy, accountancy reform, commercial law reform, or the issue of the substantial donations to political parties made by business (Roundtable businesses prominent among them)'.

Perhaps one explanation for this puzzle is to suppose that the members of the Business Roundtable did not represent any sectional interest at all. They represented the interests of the 'top 40 or 50' chief executives in the country and recognized that a global whirlwind of social, political, economic and technological change was generating unprecedented opportunities to boost the power, prestige and pay of whoever occupied the top executive echelon in the private and public sectors of the national economy. The 'demise of the corporate man' in English-speaking nations since the 1980s has been vividly described by Sampson (1995) who argues that in an environment of accelerating computerization, intense global competition, financial deregulation, and the 'leveraged buyout', 'downsizing' and 'delayering' of corporate bureaucracies by 'corporate raiders' on a crusade to advance the short term profit maximization of the giant insurance companies and pension funds who own the bulk of shares in modern companies, there has been an upward spiral in the demand for a new breed of chief executive.

This new executive is someone who can 'make the tough decisions', who can provide 'leadership', and exert leverage over the behaviour of the core of specialist 'knowledge workers' (Drucker, 1993) who remain in organizations after they have been stripped of multiple layers of middle management. The market for this new breed has been described by Frank and Cook (1995) as a 'winner take all market' in which competition for a limited number of positions can cause a 'hyperinflation' of the pay packages of those who can lay claim to being the best performers. These organizational 'superstars' experience 'solidarity benefits', not just in interacting with one another , but with other 'key players' in government and politics who, like them , have to make 'tough decisions' which effectively remove the job security of a greater and greater percentage of the people who are affected by them.

Implementation Through Change Agents

In New Zealand, the Business Roundtable provided the forum within which interactions between members of the 'New Establishment' (Easton 1997) could take place. This institution played an important role in the implementation as well as the advocacy of reforms. From its pool of members, there emerged the small group of change agents who 'moved among key institutions, putting reforms in place and preventing bottlenecks' (Bollard, 1994, p.91). Kelsey (1995) refers, in particular, to the way these tasks were performed by like-minded executives such as Rod Deane, Graham Scott, Roger Kerr, Ron Trotter, John Fernyhough and Alan Gibbs who moved from one top job to the next. They tended to recommend one another to fill positions either in control agencies, such as the Treasury, the Reserve Bank and the State Services Commission (which oversaw state sector reform), or in the newly restructured former government departments and enterprises. The way this tight circle sought to promote one another to key positions was neatly summarized by Hubbard (1992, p.14).

> Rod [Deane] helped Roger [Kerr] get the Roundtable job; Roger helped Rod get the Electricorp position. Roundtable stalwart Ron Trotter has held a bewildering number of positions under Labour as well as National. This is a like-minded elite which is always taking in each other's washing.

Once these change agents had penetrated a particular public organization, they sought, as far as possible, to prevent its former leaders from using their specialized knowledge to capture the change process and steer it in ways which protected their interests or views about its desired outcomes.

Spicer (1995) describes the extreme measures the change agents were prepared to take to avoid this type of capture as they sought to restructure state-owned enterprises (SOEs) along the lines mandated by the SOE Act of 1986. Rather than seeking to consult with the groups affected by this restructuring, the chief executives who were appointed to oversee its implementation typically set up task forces in separate offices 'away from the day-to-day pressure and scrutiny of existing management ... with a "blank sheet of paper" to develop a new structure for the organization' (Spicer 1995, p.31).

Once the decisions about restructuring had been made, the change agents moved quickly to implement them to remove *ex ante* uncertainty about the identity of losers and to isolate the identifiable losers from the remaining employees and service users. They recognized that laid-off workers would be removed from workplace interaction and would find it difficult to mobilize any form of collective resistance to their dismissal. They expected that as the remaining workers became more confident that they could survive the restructuring, they would be more be likely to co-operate constructively with the new management. To reshape the culture at the senior levels of these organizations, some CEs took the radical step of requiring all managers to reapply for their positions. In this way they sought to rapidly build up a management team comprising senior managers drawn from outside the organization as well as relatively junior staff who were not only expected to be less resistant to change but also to welcome the opportunity to leapfrog their more senior colleagues into management positions. Through strategic 'infiltrations' the CEs sought to build a following at all levels of the organization so that a commercial culture could be developed in which workers could be trusted to be alert to and responsive toward opportunities to provide its core services more efficiently.

The Divison of Labour in the Supply of Policy Leadership

A clear divison of labour thus appears to have occurred between the leadership tasks performed by the members of New Zealand's reformist network. The Treasury and the Business Roundtable both performed advocacy and agenda-setting tasks. However, the more detailed policy formulation tasks appear to have rested with the Treasury. This control agency also sought to evaluate reform proposals not so much according to their consequences but in terms of their consistency with the overall direction of the reform process. It therefore played a leading role in the institutionalization of the new government failure paradigm. The political tasks involved in sequencing the reforms in a way to mitigate potential resistance and driving reformist legislation through a relatively small number of 'veto points' at cabinet, caucus and parliamentary level rested with key reformists in cabinet such as Douglas, Richardson and their allies. To ensure that the implementation of the reforms followed the intentions of these reformers, change agents drawn from the membership of the Business Roundtable were placed at the head of newly created public agencies. They supplied the leadership required to transform these organizations along commercialist lines and, where possible, prepare them for ultimate privatization. The implications that can be drawn from this experience concerning the nature and role of policy leadership in paradigmatic policy change must now be considered by way of conclusion to this chapter.

5.6   CONCLUSION

The New Zealand experience suggests that the tasks of policy leadership required to institutionalize a new policy paradigm must be collectively supplied. A network of policy leaders must be formed which seeks to place its own members in positions of leverage over the agenda-setting, formulation, decisonmaking, implementation and evaluation stages of the reform process. This concept of leadership ties in with much of the modern writing on the subject which tends to emphasize the collective dimension of this phenomenon. Less credence appears to be given nowadays to the 'great person theories of history' that were popularized in the nineteenth century by Carlyle (1841) and James (1880). As Bryson and Crosby (1992, p.32) have pointed out:

> In a world where shared power is more effective than individual power, the tasks of leadership must be widely shared. No one person can embody all the needed qualities or perform all the tasks. People will pass into and out of leadership roles; a person may be a leader on one issue and a follower on others. This year's leader on a particular issue may even be next year's follower on the same issue.

This leadership-based explanation of paradigmatic policy change straddles the typology of explananda set out by Hood in his book *Explaining Policy Reversals*. Hood (1994, p.4) proposes that there are four types of explanation for 'policy reversals':

(i) The idea that policy reversal comes mainly from the force of new *ideas*, which succeed in upsetting the *status quo* in some way (through experimental evidence, logical force or rhetorical power).

(ii) The idea that policy reversal comes mainly from the pressure of *interests*, which succeed in achieving changes that suit their purposes.

(iii) The idea that policy reversal comes mainly from changes in social '*habitat*' which make old policies obsolete in the face of new conditions.

(iv) The idea that policy reversal comes mainly from 'inside', with policies and institutions *destroying themselves* rather than being destroyed from the outside.'

This writer acknowledges, though, that these processes may be interlinked and that the distictions between them may be more blurred than his typology suggests. In particular Hood (ibid., p.7, p.11) argues that an emphasis on 'the role of packaging rather than content in explaining how economic policy ideas become persuasive' and an appreciation of the role of policy entrepreneurship make it harder to distinguish between ' "ideas", "interests" and "social contexts" as sources of policy dynamism'. This would seem to be true of the type of leadership network discussed in this chapter. The 'entrepreneurial' members of this network seem to have packaged a stream of ideas into a policy paradigm that served the interests of an emergent source of authority so that they could be ready to take advantage of the opportunities generated by a combination of institutional inertia and a changing global environment to advance a policy quest that embodied particular ideas and benefited particular interests.

While leadership is clearly a significant factor in the political economy of policy reform it has traditionally been neglected as a subject of inquiry by the mainstream economics profession. However, recent developments in economic theory have, however, made this neglect less tenable. The relationship between leadership and economic theory and the directions which economists could take in explaining the phenomenon of leadership will be now be considered in Chapter 6.

6 Economics and Leadership Theory

6.1 INTRODUCTION

The phenomenon of leadership has been the subject of a considerable body of literature in the humanities and certain branches of the social sciences. Traditions of inquiry into leadership have been particularly prominent in philosophy, politics, anthropology, psychology, sociology and history. Moreover, insights from all these traditions have been integrated into studies of management and organizational behaviour that have been of both an academic and popular nature. A particularly comprehensive and useful survey of these studies is provided by Bass (1990).

The considerable interest other disciplines have shown in leadership makes the relative neglect by economists of this phenomenon all the more striking. The purpose of this chapter is to attempt an explanation of this neglect in terms of the difficulties economists must face when they seek to address the three main issues raised in the broader literature on leadership from the relatively narrow perspective of conventional economics. What then are these issues? How relevant are they to the economics profession? What attempts have economists made to analyse leadership? How should the standard assumptions of conventional economics be modified to allow a greater consideration of the issues raised in the leadership literature? These questions will be addressed in this chapter before Chapter 7 goes on to examine an important new line of development in economic theory that is likely to remove many of the problems encountered in formulating an economic theory of leadership.

The chapter itself is divided into five main parts. Section 2 examines the three central issues raised in the leadership literature, namely the significance of leadership, the distinctiveness of leadership and the possibility of moral leadership. Section 3 investigates the relevance of questions of leadership to economists and section 4 deals with economic theories of leadership. Section 5 considers some of the implications of leadership for economic discourse, not least Hirschman's (1985) arguments and the question of economics and hermeneutics. The chapter ends with some brief concluding remarks in section 6.

6.2 THREE ISSUES REPEATEDLY RAISED BY LEADERSHIP THEORISTS

Three major issues are repeatedly raised in the leadership literature. Two of these are positive in nature. They concern the significance and distinctiveness of leadership. The third issue is normative and is concerned with the possibility of moral leadership. The treatment by the leadership literature of these three issues will be considered in this section.

The Significance of Leadership

A central concern in the leadership literature is with whether or not leadership plays a significant role in catalyzing intentional historical transformation in institutions and social groups. Leaders are often claimed, by both themselves and their followers, to be authentic agents of social progress, improving the performance (according to their own criteria) of the societies, organizations or groups which look to them for leadership. A substantial literature has developed which has been directed towards authenticating this type of claim. Bass (1996, p.22) argues that 'countless surveys can be cited to support the contention that leaders make a difference to their subordinates' satisfaction and performance ... (and) ... in whether their organizations succeed or fail'. Although most of these studies have focused on business organizations, a number have advanced evidence for the quality of leadership being the 'x-factor' accounting for variations in indicators of the performance of schools (Sylvia and Hutchison, 1985), churches (Smith, Carson and Alexander, 1984) and military units (Gal and Manning, 1984).

The major sceptical response to claims made about the historical significance of leadership has been associated with various 'attributional' theorists. From their perspective, followers attribute effects due to historical, economic and social factors to leaders, as in romantic fiction (Meindl and Ehrlich, 1987). Improvements in the performance of individuals, organizations and nations are thus determined by other factors, but leaders are credited with what happened after the fact (Pfeffer, 1977). An extreme version of this view has been expressed by Gemmill and Oakley (1992, p.115) who argue that leadership is essentially a reification or 'iatrogenic social myth' which arises from a 'search and wish for a messiah (leader) or magical rescue (leadership) which intensifies at times of deepening social despair and massive learned helplessness'.

The Distinctiveness of Leadership

A second major concern in the leadership literature is with whether or not leadership is a distinctive form of social influence insofar as leaders affect the intrinsic and not just the extrinsic motivation of their followers. This distinction relates to whether the rewards or sanctions that influence the behaviour of leaders and followers are external or internal to the quest in which they collectively participate. These persons can be said to be intrinsically motivated when they receive no apparent reward except participation in the quest. The main question here can be phrased as follows: 'Should leadership be distinguished from other directive or "steering" activities such as management, administration or "political entrepreneurship" which use extrinsic rewards and sanctions, of both a pecuniary and non-pecuniary nature, to influence the behaviour of individuals and groups?'

Leaders may be in a position to exercise 'reward power' by using extrinsic rewards to induce subordinates to perform the tasks they set them, or 'coercive power' by administering a set of extrinsic penalties for non-compliance with their directions. They cannot be said to be exercising leadership *per se* if they choose to exercise only these forms of power. Less obviously, the power to influence followers does not essentially arise from the social division of knowledge. Leader–follower relationships can be distinguished from those arising from the superior expertise or knowledge of one party, such as teacher–pupil, adviser–client or doctor–patient relationships. Leaders may be in a position to gain access to and process more information than their followers but, in exercising leadership, they are not simply attempting to change their behaviour by supplying them with information they do not have. Leadership more essentially involves influencing the intrinsic motivation of followers through processes of 'internalization' and 'identification' (Kelman, 1958).

Leaders influence followers through internalization when they amplify values and beliefs that are shared by both leaders and followers. These values and beliefs will relate to the worth and possibility of the future states they are striving to realize and their amplification will enhance follower commitment to strive toward their realization. Leaders influence followers through identification by consciously engaging in behaviours that reinforce and strengthen the sense of personal identification and loyalty which followers place in them. As a result, followers can be more intrinsically motivated to make and sustain commitments as an expression of their belief in the personal worth of their leaders. It is difficult to empirically separate these two types of social influence but some writers, notably Downton (1973) and Howell (1988) have argued that 'inspirational' can be distinguished from 'charismatic' leadership in that it gives primary emphasis to influence through internalization rather than identification.

The impact leaders have on the intrinsic motivation of followers through both processes has been elaborated in theories of transformational leadership. They tend to follow Burns (1978, p.3) in distinguishing between 'transactional' leaders who 'approach followers with an eye to exchanging one thing for another' and 'transformational' leaders who seek to satisfy higher needs, in terms of Maslow's need hierarchy, and engage the full person of the follower. These theories emphasize the role of leadership in the transformation of preferences, both those of the leader and those of the followers, although leaders are typically distinguished because they influence more than they are influenced. The leadership role is that of 'an educator, stimulating and accepting changing world views, redefining meanings, stimulating commitments' (March and Olsen, 1984).

The claim that leadership essentially involves influencing the intrinsic motivation of followers can be contested from a 'social exchange' perspective (Blau, 1964). From this perspective the leader–follower relationship only differs from other exchange relationships in terms of the commodity which is being exchanged. Leaders and followers exchange a number of non-material commodities, but the most basic one would appear to be trust.

Leader–follower relationships are clearly founded on reciprocal relations of trust and commitment. They can emerge from a social division of labour in which the members of a group place their trust in a leader to perform the specialized functions of representing them in their external relations and co-ordinating their activities through the allocation of trust. In allocating tasks, roles or functions to group members, the leader is in a position to signal the level of trust that is being placed in them. In this situation followers may have extrinsic motivation to behave in a way which vindicates the trust placed in them since this may induce leaders to entrust them with higher status tasks, functions and roles. Cultivating the trust of a leader may be seen as a means toward acquiring greater status and even as a route toward achieving future leadership. However, followers may conceal this extrinsic motivation from leaders and behave in a way which signals their personal identification with them and internalization of their values. Just as the authenticity of a leader's claims can always be questioned, so too can the authenticity of a follower's apparent intrinsic motivation.

The view that leadership is something which is attributed *ex post* or claimed *ex ante* does not necessarily render it a 'myth' unworthy of investigation, but rather highlights the inseparable relationship between the practice and interpretation of leadership. This relationship arises because the 'interpretations', 'claims' and 'attributions' made with regard to particular instances of leadership can affect behaviour since the people who make them may also be striving to authenticate them. Leadership can therefore be conceived as being constituted both by the claims made about it and the striving of leaders and followers to authenticate these claims in a 'public space' of questions concerning their authenticity. The claims made about leadership in theory will thus represent the type of claims which leaders and their followers strive to authenticate in practice.

The Possibility of Moral Leadership

A third major concern in the leadership literature is with the possibility of moral leadership or, to put it differently, with whether there are criteria, other than effectiveness, according to which leadership can be evaluated. This issue is implicit in the distinctions that are repeatedly made in this literature between styles of leadership which are 'democratic', 'participative', 'group developing', 'relations-centered', 'supportive' and 'considerate' on the one hand, and those which are 'authoritative', 'dominating', 'directive', 'autocratic', 'task-oriented' and 'persuasive', on the other hand. Bass (1990, p.33) suggests that 'it is possible to encapsulate many of these typologies into the autocratic versus democratic dichotomy'.

It is possible to distinguish two claims that are made by writers who emphasize this dichotomy. On the one hand, they are simply claiming that one type of leadership is more effective than the other in terms of realizing the leader's intentions or that the relatively effectiveness of the two types is situation-dependent. On the other hand, they may make a normative claim: namely, that the democratic style of leadership is more moral since it shows a greater respect for the dignity and moral autonomy of followers.

From a liberal perspective based on deontological, Kantian foundations, however, even the morality of democratic leadership may be called into question. Kantian liberalism stresses the dignity and inviolability of persons and questions the legitimacy of any social relationship which fails to respect their moral autonomy by requiring them to alienate it in some way. No end, no matter how worthy, can legitimate this alienation. No degree of consent by the agents involved can legitimate the alienation of moral autonomy either. This is because, from a Kantian perspective, moral autonomy is that human capacity which commands the respect of ourselves and others. It is therefore inalienable.

For liberals who hold a 'strong' concept of moral autonomy (Kuflik, 1984), followers must, to some degree, compromise or alienate their moral autonomy when they look to leaders to motivate them to commit themselves to a particular quest. If they are to be morally autonomous agents they must 'lead their lives from the inside' (Kymlicka, 1989) and therefore have the 'final word' on the principles that shape the direction of their lives. This seems to exclude them from becoming followers since a follower not only accepts the legitimacy of a leader's claim to have the 'final word' on the shared values of a group but actually looks to the leader to perform this function.

However, according to a weaker concept of moral autonomy, leader–follower relationships can be moral provided that leaders do not expect, nor do followers give, an ultimacy to their leadership or quests. To claim this ultimacy would be to demand total commitment from both leaders and followers and to promise total fulfilment even if all other claims on their lives have to be subjected to this commitment. It would demand that followers place their 'faith' – in the sense defined by Tillich (1956, p.1) as 'the state of being ultimately concerned' – in their leaders and their quests.

This seems to be a fundamental moral objection which can be levelled at the relationships 'charismatic' leaders, such as Adolf Hitler, Charles Manson and Jim Jones formed with their followers. In his book *Charisma*, Lindholm (1990) uses a synthetic theory of charismatic leadership which brings together insights derived from Nietzsche, Weber, Durkheim, LeBon and Freud to explicate common features of the charismatic relationships these three leaders formed with their followers. Lindholm (1990) makes it clear that when such a group is faced by a combination of external failure and internal 'betrayal', mass suicide may emerge as the only option for that core of ultimately committed followers who have placed their faith in their charismatic leader.

It would seem to be significant that the charismatic leaders concerned all sought to disengage their followers from any tradition or sense of history they might share with outsiders so that the faith of these devotees could be placed in their leadership alone. Their capacity to do this was enhanced because their followers were largely drawn from a social milieu in which, to some extent, forms of life had been dislocated, roots unsettled and traditions undone. Sandel (1984, p.7) has argued that, 'in our day, the totalitarian impulse has sprung less from the convictions of confidently situated selves than from the confusions of atomized, dislocated, frustrated selves, at sea in a world where common meanings have lost their force'.

However, a concept of moral leadership must do more than show how the totalitarian tendencies of charisma can be avoided. It must also show

how the commitments made in moral leader–follower relationships can make a positive moral contribution to the lives of the persons concerned. It must allow scope for a type of leadership which, as Burns (1978, p.4) suggests 'converts followers into leaders and may convert leaders into moral agents'.

Perhaps more than any other writer on leadership, Burns has sought to provide a humanist concept of moral leadership. He acknowledges an intellectual debt to humanist psychologists, such as Adler and Maslow, and stresses the importance of a Kantian concept of human dignity. For Burns (ibid.), the *forte* of moral leadership is that it 'emerges from and always returns to the fundamental wants, needs and values of the followers'.

This presumes that a uniformity of hierarchies of values and needs exist across cultures. Burns (ibid., p.30) supports this notion by referring to the way 'researches in the field of moral development have uncovered remarkable uniformities in hierarchies of moral reasoning across a number of cultures'. A moral leader must not, however, merely preach moral development but should take the responsibility for bringing about the social changes which enable his followers to meet higher needs and realise higher values. The moral legitimacy of such leadership must, according to Burns (ibid.), be grounded in conscious choice among alternatives. In responding to leaders, followers should therefore have adequate knowledge of alternative leaders and quests and the capacity to choose among these alternatives.

Burns (ibid.) is careful to ensure that his conception of moral leadership excludes pathological leaders such as Hitler. He argues that Hitler could never be regarded as a moral leader since he failed to (i) realize 'modal values of honor and integrity' in a way which advanced 'fundamental standards of good conduct in humankind'; (ii) achieve 'end-values of equality and justice'; and (iii) effect a progression in the lives of his followers through a hierarchy of needs and values. By contrast Burns (ibid., p.429) declares Gandhi and Franklin D. Roosevelt to be genuinely moral leaders since while they were initially locked into relationships that were 'closely influenced by particular local, parochial, regional, and cultural forces' they were able to 'find a broadening and deepening base from which they could reach out to widening social collectivities to establish and embrace "higher" principles and values'.

Burns (ibid.) has thus formulated a mature theory of leadership in which the issues of the significance, distinctiveness and morality of leadership are treated as being ineradicably intertwined. The relevance of these issues to economic discourse must now be considered.

6.3   THE RELEVANCE TO ECONOMICS OF LEADERSHIP

The political economy of policy reform, the theory of collective action and the economics of organizations constitute three rapidly developing areas of contemporary economic thought in which the issues raised by leadership theorists appear to have a striking relevance. This section will focus on the the political economy of policy reform since it would appear that no account of this phenomenon can be complete unless it considers the three issues raised by the leadership literature.

The Significance of Policy Leadership

The extent of the shift from a policy paradigm which focuses on problems of market failure to one which seeks to limit and reduce government failure is indicated by the way in which the burgeoning literature on the global wave of policy reform, which has gathered momentum since the early 1980s, focuses less on the rationale for this shift than on the reasons for the observed unevenness in its implementation. One factor that is often cited as contributing to this unevenness in implementation is the strength and effectiveness of the policy leadership exercised by the governments concerned.

The significance of leadership was highlighted in a 1993 colloquium sponsored by the Washington-based Institute for International Economics which brought together a group of high-ranking officials who had been key players in designing and pushing through reform programmes in their particular countries. The purpose of this colloquium was to discuss those factors that had contributed to the successful implementation and consolidation of these programmes. Among the factors cited most often were the need for 'visionary leadership and for a coherent economic team' (Williamson 1994, p.589). A similar conclusion was independently reached by Krueger (1993, p.9) who writes that:

> The adoption of the same economic policies in response to the same economic circumstances will … have different consequences under a politically strong leadership of a government with a well-functioning bureaucracy capable of carrying out the wishes of the leadership than it will when … a weak leadership of a coalition attempts to do the same things in circumstances where bureaucrats believe that they can generate support for opposition to those policies.

Dunham and Kelegama (1997, p.179) have even gone as far as to argue that leadership can function as a substitute for weak governance so that 'when the state is not strong as in the case of contemporary Sri Lanka – where it is neither sufficiently cohesive nor sufficiently disciplined to implement economic policy effectively – the capacity for economic reform and for better governance is likely to be a function of political will. Political authority and strong political leadership become the crucial issue'.

Although there is little indication that the contributors to the policy reform literature have engaged much with the broader tradition of inquiry into leadership, they do seem to have formed a concept of leadership which is similar to that developed in one of the strands of this tradition. This strand distinguishes between 'trait theories' of leadership that try to identify the individual traits that distinguish leaders from other people and 'situational theories' that seek to specify the situational factors that provide such leaders with the opportunity to exercise leadership. Trait theories can be viewed as describing aspects of the supply-side of leadership while situational theories describe its demand side. 'Personal–situational' theories thus attempt to bring the demand and supply sides together by insisting that, in any given case, a combination of situational and personal elements needs to be considered.

The hypotheses which Williamson (1994) has proposed about the factors that can generally influence the opportunity newly-elected reform-minded governments have to implement their programmes can be viewed as a list of the situational factors which can give rise to a demand for 'strong' or 'visionary' policy leadership. These include: (i) the 'crisis' hypothesis which holds that public perception of a crisis is needed to create the conditions under which it is politically possible to undertake extensive policy reforms; (ii) the 'mandate hypothesis' which holds that the size of the government's winning majority may be interpreted as giving it the mandate to introduce the reforms it campaigned for; (iii) the 'honeymoon hypothesis' which holds that incoming governments enjoy a period during which the public will give them the benefit of the doubt and blame any sacrifices and difficulties on its predecessor; and (iv) the 'weak discredited opposition hypothesis' which holds that comprehensive reform is made easier by the presence of a fragmented and demoralized opposition which is identified with past policy failures.

Moreover, as Chapter 5 made clear, the climate of uncertainty and puzzlement which prevails after the breakdown of authority of a dominant policy paradigm may constitute an overarching situational factor in which most of these conditions are likely to be met. Chapter 5 also suggested that the essential trait policy participants look for from reformers who seek to exercise policy leadership is a commitment to advance a quest to reconstruct public policy on the basis of a new paradigm that is both coherent and authoritative. This commitment will give these leaders the 'tunnel vision' required to formulate a clear set of coherent goals from their underlying paradigm. It will also give them the willingness to use their own authority and political skills to overcome and circumvent the resistance to reform generated by special interest groups; to bring bureaucrats into line; to lead public opinion by taking firm positions on contentious issues; and to 'stand before the bar of history' and be held to account for their persistence in striving to institutionalize this policy paradigm.

Any theory of the supply-side of policy leadership must explain how this commitment is formed and how it can be influenced and strengthened through the interactions which occur in leader–leader and leader–follower networks. The distinctiveness of leadership as an influence process would thus need to addressed.

The Distinctiveness of Policy Leadership

It is perhaps an indication of the nascence of the literature on the political economy of policy reform that it has tended to focus more on the significance than the distinctivness of leadership. However, if Rodrik's (1996, p.10) claim that 'no other area in economics or political science that I can think of has spawned so much interdisciplinary work' is accepted, then it is unlikely to be long before the collaborators involved draw on those areas of research in the broader field of public policy which are explicitly concerned with the latter issue.

The enormous body of 'implementation research' that has been generated since the seminal work by Pressman and Wildavsky (1973) may be particularly helpful in this regard. In a survey of this research, Sabatier (1986, p.268) suggests that 'top-down' approaches have reduced the 'sufficient and necessary conditions for effective implementation' to a manageable set of variables. This includes (i) clear and consistent objectives; (ii) adequate causal theory; (iii) the structural limitation of 'veto points'; (iv) committed and skilful implementing officials; (v) support of interest groups and sovereigns; and (vi) the absence of changes in socioeconomic support that may substantially undermine political support or the causal theory.

The case study of the 'New Zealand experiment' presented in Chapter 5 indicated the attention reformers in this country have paid to these variables. In particular, it highlighted their shared commitment to advancing a policy quest derived from a particular policy paradigm and the way they formed a network of change agents who sought to transform public agencies by restructuring them and building within them a network of followers who would share the same commitment.

Autocratic versus Democratic Policy Leadership

While the philosophical issues relating to the possibility of moral leadership have not been explored to any depth in the political economy of policy reform, this literature has concerned itself with the type of autocratic–democratic dichotomy found in the writings of leadership theorists. Indeed, Rodrik (1996, p.32) has pointed out that 'a fundamental fault line that divides the contributors to this literature is the issue of how participatory reform politics should be'.

In a case study of the reform 'blitzkreig' launched in Poland in January 1990, Przeworski (1993, p.173) documents how public confidence in representative institutions like political parties, the government, and the Sjem eroded to the point where 'two years after the transition to democracy, Poland was a country in which the three institutions in which people had the most confidence were the army, the church and the police'. From this experience he draws the lesson that (ibid., pp.9–10): 'the autocratic policy style characteristic of Washington-style reforms tends to undermine representative institutions, to personalize politics, and to generate a climate in which politics becomes reduced to fixes, to a search for redemption. Even if neo-liberal reform packages make good economics, they are likely to generate voodoo politics.'

A similar lesson has also been drawn by critics of the New Zealand experiment such as Kelsey. She points out that it has left a disturbing legacy in the form of 'a deep-seated scepticism about electoral politics and parliamentary democracy' (Kelsey, 1995, p.297) and the alienation of groups who have borne the burden of a structural adjustment which has been dictated from above by an elitist network of reformers.

The issue of whether a tradeoff exists between the degree reformers succeed in implementing and consolidating their programmes and the degree to the reform strategy strengthens or preserves confidence in democratic institutions is clearly an important one for political scientists. To the degree that economists continue to collaborate with them in this area, they too may have consider the significance of this tradeoff.

It is one thing to highlight the distinctiveness of leadership in terms of its capacity to build social networks with members who come to share a commitment to a particular quest and to question whether or not this is a process which strengthens democratic institutions. It is quite another thing, however, explain how this can be done. The extent to which economic theory has laid the foundations for this explanatory task must now be considered.

6.4   ECONOMIC THEORIES OF LEADERSHIP

There are relatively few economic theories of leadership on which economists can build in addressing the issues discussed in the previous section. However, some recognition of the significance of leadership can be found in rational choice theories of collective action.

Leadership in Theories of Collective Action

In his seminal work in this area, Olson (1965) suggested that leaders exist to provide selective incentives that solve collective action problems. A classic example of this is provided by the Automobile Association. In many countries the national leaders of this organization have been able to build up a large membership, not by engaging them in a shared commitment to advance the interests of automobile owners, but by offering a range of discounts and services which accrue exclusively to members.

This approach was elaborated upon by Frohlich, Oppenheimer and Young (1971) who proposed that social leaders can found and expand organizations and seek collective benefits for interest groups in exchange for organizational and financial resources from organization members. The members of the group, who enjoy the collective and private benefits that leaders provide, have an incentive to accept and contribute to the beneficial position of the leaders, giving them their support or votes.

Calvert has gone even further to generalize the significance of leadership in these models. He suggests that leadership finds its basis in problems of social co-ordination. It is the means by which social groups attempt to realize gains from co-operation, co-ordination and efficient allocation. These problems are recurrent but are likely to vary from one situation to the next. This makes decentralized solutions difficult and provides the rationale for leadership. Calvert (1992, p.7) then uses game theory to show that the 'solution of such overarching problems makes leadership possible in the basic problems in which social gains are available including activities such as organizing, sanctioning, communicating, and allocating'. Moreover, he demonstrates that the stability of leadership is based on the group's need to solve co-ordination problems so that the leader has the discretion or 'power' to engage in sub-maximal pursuit of group goals.

A similar game-theoretic approach has been followed by Colomer. He argues that while the Prisoner's Dilemma structure may be used to formalize a 'horizontal' interaction between the members of a group, the 'vertical' interactions between leaders and followers can be more appropriately understood if they are modelled as a 'Battle of the Sexes' game whose equilibria are found in outcomes in which players do not coincide in their choices. Colomer (1995, p.225) claims that his analysis 'supports the conclusion that leadership can explain the creation of organizations for collective action and that leadership effects reinforce the differences in the relative strength of different kinds of groups'.

While these theories of collective action highlight the significance of leadership, they do not follow the broader tradition of inquiry into leadership in delineating its distinctiveness. This is because they tend to treat the interactions between leaders and followers as strategic and extrinsically motivated. Accordingly, they do not thus allow scope for leaders to influence the intrinsic motivation of followers through processes of internalization and identification.

Casson's Theory of Leadership

In his book *The Economics of Business Culture*, Mark Casson (1991) not only makes a strong claim about the significance of the quality of leadership as a factor that can affect the performance of economic institutions, but also relates this significance to the distinctive way in which leadership can counteract agency failure.

The central insight of Casson's theory seems to be that if principal–agent relationships can be transformed into leader–follower ones in which followers are intrinsically motivated to advance the leader's quest, then there may be significant scope for reducing the types of agency cost identified by Jensen and Meckling (1976) (referred to in Chapter 4). Significant savings in these costs may occur if principals forego a contractual approach to governing their relationships with agents and instead choose to exercise leadership by developing a distinctive culture which transforms them into followers who can be trusted to observe norms which govern their intrinsic motivation to carry out the tasks and functions delegated to them. The significance of this moral and cultural dimension to agent behaviour is only alluded to in the new institutional economics and agency theory. However, it has been transported to centre stage in the 'economics of business culture' formulated by Casson (ibid.).

According to Casson, leaders can reduce agency failure through either (i) more intensive monitoring of the individual performance of group members or (ii) more intensive 'moral manipulation'. The latter involves the use of 'moral rhetoric', addressed to the group as a whole. It aims to establish a group norm for moral commitment which indicates the extent to which members can expect to place their trust in one another. Casson (ibid.) justifies his treatment of these options as mutually exclusive along similar lines to Frey (1994). The basic argument is that if principals seek to strengthen the extrinsic motivation of agents by making their rewards or sanctions more contingent on their individual performance, their intrinsic motivation will be 'crowded out' since (i) agents may have a reduced degree of discretion to exercise moral responsibility and behave in a trustworthy way, and (ii) the strengthening of monitoring mechanisms often involves an implicit withdrawal of trust.

Casson (ibid.) suggests that the utility functions of followers will include both material and emotional components, with the parameters of the latter being susceptible to moral manipulation by the leader. Thus, the guilt a follower associates with failing to comply with the group norm for moral commitment will be affected by a combination of his or her innate moral sensitivity and the 'intensity of manipulation' applied by the leader. It follows that even if a follower faces a material incentive to break the group norm, this person will still comply with it if the disutility of guilt exceeds utility associated with such material incentives.

Now, if each follower faces a given material incentive to break a commitment to the group norm, then there will exist a threshold intensity of manipulation below which even the most morally sensitive follower does not experience sufficient guilt to make keeping the commitment worthwhile. Casson argues further that, once this threshold is passed, the benefits of raising the intensity of manipulation will be subject to diminishing marginal returns, since its impact will be felt more and more by people who have already decided to comply with the group norm and less and less by the remainder of relatively insensitive 'hard cases' for whom non-compliance is still an option.

There will be fixed and variable costs to raising the intensity of manipulation. These will depend on the charisma of the leader, the cost of media services, and the level of trust in the culture in which the group is imbedded. While these costs will vary between groups, it is assumed that each leader will know the constant marginal cost function which applies the particular group concerned. Since the leader will also know the shape and position of the declining marginal benefit function this person will be able to set the optimal intensity of manipulation where marginal benefit equals marginal cost. This optimum will be associated with a particular level of agency failure, the cost to the leader of which can be added to the total costs of achieving an optimal intensity of manipulation to ascertain whether manipulation is less costly than monitoring.

Casson (ibid.) is able to derive a number of predictions from his model of rational leadership. In particular, he is able to identify situations which are likely to affect the choice between monitoring or manipulation. Monitoring is likely to be favoured where leaders lack charisma or face high media costs or where followers are subjected to hazardous or strenuous work since, in all these cases, the costs of manipulation are likely to be high. However, manipulation may become more appropriate where the performance of followers is difficult to measure. In intellectual work or in the 'craft' and 'coping' activities performed in the public sector where work tends to be 'unobservable' (Wilson, 1989), leadership would seem to be an attractive option.

Casson's model represents one of the most notable attempts to date to address both the significance and distinctiveness of leadership within a model which uses the standard economic tools of constrained optimization and game theory. There are, nonetheless, some aspects of incoherence in his model which will be considered in Chapter 7. Before this can be done, it is necessary to consider whether some of the modifications to standard economic assumptions that have been proposed by various economic revisionists may make leadership a more tractable concept for economic theorists.

6.5   SOME HELPFUL COMPLICATIONS FOR ECONOMIC DISCOURSE

Perhaps a major reason why economists have traditionally tended to steer away from studying leadership is because they have recognized that leadership is essentially concerned with preference change. For leaders to be able to influence the behaviour of followers without resorting exclusively to extrinsic rewards or sanctions, they must be able to influence or change their preferences. The processes according to which preferences are formed and transformed have, however, typically been treated as a 'black box' that lies outside the domain of economic inquiry.

In a now-famous article Stigler and Becker (1977) criticized the neglect by economists of phenomena which apparently involved preference transformation. They argued that these phenomena could be explained in terms of a change in the 'shadow prices' of the inputs households deploy to 'produce' the commodities that enter as arguments in well behaved and stable utility functions. A Beckerian-type approach to modelling leadership will be briefly considered in Chapter 7.

Hirschman's 'Complications to Economic Discourse'

Hirschman has taken issue with notion that the methodological principle of parsimony determines that economists should always ignore, or attempt to explain away, preference changes. He suggests that 'parsimony in theory construction can be overdone and something is sometimes to be gained by making things more complicated' (Hirschman, 1985, p.8).

One complication that Hirschman proposes is that economists should recognize that there are 'two kinds of preference change' (ibid.). They would therefore acknowledge that individual preferences do not only change due to 'wanton', unreflective and unpredictable shifts in tastes, but also due to reflectively monitored commitments to realize 'second order values'. Hirschman (ibid., pp.10–11) accepts that the first type of preference change is 'inscrutable, capricious ... (and) of little analytical interest'. He, nevertheless, contends that changes in values should not 'be downgraded to the wanton kind by assimilating them to changes in tastes' since they 'do occur from time to time in the lives of individuals, within generations, and from one generation to another, and that those changes and their effects on behavior are worth exploring – that, in brief, *de valoribus est disputandum*'.

In directing attention to the 'distinctively human capacity' to reflexively form 'second order' 'metapreferences' about the way we want our preferences to be shaped by our values, Hirschman (ibid.) drew from the seminal analyses of this issue by Frankfurt (1971) and Sen (1977). In an earlier book, Hirschman (1982) argued that second order metapreferences would only be relevant in those situations of dissonance where individuals were wrestling with decisions about whether or not to keep or break commitments in respect of which they had experienced an accumulation of disappointments. This situation is clearly relevant to studies of leadership, since an important function of leaders would be to supply followers with 'reasons' that reinforce their second order metapreferences to sustain their commitments to a special group, an individual leader or a particular quest.

Another complication suggested by Hirschman (1985, p.11) is that economic discourse should recognize that there are 'two kinds of activities' in which human agents can engage. The first kind has historically tended to monopolize the attention of economists. It is the type of instrumental activity that 'carries with it a neat distinction between process and outcome, inputs and outputs, or costs and revenue'. The motivation to engage in such activities is essentially extrinsic since 'from the point of view of the individual participant in the process, a seemingly similar distinction can be drawn between work or pay or between effort and reward' (ibid.).

A second kind of activity that has been largely neglected by economists is the expressive, non-instrumental type engaged in by individuals in 'the pursuit of truth, beauty, justice, liberty, community, friendship, love, salvation, and so on' (ibid., p.12). In this type of expressive activity, a 'fusion of striving and attaining' occurs as individuals 'savor in advance' the realization of their quest. This not only compensates them for 'the uncertainty about the outcome, and for the strenuousness or dangerousness of the activity' but can act as a disincentive to free-riding. Hirschman (1982, p.86) pointed out that:

> Since the output and objective of collective action are ... a public good available to all, the only way an individual can raise the benefit accruing to him from the collective action is by stepping up his own input, his effort on behalf of the public policy he espouses. Far from shirking and attempting to get a free-ride, a truly maximizing individual will attempt to be as activist as he can manage.

If the scope of economic discourse could be expanded to encompass expressive activities, then it could also grasp the distinctiveness of leadership since the intrinsic motivation leaders and followers derive from striving to advance particular quests would seem to be crucially related to the 'in-process benefits' (Buchanan, 1979) experienced through participation in these collective activities.

Economics and Hermeneutics

Berger (1989) has suggested that expressive behaviour could be brought within the reach of economic models if they allowed some scope for the type of 'hermeneutical' concept of human agency advanced by the political philosopher Charles Taylor. According to Taylor (1985, p.41), an agent can be conceived as being in a 'world of meanings that he imperfectly understands' so that the essential task 'is to interpret it better in order to know who he is and what he ought to seek'.

Attention is, nevertheless, a scarce resource. Accordingly, there is a limit to the number of issues that people can attend to at any time and they must decide how they are going to allocate their scarce attentional capacity. This decision cannot be made by calculating the costs and benefits of alternative deployments of attention since this type of utility calculus will divert their attention from issues that are either urgent or significant (Berger, 1989, p.219).

Language plays a key role in the deployment of attention. According to Taylor, it can perform both formulative and expressive functions. It can make explicit what was previously implicit, it can focus the attention of both the agent and his or her interlocutors on the significance of an issue, and it can express how much the agent is moved by the significance of this issue. In performing these functions, language can evoke what Taylor calls 'subject-referring' emotions. These include 'our sense of shame, of dignity, of guilt, or pride, our feelings of admiration and contempt or moral obligation, of remorse, of unworthiness and self-hatred (and less frequently) of self-acceptance' (Taylor, 1985, p.59). They can only be experienced if a certain 'import' or significance is ascribed to the situations which give rise to them. This constitutes more than a subjective reaction to an objective situation since as Taylor (ibid., p.54) puts it, 'to ascribe an import is to make a judgment about the way things are which cannot be reduced to the way we feel about them'.

Subject-referring emotions have to incorporate a degree of articulation in order to open a person to the imports involved. To recognize that these emotions are bound up with a process of articulation, is to acknowledge that, at any time, they will be at least partly constituted by their latest articulation and that further articulation may change the nature of the emotions being experienced. An emotion such as guilt is therefore not commensurable with those goods which have an objective existence independent of interpretation. The relationship between this emotion and the other consequences associated with breaking a commitment cannot therefore be treated as a simple trade-off between the material and emotional components of individual utility functions along the lines suggested by Casson (1991).

The expressive power of language, its capacity to express and evoke subject-referring emotions will depend, at least partly, on the extent to which it is validated by commitment. It is often not sufficient for an agent to be moved by the significance of an issue and to express the subject-referring emotions it evokes: this person may also seek to show how much he is moved by its significance by making expressive commitments. As Kelley (1972, pp.52–3) has put it:

> There is as realistic an economy in the realm of meanings as in commodities, but the currency is different. In both cases, it obtains its value from the guarantees that undergird it: what has been invested in it, what backs it up. In the realm of meaning that backing, that guarantee or validation, is a personal and social earnestness shown in the investment by real people of time, money, effort, reputation and self in the meaning and movements which bears it.

There is clearly a close link between leadership and language. This has been recognized by Casson (1991) who characterizes leaders as having to choose between 'monitoring' and 'manipulation through moral rhetoric'. More generally, it would seem that the formulative and expressive power of langauge enables leaders to perform what many writers see to be their major function of articulating and focusing attention on a group vision. With regard to this function Bennis and Nanus (1985, p.96), have observed that:

> The leader may have been the one who chose the image from those available at the moment, articulated it, gave it form and legitimacy, and focused attention upon it, but the leader only rarely was the one who conceived the vision in the first place.

However, by repeatedly signalling through language (and other non-verbal means) that their own attention is focused on advancing a quest toward the realization of a particular vision, leaders can evoke subject-referring emotions in their followers and thereby induce them to commit themselves expressively to advancing the same quest. Bennis and Nanus (ibid., p.28) observe that:

> Leaders ... visions ... are compelling and pull people toward them. Intensity coupled with commitment is magnetic. And these intense personalities do not have to coerce people to pay attention; they are so intent on what they are doing that, like a child, completely absorbed with creating a sandbox they draw others in.

The attention signals of a leader with this engaging quality must comprise a large proportion of the signals they communicate since, as Peters and Austin (1985, p.270) note, 'its a matter of the quantity of attention paid to the matter at hand rather than the quality, odd as that statement may sound.'

A hermeneutical approach does thus seem to provide a promising perspective from which the distinctiveness of leadership can be appreciated. In addition, many of the moral objections to leadership *per se* fall away when it is viewed from this perspective. Followers do not necessarily surrender their autonomy when they look to leaders to 'have the final word' in articulating and expressing the significance of their quest in a way which simply makes explicit their own sense of its significance. This sense of significance is implicit, inchoate, and only partly articulated, and the leader can help make it clearer and to focus attention on it more sharply. Moreover, the leader's interpretations must not only resonate with the follower's sense of the particular quest's significance but also with what Taylor (1985, p.40) calls their 'deepest, unstructured sense of what is important, which is as yet inchoate' and which they 'are trying to bring to definition'.

According to Berger (1989), the hermeneutical concept of agency advocated by Taylor (ibid.) should appeal most to revisionist economists who stress the 'normative–affective' and 'bounded rationality' dimension of decisonmaking (see, for example, Etzioni, 1988; Simon, 1983). It should thus gain more credence among mainstream economists if a general way could be found to incorporate the emotions into the tool kit of economists. An important recent survey article by Elster (1998) provides a detailed consideration of this issue. Chapter 7 will consider the main lines of Elster's argument in addressing a number of questions it raises in relationship to leadership. Before this can be done the main arguments of this chapter need to recapitulated by way of conclusion to this chapter.

6.6   CONCLUSION

For any theory of leadership to address the issues that have been repeatedly raised in the long tradition of inquiry into this phenomenon, it must be framed in such a way that the significance, distinctiveness and morality of leadership can be adequately considered. Despite the significance of leadership having been highlighted in the growing literature on the political economy of policy reform and notwithstanding the fact that the issues of the distinctiveness and morality of leadership are clearly relevant to this field of inquiry, mainstream economics has been constrained from developing an economic theory of leadership by its reluctance to examine the expressive dimension of human behaviour. An economic theory of leadership which explicitly deals with this dimension by examining the way leadership influences a particular type of emotion will be formulated in Chapter 7.

7 An Economic Theory of Hope and Leadership

7.1 INTRODUCTION

In an important survey article, Elster (1998) has posed the following question to the economics profession: 'How can emotions help us explain behavior for which good explanations seem to be lacking?' In order to address this issue, Elster has explored the field of emotion theory in psychology to find the answers it provides to a number of subsidiary questions. These include the following: (i) 'What emotions are there?'; (ii) 'What are emotions?'; (iii) 'Can we choose our emotions or can we only choose to seek out or avoid situations that give rise to particular emotions?'; (iv) 'How do we induce particular emotions or inculcate particular emotional dispositions in others?'; and (v) 'Can emotions improve decisionmaking?'

In answer to the last question, Elster (ibid.) points out that emotions can function as 'tiebreakers', enabling agents to make decisions where rational choice theory is indeterminate. He also refers to Damasio's (1994) research in neurobiology which finds that patients who have experienced damage to their frontal lobes lose their capacity to make decisions. This is because they cannot perform the basic agenda-setting function of screening issues according to their urgency and significance, since it is the emotions that enable 'normal' people to spontaneously react to, and focus their attention on, issues that are urgent and significant.

Without explicitly acknowledging any connection, Elster comes close to the hermeneutical approach to decisionmaking discussed in Chapter 6. This is apparent in his rejection of the notion that emotions can be incorporated as psychic costs and benefits in individual utility functions in favour of an approach which he sums up as follows (Elster, 1998, p.73):

> The role of emotions cannot be reduced to that of shaping the reward parameters for rational choice. It seems very likely that they also affect the ability to make rational choices within those parameters. This dual role of the emotions – shaping choices as well as rewards – has analogues in pain, addictive cravings, and other visceral factors. As in these other cases, the claim is not that the emotions fully determine choice, or that there is no tradeoff between emotional rewards and other rewards.

Rather, it is that the tradeoff itself is modified by one of the rewards that is being traded off against the others.

Chapter 6 outlined the difficulties involved in adequately explaining leadership from a conventional economics perspective. This chapter will draw from some of the insights contained in Elster's article to show that leadership represents a classic case of a phenomenon that can only be adequately explained by taking into account the distinctive effect of the emotions on human behaviour. It will seek to address a number of the questions that arise with regard to the relationship between the emotions and leadership. These include: (i) 'What emotions do leaders specifically seek to influence?'; (ii) 'What are the characteristic features of this emotion?'; (iii) 'How can it be influenced in a way that makes leadership more effective by strengthening the relationship of trust that emerges between leaders pursuing the same goals and between these leaders and their followers?'; (iv) 'What role does social interaction play in facilitating these relationships of emotional influence?'; and (v) 'How can these networks overcome the resistance that arises within and between the organizations that they are seeking to steer in a particular direction?'

The chapter itself is divided into four main areas. Section 2 focuses on the complex interelationships between leadership and hope and the behavioural motivations induced by hope. Section 3 advances a theory of leadership as a dissonance reduction mechanism. Section 4 examines how a policy leadership network can play a crucial role in effecting a paradigmatic process of policy change. The chapter ends with some brief concluding remarks in section 5.

7.2   HOPE AND LEADERSHIP

The point of departure for the theory of leadership presented in this chapter is that *hope* constitutes the emotion that leaders strive to influence. It thus differs from Casson's (1991) theory of leadership which equates this phenomenon with the 'moral manipulation' of shame and guilt. However, as Elster makes clear, the intention to induce shame and guilt through manipulative rhetoric is incoherent. He generalizes this concept in the following way (Elster, 1998, p.58):

> By an incoherent intention I mean the intention to induce emotion X by behavior that would induce X if it was spontaneous but that induces emotion Y if believed to be motivated by the intention to induce X.

Thus, for example, if followers come to believe that their leaders are trying to manipulate their emotions of shame and guilt they may become angry at these leaders and experience a build-up of resentment toward them that would undermine their willingness to look to them for leadership. Alternatively, they may direct their anger at themselves and experience a build-up of disappointment that erodes their commitment to strive for the advancement of a particular quest. In either case, the manipulation of emotions such as guilt and shame can have counterproductive consequences. Moreover, as Elster (ibid.) points out, 'although a person with an incoherent intention may try to get around this problem by hiding his motivation, this requires an effort that should itself be counted as a cost and may in a given case be hard to achieve successfully.'

However, if leadership is conceived as involving the influence by leaders of the emotions of hope possessed by the members of a particular group, then these problems of incoherence will not arise. Followers are unlikely to be angry with leaders who succeed in strengthening their hopes. Moreover, to the extent that leaders succeed in doing this they will enable followers to counter the disappointments they experience during the course of their engagement on a particular quest. Generally, people are drawn to interact with other people who strengthen their hopes. Indeed, leadership can be conceived as the collective activity that develops social networks within which the shared hopes of members can be strengthened through their repeated social interaction. There would thus seem to be scope for deriving a greater insight into the distinctive nature of leadership through an analysis of the nature of hope and its potential effect on human action and interaction.

What is Hope?

Hope would seem to unambiguosly qualify as an emotion. Elster (ibid., p.48) brackets it, along with fear, as an emotion that is 'generated by the thought of what may happen'. In this regard, it can be distinguished from (i) various social emotions like 'anger, hatred, guilt, shame, pride, pridefulness, admiration, and liking'; (ii) the 'counterfactual emotions' of 'regret, rejoicing, disappointment, [and] elation'; (iii) emotions generated by 'things that have happened' such as joy and grief; (iv) 'emotions triggered by the thought of the possessions of others' like envy, malice, indignation and jealousy; (v) emotions that 'do not fall neatly into any category' such as contempt, disgust and romantic love; and (vi) 'borderline or controversial cases' which 'include surprise, boredom, interest, sexual desire, enjoyment, worry and frustration'.

It is the future orientation of hope that establishes the link between hope and leadership. To engage people in a quest to change history in a particular direction, leaders must strengthen the hope they have that they can somehow contribute to history following this future course. Hope would also seem to exemplify what Taylor (1985, p.54) termed a 'subject-referring emotion'. People must not only hope but they must be prepared to give reasons for their hope – or as Taylor puts it they must be prepared 'to ascribe an import … to make a judgment about the way things are which cannot be reduced to the way we feel about them.'

Along with the other emotions, hope can be distinguished from non-emotional mental states by six features, namely 'cognitive antecedents, intentional objects, physiological arousal, physiological expressions, valence, and action tendencies' (Elster, 1998, p.49). This scheme may be simplified, somewhat, by the proposition that hope is constituted by (i) particular beliefs about a particular quest or relationship (this combines the cognitive antecedent and intentional object features of this emotion); (ii) an observable level of emotional energy generated by these beliefs that can be invested in social interactions (this conflates the physiological arousal, physiological expression and valence aspects of hope); and (iii) by a particular type of action tendency that is engendered by the antecedent beliefs and investment of emotional energy. These features of hope must be examined in more detail.

The Beliefs that Trigger and Sustain Hope

Hope can be viewed as arising from two core beliefs. The object of these beliefs will be the process of striving that people engage in when they are seeking to advance a quest or sustain a relationship. This object is clearly germane to leadership since leaders typically seek to engage people on particular quests by drawing them into networks whose members share a commitment to advance these quests. There are, of course, other relationships that can become the object of hope. Samuel Johnson, for example, described the second marriage of a friend as 'the triumph of hope over experience' (Sutherland, 1989, p.193).

The first belief that triggers and sustains hope is the belief that the advancement of a quest or the maintenance and strengthening of a relationship is 'neither impossible nor inevitable' (ibid., 1989, p.195). This belief does not have to be based on probabilistic calculation. A commitment to a particular quest or relationship is often made under conditions of 'bounded uncertainty' such that its consequences cannot be probabilistically calculated – they can only be imagined (Shackle, 1973, p.62). In the

case of the reformists discussed in Chapter 5, it would seem to be sufficient that they believe that they have the 'policymaking capacity' (Moon,
1995) or 'waypower' (Snyder, 1994) to effectively react to the obstacles
and resistance generated by their opponents by devising and pursuing
alternative ways to advance their quest.

The second belief is that the advancement of a quest or 'reproduction'
of a relationship is 'worthwhile' or 'important' in the sense that it is 'worthy
of pursuit in a special way incommensurable with other goals we might
have' (Taylor, 1985, p.135). The process of placing our hope in certain goals
seems to involve an investment or commitment of self to the realization
of these goals.

Kingdon's (1984) characterization of certain policymakers as having
'pet' solutions or 'problems' that they advocate every time the 'garbage
can' of a particular issue 'rises to prominence on the policy agenda' indicates a degree of identification that stems from a belief in the worth or
importance of these problems or solutions. These advocates have more
than an 'inarticulate desire' that their goals be realized. In articulating the
worth of their goals or relationships in response to questions about their
significance, they identify with them, in the sense that their public identity
is, at least partly, constituted by the positions they take about them in
'public space' (Taylor, 1989). It follows that people can strengthen their
own sense of identity by interacting with other people who share the same
hopes since during the course of such interactions they are likely to be
given more articulate reasons for committing themselves to the realization
of the objects of these hopes.

The beliefs that trigger hope do not just have to be placed in specific
quests or relationships. They can be more generally related to the type
of quest that, according to Alisdair MacIntyre, constitutes the 'good life'.
MacIntyre (1981, p.219) thus proposes that 'the good life for man is the life
spent seeking for the good life for man.' This overarching quest can encompass the whole life of a person so that any particular quest or relationship
undertaken during this life can only be undertaken as a partial expression of
this quest for the good life. No person can sustain the quest for the good life
without believing in its worth and possibility, without believing that there
will always be quests and relationships worth making commitments to, as an
expression of this fundamental capacity for hope. Even if a quest or relationship fails, the people who have committed themselves to it may not consider
their hope to have been completely misplaced, since through their involvement in it they may have increased their understanding of a way of pursuing
the good life. As MacIntyre (ibid.) puts it 'a quest is always an education
both as to the character of that which is sought and in self-knowledge.'

However, a person who chooses to give up hope, in the general sense, can command our sympathy or compassion, but does not command our respect. It would not be right to accept and respect this decision. It would be incumbent on all those who are in a position to influence this person to attempt to influence them to reverse this decision, to revive their sense of hope that life is worth living, that there are quests or relationships worth making commitments to, because they can potentially advance the quest for the good life.

MacIntyre's (ibid.) conception of the overarching quest for the good life intimates how leader–follower relationships can be morally legitimate provided that followers only place their specific and not their general hope in the leader and the quest. Such followers still retain their moral autonomy in the weak sense that, although they are submitting to the leadership of another person, they still have the capacity to disengage from this relationship when they loose hope in the leader's quest and can place their specific hope in alternative leaders and quests.

However, it would be immoral for a leader to expect followers to invest their general sense of hope in their quest. To do this would conflate the particular hope a follower has, in a particular leader or quest, with the fundamental hope they have that life is worth living. It would claim an ultimacy for the quest and its leader that it could not bear and could thereby lead to the pathological, totalitarian type of leader–follower relationship described in Chapter 6.

The Passion Aroused by Hope

Hope, nevertheless, involves more than a set of beliefs. These beliefs must be expressed with a degree of emotional energy or *passion* that is reflected in the characteristics of physiological arousal, physiological expression and valence described by Elster (1998). Perhaps the most immediate indicator of passion is a person's level of emotional energy. Collins (1993) has formulated a theory in which emotional energy is 'the common denominator in rational social action'. According to Collins (1993), people invest varying levels of emotional energy in their social interactions. High levels of emotional energy will be reflected in feelings such as enthusiasm and confidence while low levels are manifested, for example, by apathy and depression. However, in most interactions the emotional energy of individuals is at a 'medium level' which will be unnoticed by both themselves and those with whom they are interacting. Only people with very high or very low levels of emotional energy will pass the attention threshold at which their degree of emotional intensity becomes 'empirically visible, both in behaviour (especially nonverbal expressions and postures) and in physiology' (Collins, 1993, p.211). It is suggested that 'passion' consists in the high and observable level of emotional energy that can either draw people toward, or repel them away from, interactions in which it is generated by participants.

Leadership can be conceived as involving the development of a culture of passion to advance a particular quest within leader–leader and leader–follower networks. This passion is perhaps the most important source of the intrinsic motivation the members of these networks have to advance this quest. It provides a boundedness and common focus to the network as a whole. Such a culture is likely to foster a 'tunnel vision' among its members so that they collectively focus on striving toward the advancement of their quest and reproduction of their relationship. What then are the action tendencies produced by this culture?

The Action Tendencies Produced by Hope

In his survey of emotion theory, Elster (1998, p.47) has pointed out that:

> By and large, psychological studies of the emotions have not focused on how emotions generate behavior. Instead, they have tried to identify the proximate or ultimate causes of the emotions. To the extent that psychologists are concerned with behavior, it is usually with *action tendencies* rather than with observable actions.

These 'action tendencies' have been defined by Frijda (1986, p.70) as 'states of readiness to execute a given type of action'.

Erich Fromm (1968, p.9) has highlighted this characteristic of hope:

> Hope is paradoxical. It is neither passive waiting nor is it unrealistic forcing of circumstances that cannot occur. It is like the crouched tiger, which will jump only when the moment for jumping has come. Neither tired reformism nor pseudo-radical adventurism is an expression of hope. To hope means to be ready at every moment for that which is yet to be born, and yet not to become desperate if there is no birth in our lifetime. There is no sense in hoping for that which already exists or for that which cannot be. Those whose hope is weak settle down for comfort or for violence; those whose hope is strong see and cherish all signs of new life and are ready at every moment to help the birth of that which is ready to be born.

In a more prosaic way, Kingdon (1984) associates this same characteristic with those 'policy entrepreneurs' who 'lie in wait' for an opportunity to influence the outcomes of a policy process. These actors perform the function of 'coupling' solutions, problems and politicians together at the time when 'policy windows' open. As 'brokers' they seek to build winning coalitions in favour of proposals. As 'advocates' they must have their pet proposals or concerns ready to be pushed when the opportunity arises. They may spend years 'lying in wait' for such propitious moments to arrive. During this time they will ensure that their pet problems, solutions and theories survive in conflict and competition with alternatives, and that the policy-making community is 'softened up' to a state of receptivity to them. To do this they need to have not only technical and political skills, but also and above all, a *persistence* that depends on the reserves of hope they can draw on in striving to realize their goals.

Snyder's (1994, p.5) definition of hope as 'the sum of the willpower and waypower that you have for your goals' seems to be particularly germane to understanding the behaviour of policy entrepreneurs. From Kingdon's (1984) perspective, policy entrepreneurs are purposive agents with relatively limited goals: that is, highlighting a policy problem, advocating a policy solution, coupling a solution with a problem and so on. In the course of striving to achieve these goals, they will need to exercise (i) 'willpower' as they draw on their reserves of emotional energy or 'determination and commitment', and (ii) 'waypower' as they generate one or more effective paths to their realization. They will particularly need to exercise willpower and waypower in the face of opposition or resistance or when the path they are pursuing toward a goal comes to be blocked. The exercise of these qualities by policy entrepreneurs is exemplified by the way in which they adapt their 'pet solutions' to a changing mosaic of problems and politics. Kingdon (1984) illustrates this with reference to the case of urban mass transit in the United States which has at various times been proposed by the same group of policy entrepreneurs as a solution to problems of traffic management, environmental pollution and energy shortages.

The goals that are shared by members of the type of reformist network discussed in Chapter 5 will typically be broader than the rather limited individual goals which Kingdon depicts policy entrepreneurs as pursuing. They will typically strive to advance a policy quest by advocating comprehensive reform processes such as liberalization, stabilization, privatization and commercialization. For such a reform programme to seem appropriate, it must be coupled with a 'crisis' of sufficient magnitude, and paradigm shift of sufficient scope, to warrant a radical change in policy direction.

The goals of such reformists are thus more ambitious and the window of opportunity they are waiting for greater than would seem be the case with 'ordinary' policy entrepeneurs. Moreover, they are not independent agents. They are highly dependent on a network of like-minded policy advocates who provide one another with the backing and resources to redirect public policy. Indeed, part of the 'crouched tiger' tendencies of the members of such a network is a willingness and capacity to 'wait for one another', to allow that member of the network who is in the best position to exert leverage over the direction of policy to 'have their day in the sun' when the opportunity for this arises.

It is through the interactions that occur between the members of a network that the action tendencies that arise from their shared hopes are reproduced and strengthened. How this process occurs and the link between this process and leadership forms the subject of the next section.

7.3   LEADERSHIP AS A DISSONANCE REDUCTION MECHANISM

Elster (1998, p.64) rejects a cost–benefit model of the emotions that treats them 'as psychic costs and benefits that enter into the utility function on par with satisfactions derived from material rewards' in favour of an approach that views them both as sources of dissonance and as mechanisms of dissonance reduction. The concept of 'cognitive dissonance' was popularized by Leon Festinger (1957). It refers to the unpleasant feeling of tension individuals experience when they have to choose between alternative, mutually exclusive courses of action. Once they have committed themselves to a particular course, they will look for cognitions that support it and reduce their feelings of tension or dissonance. A classic example of this is provided by automobile buyers who, after having decided to buy a particular model, mainly read literature which confirms the wisdom of this decision.

According to Elster, 'dissonance theory is more realistic than the cost–benefit model in that it views individuals as making hard choices on the basis of *reasons* rather than on the basis of introspections about how they feel' (ibid., p.66). It can help explain the 'sticky', 'punctuated equilibrium', 'path dependent' nature of many commitments in respect of which individuals seek for reasons to sustain their commitments until a threshold is reached 'when the arguments on the other side become too strong and the rationalization breaks down' so that 'a switch in behavior occurs'. Although Elster (ibid.) points out that 'psychologists have not considered emotions as sources of cognitive dissonance and dissonance reduction', he suggests that 'there seems to be no reason why emotions could not be sources of dissonance' (p.66). The 'subject-referring emotions' referred to by Taylor (1985) would seem, in particular, to lend themselves to this approach since, according to this philosopher, they are constituted, in part, by the reasons advanced for holding them.

Elster (ibid.) proposes that if emotions can be incorporated into dissonance theory then this could lead to their incorporation into economic theory since a number of economists (such as Akerlof and Dickens, 1982; Rabin, 1994) 'are now incorporating dissonance theory into their framework'. This section will elaborate a theory of leadership as a dissonance reduction mechanism. Prior to this discussion, though, it will briefly consider an alternative Beckerian approach to modelling the relationship between hope and leadership.

A Beckerian Theory of Leadership

Gary Becker (1981) has been awarded the Nobel Prize in economics in part for his role in pioneering a 'new home economics' that enables economists to analyse 'non-market' behaviours that have traditionally been considered to be beyond their reach. The standard assumption in Beckerian models is that agents use inputs of purchased goods, time and human capital to 'produce' satisfaction from 'commodities' which constitute the actual arguments in their utility functions. These commodities can be as abstract as recreational enjoyment and health. The satisfaction individuals derive from participation in leadership networks could be treated as another such commodity. It is clear that individuals use inputs of time and goods to produce this commodity. But what is the nature of the human capital they combine with these other inputs?

In standard Beckerian models, human capital is conceived as the knowledge individuals acquire through general education and learning on-the-job. In an earlier article (Wallis, 1996), some reasons why hope can be treated as a form of human capital were advanced. Firstly, it is possible to distinguish between general and specific forms of hope in the same way that it is possible to distinguish between general and specific forms of human capital. The general capacity for hope enables people to place their hope in specific projects or relationships without necessarily attaching an ultimacy to these projects or relationships. Like general human capital, this capacity will to some degree be innate but can also to a significant degree be developed through social interaction and social influence. The specific hope which individuals have in particular projects or relationships is like the specific form of human capital that is formed 'on-the-job' through practice. This is the type of hope which individuals place or invest when they commit themselves to particular leaders, groups and quests.

Like any form of capital, the specific hope that is invested in a leadership network can be subject to processes of accumulation and depreciation. The distinctive role of leadership is to reinforce and strengthen it in the face of disappointments that can accumulate in a way which undermines it. These disappointments can arise from a number of sources. Firstly, the members of a leadership network will be exposed to disappointments associated with its quest. Due to their 'poverty of imagination' (Hirschman, 1982) they may not imagine all the obstacles to its advancement so that surprising failures and setbacks may be interpreted as disappointments. Secondly, they may experience disappointments associated with belonging to a particular group. These disappointments typically arise when group pressures to conform its norms lead to 'preference falsification' (Kuran, 1990) among its members as they over- or under-commit themselves in relation to the degree that they seek to express their hope in the quest. Thirdly, to the extent that individuals internalize group norms and form 'second order' 'metapreferences' to keep them, they will experience guilt or shame when they fail to keep the commitments that are the subject of these norms. These different sources of disappointment can clearly combine and interact with one another in a cumulative process.

In terms of a Beckerian model, changes in the stock of human capital will change the 'shadow prices' of the inputs that are used to produce satisfaction from a commodity. Where the accumulation of disappointment weakens the hope placed in a leadership network and its quest, these shadow prices will rise and induce the type of substitution effects which are very familiar to economists. This suggests that there will occur smooth and continuous adjustments of the inputs supplied to produce satisfaction from participation in the leadership network in relation to those supplied to produce other commodities (including those derived from participating in other networks). This ignores the punctuated equilibrium pattern that has been observed with regard to many types of commitment. This is reflected in the way individuals sustain their commitments until their disappointments have accumulated above the threshold at which they break these commitments and commit themselves to alternative quests and relationships (Hirschman, 1982). This type of behaviour becomes readily explicable when disappointment is treated as a source of dissonance and leadership as a dissonance reduction mechanism.

Leadership versus Disappointment

To recapitulate, leadership has been conceived in this book as a collective activity. It is an activity that is performed in a leadership network. It is directed toward strengthening the shared hopes of the members of the network so that they can be in a state of preparedness to take full advantage of whatever opportunity arises to advance their quest or to advance other members into a position from which they can contribute to this advancement. Leadership networks can be constituted by horizontal relationships between different leaders or they can be leader–follower networks in which a particular person, the leader, plays a focal role. In the latter type of network, followers look to their leaders to strengthen their hopes, while in the former type this process occurs through the repeated interactions of different members. The distinction between the two types of network is sometimes blurred since in some networks an alternation of roles can be observed with the same person assuming leadership on some issues or tasks and playing the role of a follower with regard to others.

In the case of the New Zealand reformist network described in Chapter 5, it is clear that the formulation of public policy was driven by a horizontal leader–leader network which spanned across different organizations and groups at the top while the implementation of policy was placed in the hands of change agents who sought to transform public organizations 'from the top down' through the formation of leader–follower networks. These networks differed not so much in the means they used to establish a high degree of internal cohesion as in the 'enemy territory' they were seeking to penetrate, dismantle and reconstruct. The similar means they used to establish internal cohesion, and to build up the shared hopes of their members, will be examined in this section while their external strategy will be considered in the next section.

Leadership networks provide the context within which the hopes shared by members can be strengthened through their interaction so that the dissonance associated with accumulated disappointments can be reduced. This dissonance-reducing function of interaction should ensure the continuity of leadership since it helps sustain the commitment to a particular quest of network members.

There are two ways in which network interaction can strengthen hope and reduce disappointment. Firstly, such interaction is likely to involve a mutual sharing of reasons for hope. Each member is likely to have his or her own reasons for participating in the leadership network but these will always, to a degree, be implicit, inchoate and partly articulated. They will therefore look to other to provide a clearer, more explicit articulation and to buttress their beliefs in the worth and possibility of committing themselves to the advancement of their quest. This will not only strengthen the cohesion of the network and facilitate the convergence of their hopes on a shared vision. It may also serve an 'evangelistic' function, persuading outsiders of the worth and possibility of committing themselves to the particular leadership network and its quest.

Secondly, network interaction can enhance the emotional energy or passion of its members. Collins has proposed that this type of passion can be both a product of, and a resource which can be invested in what he calls 'interaction rituals' (IRs). This 'emotional energy' will reach its peak at the climax of a 'successful' IR in which the participating group's focus of attention and common emotional mood go through a short-term cycle of increase and mutual stimulation until a point of emotional satiation is reached. The interaction will leave each participant with an 'energetic afterglow' that 'gradually decreases over time' so that individuals have an incentive to reinvest their emotional energy in subsequent interactions. It may therefore accumulate across IRs so that 'an individual may build up a long-term fund of confidence and enthusiasm by repeated participation in successful IRs' (1993, p.212). It is this fund or reserve of 'willpower and waypower', that can be drawn on by the members of a leadership network to counter the emotional component of the dissonance they experienced as a result of disappointments and to sustain their 'action tendencies' to 'lie in wait' 'like crouched tigers' for opportunities to advance their quest for one another.

To develop this type of culture in a leader–follower network, the leaders will have to structure group interactions so that they pass the thresholds of 'physical density' and 'boundedness' that are necessary for their success. The threshold of physical density is passed when at least two persons are close enough for a sufficient period of time to ensure that they can be moved by one another's passion. The threshold of boundedness may be passed when there is an expressive dimension to group interaction so that participants are expected to identify themselves as followers by expressing a passion for advancing the leader's quest.

A person who does not have this passion will find it more difficult to interact as a member of the leadership network than Kuran's (1990) theory of preference falsification seems to suggest. It will be hard to 'keep up an act', continuously 'fooling' other members about their lack of passionate intensity and, even if they succeed in this falsifying strategy, they will derive no satisfaction from a sense of belonging to this group. A culture of passion can therefore function as a selection mechanism screening out those participants who do not believe the quest to be worthy of their passion and drawing into the network those people who are willing to commit themselves passionately to it in the hope that it will prove worthy of this commitment. The boundedness of the group may be enhanced over time by the selective effect of this culture.

Leaders may ensure that these thresholds of density and boundedness are passed by structuring group interaction into a number of levels descending in status from the 'inner circle' of followers who the leader chooses to interact directly with. Access to this level of interaction will be limited to those followers in whom the leader has placed the highest level of trust. This trust will be based not just on the skills and resources which these followers can deploy in performing the tasks allocated to them, but also on the passion which they express in seeking ways to advance the leader's quest. The members of a leader's inner circle will often typically be 'autonomous' rather than 'habituated' followers (Howell, 1988). The passion that is expected of them will not be a blind zeal but a persistent focus on seeking the best means available to advance a particular quest.

Leaders can thus shape the development of their follower culture by setting the terms according to which followers compete for access to their inner circle. Moreover, they can influence the passion that is generated in this circle and which filters down the different levels of followership by enhancing the commonality of focus and emotional mood that is stimulated by IRs. Bennis and Nanus' (1985) conception of leaders as 'managers of meaning' would seem to be pertinent in this regard. Leaders direct followers' attention to the point and significance of their actions and interactions and they narrow their evaluation of this point and significance to a simple consideration of whether these activities are moving the quest in the direction intended by the leader.

Regardless of whether leadership takes place in a vertically structured or, more informal, horizontal network, it facilitates interactions which buttress and strengthen the belief, passion and action tendency components of hope. The leadership that occurs in these networks is thus a distinctive process but is it significant? It is possible to conceive of a social network that achieves a high degree of internal cohesion but makes no difference to the history of the broader social context or environment in which it is situated. The issue of the significance of leadership will be revisited by examining how a policy leadership network can play a significant role in effecting a paradigmatic process of policy change.

7.4   THE POLITICS OF LEADERSHIP

Chapter 5 described the leadership network that has played a significant role in effecting paradigmatic policy change in New Zealand. One lesson that can be drawn from this experience is that the degree to which this type of network can establish itself as a coherent source of policy leadership will not just depend on its internal cohesion. It will also depend on its external articulation and penetration – on the degree to which it is able to establish 'beachheads' within 'enemy territory' from which its members can exert leverage over the direction of public policy.

A map of the 'enemy territory' that can lie before this type of leadership network has been provided by Rhodes and Marsh (1992). According to these writers, a national 'policy space' may be occupied by a fragmented structure of 'policy networks' that 'exist to routinise relationships' between the government departments and sectional interests affected by functionally segmented areas of public policy. Rhodes and Marsh (ibid.) conceive 'policy networks' as a generic term which encompasses a continuum of types, ranging from the stable, highly integrated, vertically interdependent and exclusive 'policy community', to the more open and unstable type of 'issue network' studied by Heclo (1978).

In Britain, case studies based on the 'Rhodes model' have been made of policy networks in agriculture, civil nuclear power, youth employment, smoking, heart disease and health services, information technology and exchange rate policy (Marsh and Rhodes, ibid.). Most of these networks were found to be closer to the policy community end of the continuum. They were, to a varying degree, exclusive and elitist so that 'in each area a limited number of groups enjoyed privileged access to policymaking shaping both the policy agenda and policy outcomes' (Rhodes and Marsh, ibid., p.199). Significantly, Rhodes and Marsh (ibid., pp.196–7) conclude that such policy networks can act as a major constraint on policy change. They 'do not necessarily seek to frustrate any and all change but to contain, redirect and ride-out such change, thereby materially affecting its speed and direction.'

Reforming legislation can be viewed as part of the 'aerial attack' designed to demolish the organizational strongholds within which such policy networks can become entrenched. Public sector reform seems to play a particularly important role in this regard. A key feature of the 'New Public Management' discussed in Chapter 4 is the way it has sought to break up large bureaucratic government structures into 'single, objective, trackable and manageable units' (Hood, 1991, p.14). An aerial attack typically prepares an enemy position for assault by ground forces. In New Zealand, the ground forces of the drive for comprehensive reform were led by 'change agents' – the trusted members of the reformist network who could be moved into position at the head of government agencies so that they could strive to break up, reconfigure and wrest the reins of policy leadership from previously insulated policy communities that had formed around these agencies.

Moreover, as Chapter 5 made clear, the 'leadership' provided by these change agents will not just have a horizontal dimension. It will also have a vertical dimension as followers of these change agents seek to infiltrate and overcome the cultural resistance of the informal networks that exist within organizations. A description of these networks can be found in various 'bottom up' implementation studies of the type developed by Hjern and Hull (1982). These studies focus on the way the 'street level bureaucrats' (Lipsky, 1973), who interact directly with the public in the provision of the services of government organizations, develop 'coping' strategies to maintain their autonomy in the face of top-down initiatives to overcome their resistance and change their behaviour. Critics of the New Zealand experiment, such as Easton (1997), have identified public health as an area where the 'cultural resistance' of professional service providers has been effective in thwarting the drive toward privatization by committed change agents.

The 'clash of cultures' (Raelin, 1991) that emerged in New Zealand between the commercialist change agents appointed to manage public service agencies, such as hospitals (or crown health enterprises – CHEs – as they were renamed in New Zealand), and the professionals responsible for delivering public services has often concentrated upon the differing significance or priority that the rival cultures attached to efficiency values and 'invisible' outputs. For the commercialists, efficiency values are paramount and the propensity of professionals to pursue excellence in professional practice beyond the point where it is cost effective should be tightly controlled.

In New Zealand, this has been done through contractualist arrangements and performance monitoring systems that have compelled service providers to rigorously specify their 'outputs' as well as a 'sinking lid' policy of progressively reducing funding to public agencies to place their management under pressure to seek more cost-efficient ways of delivering these outputs. Under pressure to cut costs and ensure that 'visible', specified outputs are provided, public managers can come into conflict with professionals. This is because the professionals may not only find it more difficult to satisfy their own standards of excellence, but they have to interact with clients dissatisfied by a reduced level of assurance that their own needs will override cost-cutting imperatives and by a reduction in the 'invisible' unspecified aspects of service they receive.

The resistance generated by such professional groups can take a number of the visible, active forms normally associated with politics. However, as the 'bottom-up' implementations studies indicate, it can also take the invisible, passive form exemplified by a street-level bureaucrat who treats the intrusions of a top-down leadership network as a constraint to be coped with, rather than a set of values or beliefs to be internalized.

No discussion of leadership can be complete without a discussion of the resistance it can potentially generate. No matter how high the degree of internal cohesion and external articulation and penetration achieved by a leadership network, it may still fail to 'make a difference' if it cannot circumvent, overcome or come to terms with the sources of resistance it provokes. The next chapter will consider the nature and purpose of the 'reactionary' patterns of rhetoric which can sustain this resistance in the face of the advances of a 'progressive' leadership network. The main arguments of this chapter are recapitulated by way of conclusion.

7.5   CONCLUDING REMARKS

This chapter has developed a theory that highlights the distinctiveness of leadership. This distinctiveness is derived from the distinctive emotion – hope – that can be developed through interaction in leadership networks. The interaction between agents who share the same hope is likely to build up the beliefs, emotional energy and action tendencies that underlie, sustain and are expressed by this emotion. Moreover, this social process of strengthening hope should counter the dissonance members experience as a result of their disappointments. This should also sustain their own commitment to advance the network's quest and enhance the internal cohesiveness of the network as a whole. A cohesive network with a committed membership should expand as it engages new members who may be predisposed to make new commitments as a result of their disappointments with other quests and relationships.

For an internally cohesive leadership network to make a difference it must be able to penetrate and reconfigure those networks that are likley to resist its forward thrust. The resistance generated by these networks is, nevertheless, unlikely to be purely reactive. In the course of resisting they are likely to develop a cohesion of their own and to advance reasons for resisting that not only strengthen the hopes of their own members, but also weaken the hopes of the forces of 'progressive' leadership. Since hope is an emotion that is based on reason, any discussion of paradigmatic policy change that takes the role of hope into account will also have to take into account the patterns of rhetoric that emerge in the struggle between the advocates and opponents of radical reform. The link between hope and rhetoric will thus form the subject of Chapter 8.

8 The Rhetorical Patterns in Paradigmatic Policy Change

8.1 INTRODUCTION

In his book *The Rhetoric of Reaction*, Albert Hirschman (1991) argues that each major advance in the development of citizenship in Western democracies – from civil to political to socio-economic citizenship – has provoked a strong reaction in which the opponents of reform have 'unfailingly' advanced a few common or typical arguments. Hirschman denotes these three lines of argument as 'the perversity thesis', the 'futility thesis', and the 'jeopardy thesis'. Although he relates these theses to the question of the development of citizenship, he makes it clear that they can apply to any reform that constitutes a radical change (or paradigm shift) rather than an incremental adjustment to the previous policy configuration.

According to the perversity thesis, a radical reform may have perverse consequences in the sense that it can exacerbate the condition the reformers are seeking to remedy. The futility thesis predicts that reform will bring about no significant transformation; that it will 'simply fail to make a dent'. Finally, the jeopardy thesis holds that the cost of the proposed reform is too high since it will damage some vital traditional capacity or endanger some previous, hard-won historical achievement.

This chapter will focus on the way these theses and their 'progressive counterparts' have been deployed in the debate that has surrounded the implementation of the 'New Public Management' (NPM); a doctrine we examined in some detail in Chapter 4. It should be borne in mind that the process of institutionalizing NPM forms only one component – that is commercialization – in a comprehensive reform programme that seeks to advance processes of liberalization, stabilization, privatization and commercialization (LSPC) in response to pervasive problems of government failure. However, as Chapter 7 made clear, the struggle to advance a paradigmatic process of policy change will be fought out in one policy subsystem after another as a reformist leadership network seeks to penetrate and displace the policy networks that can dominate policymaking in particular subsystems for prolonged periods. Accordingly, much can be learned from a study of the arguments and counter arguments that are advanced in a particular policy subsystem in which a reformist network is striving to effect paradigmatic change.

In examining the patterns of argument that have emerged in the policy subsystem that is concerned with the administration of the core public sector, this chapter will try to address a number of questions. Why can the type of policy change involved in the implementation of the NPM be viewed as being paradigmatic in nature? What have been the jeopardy, perversity and futility arguments levelled against this paradigmatic policy change? What have been the progressive counterparts to these arguments? To whom have these different lines of argument been typically directed? Why does a recognition of the importance of hope and leadership in policy-making focus attention on these patterns of rhetoric? What rival notions of the public interest underlie the main rhetorical positions and shape the rhetorical strategies of the main protagonists? And finally, is there any solution to the rhetorical intransigence that Hirschman (1991) suggested can emerge in a policy community that factionalizes itself on the basis of these arguments, counterarguments, and rival conceptions of the public interest?

The chapter itself is divided into five main sections. Section 2 examines the paradigmatic nature of NPM. Using Hirschman's (1991) tripartite taxonomy of the perversity, futility and jeopardy theses, section 3 focuses on reactionary rhetoric in criticisms of NPM. Section 4 deals with the rhetorical strategies deployed by hope-based leadership networks. The chapter ends with a concluding argument in section 5.

8.2   THE PARADIGMATIC NATURE OF NEW PUBLIC MANAGEMENT

As we have seen in Chapter 4, it has been widely acknowledged that the implementation of the 'broadly similar set of administrative doctrines' (Hood, 1991) often referred to as 'New Public Management' (NPM) reflects a paradigm shift in the theory and practice of public administration. This development has thus been heralded as a move to a 'post bureaucratic' paradigm (Aucoin, 1990; Barzelay, 1992; Kernaghan, 1993; Yeatman, 1997) or from bureaucratic to entrepreneurial government (Osborne and Gaebler, 1993) or as a replacement of the set of values underlying traditional public administration (Hood, 1991).

It can be argued that NPM falls into the category of what Hall (1993) has termed a 'policy paradigm'. The type of policy change involved in the shift to this paradigm therefore accommodates more than a 'first order' change in the settings of policy instruments or a 'second order' change in the instruments or techniques used to achieve policy goals. It also involves a radical 'third order change' in the hierarchy of goals in the policy subsystem concerned with public administration, in the overarching terms of policy discourse, and in the interpretive frameworks that shape policy-makers' understanding of the problems that they are capable of solving.

In Chapter 4 we argued that as a policy paradigm, NPM was derived from and yet remains distinct from the stream of theories that shaped its development. We noted that Hood (1991, p.4) viewed NPM as a 'marriage of two different streams of ideas' – (i) the 'new institutional, economics' that has been built on the foundations laid by public choice, transaction cost and principal–agent theory and (ii) 'managerialism' based on the 'ideas of "*professional-management*" expertise as portable, *paramount* over technical expertise requiring high *discretionary power* to achieve results ("free to manage") and *central* and *indispensable* through the development of appropriate institutions and the active measurement and adjustment of organizational outputs.'

Chapter 5 discussed the way policy advisers tend to screen out ambigui-ties and blur fine distinctions in constructing a policy paradigm. It is not surprising, therefore, that various writers have detected various inconsis-tencies and sources of incoherence between the two main theoretical streams that have been drawn from in the development of NPM, as we have argued in Chapter 4. The inherent policy pessimism of a new institu-tional economics that typically highlights the conditions of nonmarket supply, which generate nonmarket failure, does not always sit easily with the intrinsic optimism of a managerialism that views best practice manage-ment techniques as a generic solution to organizational problems in both the private and the public sector. Moreover, as Hood has observed, 'free to manage', is a rather different slogan from 'free to choose'. The two can conflict, particularly when the NPM revolution is led from above (as it was in the UK) rather than from below. Some clear differences can there-fore be discerned in the shape NPM took in different countries where the relative dominance of the two theoretical streams varied. Hood (ibid., p.6) has put this argument as follows:

> In the unique circumstances of New Zealand, the synthesis of public choice, transaction cost theory and principal–agent theory was predomi-nant, producing an analytically driven NPM movement of unusual coherence. But in the UK and Australia, business-type managerialism was more salient producing a more pragmatic and less intellectually elegant strain of NPM.

A deep structure of core beliefs and values can nevertheless be dis-cerned in all these strains of NPM which set them clearly apart from the deep structure of the 'bureaucratic', 'traditional' or 'progressive' paradigm that they have sought to replace. Hood locates this deep structure in the administrative rather than political value judgements made by the advocates of NPM.

As we noted in Chapter 4, Hood (1991, 1994a) identifies three clusters of core administrative values: (i) the 'sigma' family of values that emphasize economy and frugality in resource use, and which can be pursued through reforms that restructure public agencies so that resources can be more closely matched with narrowly defined tasks and functions; (ii) the 'theta' family of values that underlie a commitment to honesty and fairness, and the prevention of distortion, inequity and abuse of office through the routinization of appropriate procedures and the delineation of the duties attached to different roles; and (iii) the 'lambda' family of values that focus on enhancing the resilience of public agencies through a quest to transform them into 'learning organizations' capable of adapting rapidly and avoiding system failure in the face of unforeseen threats, challenges and crises.

Although Hood (1991, p.15) accepts that 'these three sets of mainstream administrative values overlap over some of their range' he identifies NPM with a commitment to realize 'sigma values' even where this may eventually make public agencies less capable of realizing the others. It thus constitutes a radical break from a policy paradigm which tended to privilege 'theta' and 'lambda' value clusters over the sigma-related one.

The historic achievement of this predecessor bureaucratic paradigm or Hood's (1994, p.125) 'Progressive-Era Public Administration' (PPA) lay in the way it addressed problems of 'partisan patronage and *ad hoc* meddling' by politicians in public administration. It did this by separating politics and administration and establishing procedures which ensured that administrative decisions could be made in a professional manner by a 'Jesuitical Corps' of public servants. As a result of their fixed salaries, promotion on merit and permanence of tenure, it can be argued that they could be trusted to behave in a more appropriate, professional manner than short-term appointees whose tenure and levels of remuneration could be determined by their political patrons.

The institutionalization of this bureaucratic paradigm was effected through the development of a comprehensive legal-administrative framework of public law and a distinctive public service culture characterized by a commitment to theta-values of fairness and rectitude. However, at the same time as an appreciation of this culture came to be limited more and more to practitioners, various writers, bringing an outsider perspective to the field of public administration (often derived from economic and management theories), highlighted various anomalies and problems with the bureaucratic paradigm. These were associated with its inflexibility and tendency to generate red tape and organizational slack. These problems achieved a greater resonance in the environment of fiscal austerity that prevailed in the late 1970s and early 1980s, particularly in English-speaking nations within which there was an increasingly strident political demand for governments which provided more but cost less (Peters, 1996b).

However, NPM did not stand alone as the only alternative to the old paradigm. Some popular writers, such as Osborne and Gaebler (1993), have tended to advocate an incoherent blend of economic rationalism and post-modern perspectives on 'breaking through bureaucracy'. Others, such as Yeatman (1997), have been more careful to distinguish the post-bureaucratic emphasis on participation, empowerment, decentralization and equality of opportunity with NPM's primary focus on the 'three Es' of effectiveness, efficiency and economy. Nevertheless, there are definite indications that public administration is emerging from this stage of 'paradigm fragmentation' (Howlett and Ramesh, 1996) to a situation in which NPM is being institutionalized as the hegemonic policy paradigm. This has been particularly apparent in the English-speaking nations with the public sector reforms of the late 1980s in New Zealand and Australia and the 'Next Steps' Initiatives in the UK reflecting the ascendancy of NPM.

Once a paradigm has established its ascendancy in this way, its opponents must be prepared to sustain a prolonged, persistent and consistent line of criticism in the hope that this will eventually erode its authority. The manner in which the criticisms of NPM have tended to follow the three reactionary theses identified by Hirschman (1991) will be examined in the next section.

8.3 THE THESES OF REACTIONARY RHETORIC IN CRITICISMS OF NPM

A number of articles, largely critical of NPM, have been published over the last five years in three leading public administration journals, namely the British *Public Administration*, the American *Public Administration Review*, and the *Australian Journal of Public Administration*. We now attempt to identify the jeopardy, futility and perversity arguments apparent in the literature that has been critical of NPM-style public sector reforms.

The Jeopardy Thesis in Criticisms of NPM

The jeopardy thesis is most apparent in the claims by traditionalists that the 'outsiders' who advocate the institutionalization of NPM have failed to adequately appreciate the historic achievement and enduring value of a unified public service characterized by a high degree of interagency co-operation and a strong professional culture among career civil servants. Hood (1994, p.130) has observed that 'the belief that public service needs to be uniform and inclusive to be accountable' has been replaced by a belief that 'flexibility, independence and lower transactions costs require loosely specified employment contracts and open-ended provision'. The tendency has therefore been to allow the tasks and associated organizations of modern government to become disaggregated, resulting in what Thynne (1996, p.49) calls an 'atomised component management'. According to Self (1995, p.341), this 'strongly impedes co-operation between agencies, especially of an informal kind, or the adoption of common policies and standards, except where clearly imposed from above.' The capacity of governments to seek co-ordinated solutions to problems such as unemployment, poverty and environmental degradation may thus have been eroded.

Another recurrent criticism of NPM is that it may jeopardize the professional culture of the public service. Its emphasis on financial economy and prompt service delivery may cause service providers to 'cut corners' and discriminate against 'hard cases'. Self (1995, p.340) has argued that 'equitable treatment of individuals in social services and in many forms of regulation depends on professional standards and integrity which cannot be measured but which can be administratively nurtured or frozen out.'

Moreover, the emphasis by NPM on the separation between politics and management may erode the capacity of public servants to provide 'free and frank advice' based on a dispassionate assessment of the 'public interest'. Such an assessment would involve the type of balanced consideration of the values, obligations and interests affected by particular situations that would be difficult for public servants to make if their duty to be loyal to the government of the day was not combined with a certain degree of professional autonomy. From a traditional perspective then, the relationship between, say, a senior civil servant and a cabinet minister is more akin to that between a barrister and a client than that between an agent and a principal (Martin, 1991). By dismantling the career public service in countries like New Zealand, and removing, at least to some degree, employment features such as fixed salaries and permanence of tenure, NPM may have reduced the autonomy of public service so that they are less capable of providing free and frank advice. One of the important institutions that sustains the system of checks and balances that characterize distinctively democratic policy processes may thus have been weakened.

This argument has been extended to address the way in which the NPM has had the effect of simplifying multiple stakeholder situations by creating two-party relationships between the 'chief executive' of public agencies and the cabinet ministers with a direct responsibility for the departments in which these agencies function. According to Thynne (1996), this erodes the pluralist basis for a legitimate democratic policy process since these relationships can be 'moulded and dominated by the executive which inevitably has the upper hand given its position of power and authority'. In addition, he has argued that these 'satellitic arrangements are such that key aspects of public administration and management are effectively shielded from the interplay of parliamentary politics and lie beyond the scope of judicial review in terms of both processes and outputs' (Thynne, 1996, p.51).

Jeopardy arguments are not just backward-looking, focusing only on the affect NPM has had on previously accumulated social capital or on the balance of power between the different branches of government. These arguments also tend to look forward, highlighting the way NPM may attenuate the capacity of governments to respond effectively to future demands on them.

A frequently made criticism of NPM is that a focus on improving efficiency and lowering unit costs could be 'used to cover up lack of investment and the effective renewal of public service infrastructures' (Hood, 1994, p.249). Hood goes further to point out that the drive by advocates of NPM to remove every source of organizational slack, including these which arise from maintaining safety level reserves of inputs and back-up systems, may reduce the capacity of public organizations to respond flexibly to adverse shocks and maintain their operations during crises. From this perspective, a componentized management system is less robust and resilient and tends to reproduce a workforce which finds it difficult to share information, admit errors and engage in systemic rather than narrowly compartmentalized thinking.

Perversity Arguments Against NPM

Proponents of the jeopardy thesis tend to highlight ways in which reforms have a damaging effect on values and institutions that are typically overlooked or under-appreciated by reformers. By contrast, the focus of the perversity thesis is usually on the possibility that the reforms may actually leave a policy sphere worse off in terms of values explicitly espoused by the reformers.

This line of criticism is not hard to find in the public administration literature. Thus, while NPM is often hailed as a means to reduce the costs of public service provision, a number of writers have identified those types of cost that might rise in a way that offsets its intended cost-savings. For example, Hood (ibid., p.251) has suggested that if NPM is to be interpreted as part of a shift from high-trust to low-trust relationships in the public sector, 'it might raise the transactions costs involved in monitoring the performance of public service employees who were previously trusted to behave in an ethically appropriate manner.'

Broadbent and Laughlin (1997, p.490) have raised the possibility that the high implementation costs associated with NPM – the 'publicity hype', the 'costly consulting advice' and above all the public money poured into the 'creation of a new management elite who have little direct involvement in the actual services offered by the public sector' may swallow up whatever economies are achieved by NPM-type reforms. In addition, Broadbent and Laughlin (ibid., p.480) point out, particularly with reference to the application of NPM to the health sector in the UK, that professional service providers may engage in 'subtle forms of absorption of the changes so as to minimise intrusion into established values and norms of behaviour.' This absorption process can generate significant opportunity costs since it involves 'setting up small groups to "buffer" these changes and thus prevent members of those groups from undertaking other important service functions' (ibid., p.490). This exemplifies the type of coping behaviour often attributed to 'street level bureaucrats' (Hjern and Hull, 1982; Lipsky, 1973) concerned to maintain their autonomy in the face of top–down initiatives to change their behaviour.

NPM can also have a perverse impact on the second 'E' of efficiency. This can occur because 'economizing is conceptually by no means the same thing as raising efficiency and may even conflict with it' (Pollitt, 1993, p.13). Thus, if productive efficiency is conceived of as the optimal ratio between inputs and outputs, it follows that lowering inputs will only increase efficiency if it does not induce a more than proportionate fall in outputs. Where the implementation of NPM places public managers under a tighter funding and output monitoring regime they may try to realize economies in the provision of observable, monitored, outputs by cutting back their provision of less observable outputs. Public organizations that engage in a mix of production, craft and coping tasks are particularly susceptible to this type of potentially inefficient economizing. For instance, a disability agency may provide both physical aids and counselling services.

However, a cutback in funding may induce its management to reduce the provision of less visible counselling services so that the provision of physical aids can be sustained.

The public administration literature also raises the possibility that NPM can have a perverse impact on the effectiveness of public organizations. Three aspects of organizational effectiveness seem to be highlighted. Firstly, while its advocates claim that NPM-type measures such as flexible staffing, individual performance appraisal and performance-related remuneration might enhance the motivation of individuals to contribute to organizational goals, its critics point to evidence of declining morale, work-related stress and difficulties in recruiting staff to the public service (Peters and Savoie, 1994). These critics seem to be drawing the conclusion that any positive effect NPM measures may have had on the *extrinsic* motivation of individual staff has been more than offset by its negative impact on their *intrinsic* motivation. Frey (1994) has argued that theories of intrinsic motivation emphazise the impact of factors such as recognition and autonomy on the discretionary effort exercised by individuals. This discretionary effort may be withdrawn, particularly by the professionals engaged in coping activities, where their work is increased managerial monitoring and regulation. Moreover, an 'individualist' approach to staff motivation based on managerial assessments of individual performance may be inappropriate and counterproductive in those activities where performance is dependent on the quality of teamwork.

Secondly, the claim that NPM can make public organizations more responsive to their consumers has also been challenged by its critics. Thynne (1996, p.51) has even gone so far as to argue that it may have an opposite effect on consumer responsiveness since 'the more organisations become narrowly focused and "componentised" the greater the number of agencies involved in the provision of any social service and therefore the more bewildering and inaccessible the system becomes for individuals in their necessary encounters with authority.' A similar perverse effect can occur with regard to the impact of NPM on the accountability of public agencies. While the matching of resources to particular tasks may make it possible to strengthen the accountability for outputs, it may actually weaken their accountability for outcomes particularly where these are difficult to monitor. Self (1993, p.340) puts it as follows:

> Who carries the can for a decision when the power to make it is transferred from minister to department. to operating agency and then is perhaps shifted to a private contractor? Already ministers have faced embarrassment over individual decisions in the health service. Of course,

this is an old problem of Westminster-type systems but it becomes a lot more intractable under these new conditions.

A common feature of these perversity arguments is that they suggest a broader conception of the *desiderata* of NPM – economy, efficiency and effectiveness – and then suggest, often tentatively, that its impact on these more broadly conceived values may be not only ambiguous, but potentially perverse. The purpose of these arguments would therefore seem to be to induce policymakers to be more cautious in their implementation and more careful in their evaulation of these reforms.

The Futility Thesis in Arguments Against NPM

Hirschman (1991) makes much of the difference between perversity arguments and the futility thesis which holds that attempts at social transformation will simply be unavailing. He recognizes that both theses are based on the notion of the unanticipated consequences of human action with the futility thesis seeming to be the milder version, since when it is invoked 'the unintended side effects simply cancel out the original action instead of going so far as to produce a result that is the opposite of the one that was intended' (Hirschman, 1991, p.72). He nevertheless contends that the futility thesis is actually 'from the point of view of evaluating the chances of success of purposive human action ... more devastating than the perversity thesis' (ibid., p.75). This is because it demeans the significance of reform initiatives, it argues that while they might manifest themselves on the surface in a flurry of activity, and change, they have no deep and lasting effect on underlying social structures. Hirschman (ibid., p.75) puts the argument as follows:

> A world in which the perverse effect is rampant remains accessible to human or societal intervention .... In contrast, to the extent that the futility claim holds, there is no hope for any successful or effective steering or intervention, let alone for 'fine-tuning'. Moreover, such action is likely to be costly, and being an exercise in futility is surely demoralising.

In this regard, the futility thesis is more 'insulting' than the perversity thesis since it suggests that as much as things *appear* to change they actually remain the same.

One line of criticism of NPM that clearly expresses the futility thesis is the argument that it has actually 'changed little apart from the language in which senior public managers speak in public' (Hood, 1991, p.9). This argument is most prevalent with regard to the impact of new layers of management on the behaviour of street level bureaucrats and professional service providers. It has been argued, for example by Pollitt (1993, p.15), that the application of NPM to the public-health sector has, in many cases, failed to provide hospital administrators with the management tools needed to gain control over resource use in hospitals. This is because doctors have continued to assume responsibility for the most significant uncertainties within the health care and to exercise the power and discretion that this places upon them. They are often unlikely to internalize the cost-cutting imperatives associated with NPM since these may not only make it more difficult to satisfy their professional standards of excellence, but may also expose them to a backlash from clients dissatisfied by a reduced level of assurance that their own needs will be met under a more stringent rationing system.

Proponents of the futility thesis often follow what Pollitt (1993) categorizes as a critique of the realism of NPM. Thus, while it is a central doctrine of NPM that public organizations should be broken up into single objective units that can be tightly monitored for their delivery of clearly specified output, the extent to which the application of this principle can remove every source of ambiguity and conflict over the objectives of public agencies has been questioned. For instance, even in New Zealand where the principle of output-based accountability has been pushed further than almost anywhere else, there are nevertheless still some areas of government activity that it has not affected to any significant degree. In discussing the way budgetary appropriations are now being made by output less, Easton (1997, p.175) draws attention to the way the Treasury's policy advice output is specified as 'provision on the economy, including the government's overall economic and fiscal strategies and macroeconomic forecasting and monitoring.' He argues further that (ibid.):

The hard notion of an output has been reduced to a warm fuzzy, as is true for many other outputs of all the government departments. How a Parliament or minister is to judge objectively the quantity (let alone quality) of such an output is a mystery. Perhaps it is a facade to give the impression that there was some accountability or that there was greater accountability than in the past.

Despite the fact that NPM is often advocated as a solution to the problems of government failure, the various theories that share in common a concern with this phenomenon can also provide a rich source of futility arguments. As we saw in Chapter 4 this is because they tend to relate government failure to various *conditions*, such as 'ill-defined outputs', 'monopoly supply', 'uncertain, ambiguous technology' and absence of bottom-line evaluations mechanisms (Wolf, 1989, pp.51–5) that are viewed as more or less intractable features of nonmarket supply.

Public choice theory also suggests why reforms that can have such little real impact on the social evaluation of a public organization's performance should be implemented in the first place. The argument here is that NPM, in spite of its professed claims to promote the public interest, could actually be a vehicle for 'particularist advantage' (Hood 1991, p.91). In this regard, futility arguments draw from what Pollitt (1993) calls a political critique of NPM, presenting it as a self-serving movement designed to promote the career interests of an elite group of 'managerialists' rather than the broad mass, of public service customers and low-level staff (Dunleavy, 1985; Yeatman, 1987; Keleher, 1988). Hirschman has suggested that this type of political critique is more typical of the futility than the perversity thesis. He points out that (Hirschman, 1991, pp.76–7):

> The analysts who come upon a perverse effect usually are so taken by their discovery and so desirous to claim it as an event *unanticipated and unwilled by anyone* that they are inclined to credit the policymakers whose actions have led to those untoward consequences with innocence for the disasters they have caused and hence with *good intentions* that are then disappointed. To convey this idea, they use the terms 'well-meaning' and 'well-intentioned' widely and condescendingly.... With the futility thesis there is a considerable change. To the extent that those responsible for the policies are right among the beneficiaries, the suspicion arises that they are by no means all that innocent or well-intentioned. Their good faith is being questioned and it is suggested that the social justice and similar goals that serve as justifications for the policies pursued are nothing but smoke screens hiding the most selfish motives.

Progressive Counterparts to Reactionary Arguments

While Hirschman (1991) focuses on the recurrent patterns of argument that typify reactionary rhetoric, he also finds that the futility, perversity and jeopardy theses have their 'progressive counterparts'. For example, the jeopardy thesis is often countered by what he calls the 'imminent danger thesis'. This highlights the dangers of inaction and holds that reform is imperatively needed to stave off future threats to the sustainability of particular social systems. According to Hirschman (ibid., p.152) 'the jeopardy argument stresses the dangers of action and the threat to past accomplishments that action carries. An opposite way of worrying about the future would be to perceive all kinds of approaching threats and dangers and to advocate forceful action to forestall them.'

This line of argument is apparent in claims that in an environment of fiscal austerity which typifies countries struggling to address the macroeconomic imbalances linked with high levels of debt and inflation, the continued provision of public services may hinge on whether they can be made more efficient, effective and economical through the reforms associated with NPM. It is also apparent in the advice that international institutions, such as the IMF and World Bank, often give to prospective reformist governments to take advantage of the 'window of opportunity' provided by a fiscal or balance of payments crisis to push through radical public sector reforms and structural adjustment policies (Williamson, 1994).

The progressive counterpart to the 'perversity thesis' has been described by Hirschman (1991) as the 'desperate predicament thesis'. The argument that a reform can have consequences diammetrically opposite to those intended is usually made with the ostensible aim of inducing governments to be more cautious in its implementation and more careful in its evaluation. From a progressive perspective this line of argument can be deadly, despite its apparent reasonableness, since a more cautious approach may actually cause reform proposals to 'wither on the vine' or allow opponents more time to mobilize resistance to their implementation. In response to the perversity thesis progressives may therefore escalate their rhetoric to foster a climate in which policymakers come to believe that they must 'throw caution to the wind' to deal with a 'desperate predicament'. Hirschman (1991, pp.162–3) observes that 'by invoking the desperate predicament in which a people is caught, as well as the failure of prior attempts at reform, it is implicitly or explicitly argued that the old order must be smashed and a new one rebuilt *regardless* of any counterproductive consequences that might ensue. The invocation of the desperate predicament can therefore be seen as a rhetorical manoeuvre of escalation meant to neutralize and override the argument of the perverse effect' (original emphasis).

This thesis can be discerned in claims that the various types of government failure identified by the public choice literature have become so deeply entrenched in the public sector that only a radical reshaping of this sector through the institutionalization of the NPM paradigm can effect substantial improvement in its performance. The desperate predicament thesis can thus provide a justification for the emphasis on implementation rather than evaluation which Broadbent and Laughlin (1997) associate with the advancement of NPM particularly in Britain and New Zealand.

Finally, the futility thesis finds its counterpart in the 'futility of resistance' thesis that is suggested in claims that various 'global megatrends' or 'forces of history' make radical change in moribund structures such as public organizations inevitable and resistance to such change futile. This 'historicist' form of argument can be detected in claims that the implementation of NPM doctrines provide the surest path toward government adaptation and survival in an environment that is being rapidly changed by 'globalization' and the diffusion of 'the lead technologies of the late twentieth-century, Kondratriev cycle ("post industrialism", "post-Fordism") which (are) serving to remove the traditional barriers between public sector work and private sector work' (Hood 1991, p.7).

A brief summary of the three reactionary theses and their progressive counterparts insofar as they apply to the debate over the advancement of NPM is set out in Figure 8.1. However, it is necessary to move beyond the type of descriptive schema that Hirschman proposes to an explanation of why the arguments and counter arguments concerning paradigmatic policy change tend to take this form.

Reactionary Position	Progressive Position
Jeopardy Thesis The historic achievement of the bureaucratic paradigm in establishing a unified, trustworthy public service may be threatened by the drive to make it more efficient and economical.	*The Imminent Danger Thesis* The failure to make the public service more efficient and economical may threaten the future provision of public services in an environment of fiscal austerity.
Perversity Thesis Public sector reforms can exacerbate the conditions they attempt to remedy (e.g. it is possible that the NPM may make the public service less effective, efficient and economical).	*The Desperate Predicament Thesis* Government failure has become so entrenched that it can only be addressed by a radical reconstruction of the public sector regardless of any counterproductive consequences.
Futility Thesis Reforms will fail to realise the intentions of reformers (e.g. NPM will have little impact on the craft and coping activities of public organisations).	*Futility of Resistance Thesis* It is futile to resist NPM-style reforms since it is imperative that public organisations adapt to changes in the global environment.

Figure 8.1   Reactionary theses and progressive counterparts

8.4   THE RHETORICAL STRATEGIES OF HOPE-BASED LEADERSHIP NETWORKS

The three types of leadership network and the pattern of argumentation within and between them that is likely to emerge during a process of paradigmatic policy change is shown in Figure 8.2. A progressive, a reactionary and a pragmatist leadership network are likely to emerge during a process of radical, discontinuous reform. The progressive network will draw together all those policy participants who are committed to institutionalize the paradigm by pushing the reform process through to its 'logical destination'. The reactionary network may encompass all those individuals, institutions and groups who share a commitment to resist the forward advance of the reform process. The pragmatist network will be made up of those policymakers whose support for the reform process is ultimately contingent upon its outcomes or consequences. They share a commitment to sustain a policy learning capacity through the reform process, and to take into account and deliberate on the arguments and counter arguments made by progressives and reactionaries. While they may appear to be less 'vocal' and 'active' than the other players, they typically hold the balance of power so that the outcome of the 'struggle' between progressives and reactionaries will depend on to whom and, on what terms, they are prepared to lend the weight of their support.

While the members of each network are likely to have privately interested motives for committing themselves to its political activities, the 'reasons'

Leadership Networks	Progressive	Reactionary	Pragmatist
Commitment with respect to paradigm shift	Advance the process to completion	Resist the process of advancement	Sustain policy learning capacity during the process
Concept of the public interest	Quest for coherence	Quest for 'voice'	Quest for balance
Dissonance reduced by	Imminent Danger Thesis	Jeopardy Thesis	Desperate Predicament Thesis
Dissonance increased by	Futility Thesis	Futility of Resistance Thesis	Perversity Thesis

Figure 8.2   Leadership networks and patterns of argumentation

they give for their participation will typically be based on a particular concept of the 'public interest'. Progressives will usually rationalize their commitment to advance a paradigmatic reform process to its logical destination by claiming that the public interest is best served by a quest for greater policy coherence. To achieve this, the new paradigm must be institutionalized and all practices derived from the old paradigm that are inconsistent with the principles embodied in the new paradigm should be dispensed with. This is a 'straight line' criterion of policy development that sees a system of governance improving to the degree that it becomes more streamlined and less incoherent.

While a reactionary leadership network is typically drawn from those groups who stand to lose from a reform process they must look for reasons other than their own losses to rationalize their commitment to resist its forward momentum. They often find these reasons in a concept of 'good' or 'strong' democracy being served by a quest for 'voice'; that is, by a quest to draw into the policy process an increasingly greater proportion of those groups whose interests or values are affected by public decisions. This process of inclusion will in many cases be set back by a paradigmatic reform process that is pushed forward despite its tendency to concentrate the purportedly short-term costs of structural adjustment on particular groups.

For pragmatists, policy development should be governed by a quest for balance. While they may give their support to a paradigmatic reform process, and may even hand over the reins of policy leadership to radical reformers, they typically rationalize these actions as a pragmatic response to past excesses. They may also rationalize their withdrawal of support for radical reform on the grounds that the reform process is proceeding too far and too fast in a particular direction. They tend to follow a cyclical approach to policy development in which open-ended evaluation and learning from the outcomes of policies tends to ensure that no one cluster of values or interests dictates the direction of policy for too long. Since policy development during periods of 'normal policymaking' tends to be led by pragmatist leadership networks, it follows that the majority of the policy community may still defer to pragmatic norms during periods of paradigmatic change so their continued support is often a crucial factor in determining whether these processes are pushed through to completion.

Public choice theorists tend to dismiss the significance of this 'public interest' rhetoric. They view the public articulation of these 'reasons' as a device to conceal the 'real' privately interested motives policy participants have for making particular policy commitments. For example, Gordon Tullock (1975, p.42), a leading public choice theorist has argued, somewhat triumphantly, that 'the traditional view of government has always been that it sought something called the "public interest"... with public choice all this changed' so that in the discipline of political science 'the public interest point of view' is now obsolete although it 'still informs many statements by public figures and the more old-fashioned students of politics'. There are some indications, though, that public choice theorists are beginning to back off from such assertions of a single motive for human behaviour. James Buchanan, who won a Nobel Prize in economics in 1986 for applying to politics a 'rational choice' model based on self-interest argued for the need to recognize mixed motives in political behaviour. He contended that both those who conceive a world of benevolent public servants exclusively pursuing the public interest and those who 'have modelled politicans and bureaucrats as self-interested maximizers' share a 'fatal flaw' (Buchanan, 1986, p.1):

Both images are widely interpreted, by their own proponents, to be descriptors of the total reality of politics, when, in fact, both images are partial. Each image pulls out, isolates, and accentuates a highly particularized element that is universal in all human behaviour. To an extent, political agents, elected politicians and bureaucrats, as well as voters, act in pursuit of what they genuinely consider to be the 'general interest'. But also, to an extent, these political participants act in pursuit of what they estimate to be their own pecuniary interest. Each political actor regardless of his role, combines both of these elements in his behaviour pattern, along with many other elements not noted here.

It is not sufficient though to simply acknowledge that political actors have mixed motives. The type of extreme claim made by Tullock (1975) can only be adequately countered if it can be shown that the rhetoric used by these actors, the reasons they give for pursuing a particular line of action in the public interest, can be more than 'mere words'. They can actually affect political behaviour and the outcomes of political processes.

This latter view is implicit in the dissonance theory of hope and leadership presented in Chapter 7. This theory brought the 'reasons' people give for their actions to the forefront of analysis since it is these reasons that can affect the emotions of hope and disappointment that they experience in relation to their commitments and relationships. The members of the leadership networks that concern themselves with a paradigmatic policy change will follow a persistent line of argument in their interactions with one another. This is because they tend to learn that it is only by repeating the same arguments that they can steadily reduce the dissonance experienced by their own members and increase the dissonance experienced by their opponents.

For the members of a progressive leadership network, dissonance will arise from the delays, obstacles and setbacks that occur during the course of their quest to institutionalize the new paradigm as quickly as possible. To reduce this dissonance, and to strengthen the reserves of hope their own members draw on as they prepare themselves to take advantage of opportunities to advance their quest, they will tend to repeat variations of the 'imminent danger thesis' to one another. Their aim will be to strengthen their mutual conviction that it is in the public interest to push through radical reform as rapidly as possible to forestall the serious dangers and crises that will confront a decision structure that fails to effect a fundamental and dramatic transformation.

Their reactionary protagonists will at the same time seek to enhance their dissonance by interpreting delays and setbacks as evidence that radical reform in this sphere is subject to the futility thesis. The aim of these arguments will be to demoralize and demean progressive efforts at reform and weaken the commitment that holds together the progressive leadership network.

However, arguments that are essentially negative are not that effective in arousing and strengthening hope. To build hope within their own network, reactionaries will have to persuade one another of the threat to the public interest posed by the reforms. They will therefore tend to repeat versions of the jeopardy thesis to one another in order to reinforce their shared commitment to resist the forward momentum of the reform process. It has not been surprising to find that jeopardy-type arguments are particularly prominent in the public administration literature since this is directed toward 'insiders' who retain a strong residual attachment to the unappreciated values and virtues of the old bureaucratic paradigm.

To sustain their commitment to resist, reactionaries will have to withstand a barrage of arguments from progressives that attempt to persuade them that their resistance activities are futile. The offensive arsenal of the progressive network will therefore draw on the futility of resistance thesis to demoralize their reactionary protagonists. This is apparent in the somewhat breathless way in which public management 'gurus' such as Osborne and Gaebler (1993), take their readers on a lightning tour through the brave new world of globalization and exploding advances in information technology. Their aim is clearly to leave these readers with a striking impression of the futility of resisting change, in their own somewhat insulated sphere of concern, when the world is undergoing such dramatic and far-reaching transformation.

However, progressives and reactionaries are not just engaged in a rhetorical war with one another. They also need to win and retain the support of pragmatists who often tend to distance themselves from the 'sound and the fury' of this struggle. The tone and substance of the arguments they direct toward a pragmatist leadership network will therefore be quite different.

For pragmatists, a significant level of dissonance will be experienced when they allow progressives to lead a process of paradigmatic policy change. The radicalism of the progressives, their commitment to a 'straight line' quest for coherence will tend to 'rub against the grain' of pragmatists who are typically more comfortable with an incremental approach to policy change. To reduce this source of dissonance, progressives will try to convince pragmatists that incrementalism is not an option. They will persistently resort to the 'desperate predicament thesis' to reassure these pragmatists that there is no alternative to a radical reconstruction of policy and to counter the insinuations of reactionaries that reform may have perverse consequences.

Arguments based on the perversity thesis will thus, at the same time, be directed by reactionaries to pragmatists. As Hirschman (1991) points out these arguments will be more 'reasonable' in tone than the jeopardy arguments reactionaries direct to one another or the futility arguments they direct at progressives. This is because the purpose of these arguments is to increase the dissonance, or unease, pragmatists experience during a period of rapid reform. In this way pragmatists could be encouraged to insist on a more measured, balanced approach in which the evaluation of reform is restored to its place of equality with the concerns about implementation that tend to be ascendant during times of discontinuous policy change. This 'reasonable' approach, which focuses on simply raising the possibility of perverse consequences is apparent in the rhetorical strategy of the Coalition of Public Health – a network formed to resist the commercialization of public health in New Zealand. Easton (1997, p.160) describes this strategy as follows:

> The non-party coalition's initial strategy was to discredit the most objectionable aspects of the reforms by offering an alternative which appeared to meet the government's stated intentions without the extreme elements (such as profit driving of the system). The approach acknowledged the defects of the (predecessor, community elected) AHB (Area Health Board) based system (neutralising the potential criticism that the coalition was merely a front for vested interests), but argued for incremental evolution rather than radical revolution.

Despite the superficial 'reasonableness' of some of the arguments that are presented in the 'debate' about paradigmatic policy change, Hirschman has detected in the predictable pattern of argumentation that characterizes this debate a 'rhetorical intransigence' that impoverishes democratic discourse. The implications of this intransigence must be considered by way of conclusion to this chapter.

8.5   CONCLUSION

In a policy subsystem in which a reactionary network has been able to mobilize resistance of sufficient strength to neutralize the forward momentum of a progressive leadership network, a policy impasse or 'stalemate' is likely to emerge. This appears to be the current situation in the policy subsystem concerned with public health in New Zealand, with some critics of the commercialization of health, such as Easton (1997), even being prepared to herald signs of a progressive retreat. New Zealand has not been unique in this regard since most governments that have attempted to apply NPM principles to public health have encountered extraordinary resistance from both professional providers, who find it difficult to substitute a managerialist ethos for the professional ethos in which they have been trained, and from users, who tend to regard health as the last bastion of social security.

Easton (1997, p.163) views public health reform in New Zealand as a classic case of reformist futility – a 'failed blitzkreig'. Drawing once again from the 'war metaphor' he describes the state of health reform at the time of this country's first Mixed Member Proportional Representation (MMP) election as follows:

> By 1996 it was not the tactics of blitzkreig so much as trench warfare, where the government relied on its weight and momentum to force the reforms through, co-opting people as they went. But while those health professionals who were left continued to service their patients, few committed themselves to the reform. At one stage the tactic of the 'sap' appeared to be evolving, undermining the public health system by increased funding of the private system. This continues, but has not proved to be as effective as it may have seemed, probably because of the dominance of the public sector in the system and the commitment of the public to a public system.

From the perspective of both progressives and reactionaries, there seem to be different interpretations of the slowing momentum of the

New Zealand reform process in the mid-1990s and the corresponding strengthening of resistance to reform in the 'difficult' social policy areas of public health and education. On the one hand, this development has been viewed as an indication that the reform process is moving from what Haggard and Kaufman (1992) terms a stage of 'implementation' to one of 'consolidation'. A reform programme can be said to be consolidated when it is secured against future reversal. This will occur when (i) a new Downsian consensus opposed to such reversal emerges among 'leaders, interest groups, party elites and attentive publics' (ibid., p.36); and (ii) a powerful base of beneficiaries has been constructed that has a vested interest in keeping the reforms in place and strongly resisting any attempt to significantly change or abandon the new regime. In New Zealand these conditions prevail with both major political parties being opposed to reversal and with financial markets operating as 'fire alarms' should such reversal occur. Indeed, as a result of its integration into the global market economy, the New Zealand economy has come to be dominated by foreign- and New Zealand-owned transnational enterprises and finance capital that can use the threat of 'capital flight' to discourage governments from making significant alterations to the new policy regime. This situation has been acknowledged by critics of reform such as Kelsey (1995) who laments that by the mid-1990s the new regime had become 'embedded' and was unlikely to be easily discarded by future governments elected under the new MMP system.

On the other hand, although progressives generally appear to be sanguine about the unlikelihood of reform reversal, some continue to worry about the way their quest to privatize education and health and remove the last vestiges of the welfare state seems to be stalling. These concerns have been articulately expressed by Winton Bates, an American political expert, who was commissioned by the Business Roundtable to write a report entitled 'Will a coherent economic strategy be possible under proportional representation?' (1996)

Although Bates (ibid.) concludes that an 'incoherent' reversal of reform is unlikely to occur if the 'rules of the game' established since 1984 are kept in place, he does pinpoint a democratic bias toward inaction that can be exacerbated by the new electoral system. This is particularly likely to occur in respect of those policy issues for which 'there are several ideologies competing for wider public endorsement' so that (i) 'there is often a conventional wisdom or mythology which is being challenged or defended'; (ii) 'there are often opposing views of different interest groups' and (iii) 'experts may disagree on the likely consequences of alternative courses of action'. Under these conditions pragmatic governments may be 'prone to leave contentious issues in the "too hard" basket' (ibid. pp.8–9).

The conditions set out by Bates (ibid.) are, of course, those which prevail in any policy subsystem where a stable alignment of 'rival advocacy coalitions' (Sabatier, 1988) has developed. Bates predicts that government propensity toward inaction in these subsystems is likely to be even greater under MMP, since coalition governments will have to take into account the 'median preferences' of that minority party which holds the balance of power since it occupies the middle ground between the two major parties on the left and right of the ideological spectrum. Bates (1996, p.16) regards the avoidance of hard issues such as the privatization of education and health as an instance of 'leadership failure' – a reluctance by government to 'provide leadership on complex issues' since it is unable or unwilling 'to get ahead of public opinion on such issues'.

We submit that this is a narrow, essentially amoral, concept of leadership. Furthermore we propose that leadership finds its *telos* – its logical destination – in what Barber (1984) terms 'autonomous politics'. According to this writer there can only be scope for the emergence of 'autonomous politics' on those occasions when 'some *action* of *public* consequence becomes *necessary* and when men must thus make a *public choice* that is *reasonable* in the face of *conflict* despite *the absence of an independent ground*' (ibid., p.122 – original emphasis). For autonomous politics to occur, each value, belief, interest or obligation affected by a particular choice opportunity must have an 'equal starting place' and then be required to earn legitimacy by running the 'gauntlet of public deliberation and judgement' (ibid., p.137). Where conflict emerges, each side is given an adequate opportunity to make their case so that where one prevails, the other is left with the impression that they have been the subject of a reasonable process. As Barber (ibid., p.127) points out:

The word reasonable bespeaks practicality. It suggests that persons in conflict have consented to resolve their differences in the absence of mediating common standards, to reformulate their problems in a way that encompasses their interests (newly and more broadly conceived) even while it represents the community at large in a new way. 'Well, I guess that's reasonable', admits an adversary who has not gotten his way but has been neither coerced or cajoled into the agreement he has consented to. He is neither victor nor loser; rather he has reformulated his view of what constitutes his interests and can now 'see' things in a new manner.

The type of impasse or stalemate described by various commentators on the current state of the commercialization process in New Zealand could therefore be viewed, positively, as providing the opportunity for the emergence of autonomous politics. Unfortunately the social capital that is formed through a process of reasonable deliberation on conflicted issues is likely to be damaged by the 'rhetorics of intransigence' that, according to Hirschman (1991, p.168), may 'have long been practiced by both reactionaries and progressives'. This writer goes on to suggest that (ibid., pp.169–70):

A people that only yesterday was engaged in fratricidal struggles is not likely to settle down overnight to those constructive give-and-take deliberations. Far more likely, there will initially be agreement to disagree, but without any attempt at melding the opposing points of view – that is indeed the nature of religious tolerance. Or, if there is discussion, it will be a typical 'dialogue of the deaf' – a dialogue that will in fact long function as a prolongation of, and a substitute for, civil war. Even in the most 'advanced' democracies, many debates are, to paraphrase Clausewitz, a 'continuation of civil war with other means'. Such debates, with each party on the lookout for arguments that kill, are only too familiar from democratic politics as usual. There remains then a long and difficult road to be traveled from the traditional internecine, intransigent discourse to a more 'democracy-friendly' kind of dialogue

The leadership required to engage a policy community on this 'quest' must be a leadership network that strives to 'internalize politics' in the sense described by Barber (1984). Indeed a propensity to internalize politics, to encourage debate, to relax the norms of 'political correctness' (Loury, 1994), to allow the expression of dissent and to strive to and forge from conflicting views some common and yet creative conception of how the public interest is affected by the issues at hand would seem to be the hallmark of what Burns (1978) described as moral leadership. This is the force that though 'closely influenced by particular local, parochial, regional, and cultural forces' is able to 'find a broadening and deepening base' from which 'to reach out to widening social collectivities to establish and embrace "higher" principles and values' (ibid., p.429).

The task facing this type of leadership will be that much harder the longer progressives and reactionaries have engaged in the type of intransigent rhetoric that often accompanies the struggle by progressives to establish the hegemony of a new paradigm. It is made even more difficult to the degree that both sides treat the publicly-interested reasons offered by the other with suspicion as a 'smokescreen' to conceal their actual pursuit of the private interest they have in either advocating or resisting paradigmatic change. The insistent attribution of selfish motives can leave both sides with the impression that the other is unreasonable. Genuine deliberation can never take place until both acknowledge that they both have privately interested motives and public interested reasons for their policy commitments. The task of leading them through the impasse would therefore involve directing attention to the narrowness of the concept of public interest each is advocating, in the hope of engaging them both on a broader quest that incorporates and yet transcends these particularist views of the public interest.

This is a task for which pragmatists are often likely to be most suited. Bates (1996) is right up to a point. Their failure to find a way through difficult issues is a failure of leadership. What he does not acknowledge is that a leader who is moral in the Burnsian sense would strive to draw both sides forward away from the strongholds of their well-established positions rather than attempting to deprive reactionaries of the opportunity to make their voice heard.

A theory of public policy that takes into account the way rival leadership networks mobilize around competing concepts of the public interest may lead to a greater appreciation of the role an autonomous politics can and must play in forging an expanded common understanding of the public interest. The main steps this book has taken in trying to develop such a theory must be recapitulated and some of its implications pondered in the concluding chapter.

APPENDIX: 'JIHAD *vs* McWORLD'

The main conclusion reached in Chapter 8 is that the most promising way through a policy stalemate between the progressive advocates and reactionary opponents of paradigmatic change is for both sides to lay aside their rhetorical intransigence and engage in the type of 'democracy-friendly' dialogue that provides the climate within which autonomous politics can flourish as a source of deliberative judgements. However, this is not the lesson that potential reformists have drawn from the 'New Zealand experiment'. The reform strategy applied in New Zealand has been viewed as a model of how a network of 'technopols', technocrats and change agents can effect paradigmatic reform in a representative democracy where the sources of potential resistance are well-organized and articulately represented

(Williamson, 1994). It is a characteristic feature of the 'leadership' provided by the reformist network in New Zealand since 1984 that it has consistently sought to 'externalize politics'. It has done this to preclude its opponents from seizing opportunities to 'capture' the reform process and render it incoherent by steering it in a direction that could be inconsistent with the government failure paradigm that the reformers were committed to institutionalize.

In highlighting the ways in which this network has sought to pre-emptively capture the policy process in New Zealand, its domestic critics such as Kelsey (1995) and Easton (1997) have been accused of peddling 'conspiracy theories'. Quite rightly they have rejected this charge. No matter how 'reactionary' their rhetoric may appear to be, it still reflects a concern to 'have a seat at the table' of public deliberation and to offer pragmatists reasons why they should not surrender the leadership of policy development to radicals.

The New Zealand reform process has, however, provided a fruitful field of 'investigation' for authentic conspiracy theorists. This is vividly illustrated by the banner headline – 'Nazi "reforms" rip New Zealand – Australia next' – of *The New Citizen*, a publication of the Australian branch of a network led by Lyndon LaRouche, a some time USA presidential candidate and long time conspiracy theorist. A cursory scrutiny of this document conveys something of the flavour of its rhetoric (*The New Citizen*, 1997, p.1):

> The reports of New Zealand's economic success are all lies. The only 'freedom' in the country is that enjoyed by financiers and speculators to loot the stored-up wealth created by generations of New Zealanders past, just as the Nazis wrung wealth from the very bodies of their victims in the concentration camps.... As we show these health care 'reforms' are *killing people!* Thus, by the standards by which the victorious Allies *hung Nazi war criminals at Nuremberg* – that they 'knew or should have known' that their policies were responsible for mass murder – can, and must be applied to those responsible for what is now taking place in New Zealand. (original emphasis)

Apart from the unintended irony in the deployment of the Nazi metaphor by a devotee of a leader notorious, according to Stern (1996, p.76), for his frequent expression of anti-semitic sentiments, the most striking feature of this rhetoric is its absolute 'unreasonableness'. It is the language of outsiders who, having given up all hope of being able to engage in a process of autonomous politics, have focused on developing the cohesion of their own network by intensifying the emotions of anger and indignation which their members direct toward a political elite. This is the paranoid style of politics vividly described by Richard Hofstadter (1965, p.29):

> Let us now abstract the basic elements in the paranoid style. The central image is that of a vast and sinister conspiracy, a gigantic and yet subtle machinery of influence set in motion to undermine and destroy a way of life. One may object that there *are* conspiratorial acts in history and there is nothing paranoid about taking note of them. This is true. All political behavior requires strategy, many strategic acts depend for their effect upon a period of secrecy, and anything that is secret may be described, often with but little exaggeration as conspiratorial. The distinguishing thing about the paranoid style is not that its exponents see conspiracies here and there in history, but that they regard a 'vast' or 'gigantic' conspiracy *as the motive force* in historical events. History *is* a conspiracy, set in motion by demonic forces of almost transcendent power, and what is felt to be needed to defeat it is not the usual methods of political give and take, but an all-out crusade'. (original emphasis)

In a recent book, Benjamin Barber (1995) uses the term 'Jihad' or Holy War to describe this type of 'all-out crusade'. He argues that it is the type of collective activity that is engaged in by 'hate groups'. The internal cohesion of these groups derives from their shared emotions of (i) moral indignation toward the elite group that they perceive as dominating the political process and threatening their way of life; and (ii) hatred toward those identifiable groups who are disproportionately represented in this elite and who can be singled out as 'scapegoats' for its dominance. We would suggest, though, that Barber misses the mark in his suggestion that the rationale for these emotions of indignation and hatred is supplied by fundamentalist religion *per se*.

Instead we argue that the rationale for these emotions is typically derived more directly from the type of conspiracy theory referred to by Hofstadter (1965). Indeed the development of these theories and the accumulation of 'proofs' that some elite group has not slackened in its conspiratorial quest for domination not only strengthens the solidarity of particular hate groups, but also appears to be the characteristic endeavour shared in common by a wide variety of such groups. Whether the object of outrage and hatred is the 'Great Satan' of the Muslim zealot or the 'Zionist Occupation Government' of the 'Christian patriot', the 'valence' of these emotions can always be intensified by the latest twist to the group's pet conspiracy theory. Stern (1996, p.45) emphasizes this point in his study of the American militia movement:

> Go to a militia meeting and pick up the literature. There are charts of 'The Conspiracy to Rule the World', showing the House of Rothschild connected to the London's Hellfire Club, the Hellfire Club connected to Oxford, Oxford to the Bilderbergers, the Bilderbergers to the Federal Reserve, the Federal Reserve to the United Nations. (With over seventy well known and obscure American and British groups represented, you can connect the lines and follow the links between the Socialist Workers Party, the Rand Corporation, the 'House of Rockefeller', the Mafia, and the New School for Social Research.) You may also find literature from the Liberty Lobby, the Populist Party, the Christian Patriots, the Posse Comitatus, Christian Identity Groups, Bo Gritz, the John Birch Society, and the Ku Klux Klan. This rich compost of conspiracy theory and hate has fermented on the fringes of America for decades. The ideas found in all these right-wing groups have not faded away. They have been reborn as part of the militia movement. This time around, the ideas are more dangerous, for their proponents are heavily armed.

The last sentence here merits further comment. Elster's (1998) theory of emotions proposes that they affect behaviour by producing 'action tendencies'. We would suggest that the conspiracy theories disseminated by hate groups (most commonly nowadays through the Internet) can produce an action tendency toward violence. What is so disturbing about the current proliferation of these groups is that they are, to some degree, 'leaderless networks' in which individual members can commit acts of violence without necessarily being 'called' to such action by the public frontpersons. This appears to have been the case with the 1995 bombing of the Alfred P. Murrah Building in Oklahoma City. Stern (1996) reports on the way various prominent militia figures were not only able to avoid blame for this incident but were also able to place the blame squarely back on the 'Zionist Occupation Government' that figures so prominently in their demonology.

While we dispute the necessity of the link that Barber (1995) suggests exists between hate group activity and fundamentalist religion, we do, to a degree, concur with his discovery of a dialectical interplay between the processes of globalization and hate group proliferation. The connection appears to arise when the 'policy leadership' that is exercized to push through the reforms required to remove the barriers to globalization is fundamentally elitist in its aims and strategy, with the members of the reformist network striving to 'externalize politics' by removing the opportunity for other groups to 'capture the reform process' and steer it in a different direction. We would suggest that this creates the conditions in which conspiracy theories can take root, and hate groups flourish, particularly among those groups who have only recently been denied a 'voice' in the policy process. It is fascinating to observe the 'rhetorical journey' Barber has undertaken from the measured, academic reasonableness of *Strong Democracy* (1984) to the strikingly prophetic, almost apocalyptic imagery by which he conveys the dialectical texture of *Jihad vs McWorld* (1995, pp.4–5):

> The apparent truth, which speaks to the paradox at the core of this book, is that the tendencies of both Jihad *and* McWorld are at work, both visible sometimes in the same country at the very same instant. Iranian zealots keep one ear tuned to the mullahs urging holy war and the other cocked to Rupert Murdoch's Star television beaming in *Dynasty, Donahue,* and *The Simpsons* from hovering satellites. Chinese entrepreneurs vie for the attention of party cadres in Beijing and simultaneously pursue KFC franchises in cities like Nanking, Hangzou, and Xian where twenty-eight outlets serve over 100,000 customers a day. The Russian Orthodox church, even as it struggles to renew the ancient faith, has entered a joint venture with Californian businessmen to bottle and sell natural waters under the rubric Saint Springs Water Company. Serbian assassins wear Adidas sneakers and listen to Madonna on Walkman headphones as they take aim through their gunscopes at scurrying Sarajevo civilians looking to fill family watercans. Orthodox Hasids and brooding neo-Nazis have both turned to rock music to get their traditional messages out to a new generation, while fundamentalists plot virtual conspiracies on the Internet'. (original emphasis)

The substance of Barber's message nevertheless remains the same. It is that the tendencies toward Jihad can only be contained in a 'strong democracy' that allows significant scope for an autonomous politics that strives to leave participants with the impression that they have been the subjects of a reasonable process. The nightmarish scenario depicted in *Jihad vs McWorld* effectively constitutes Barber's version of an imminent danger thesis. It aims to motivate readers to commit themselves to his political vision. However, he is not a 'lone voice crying in the wilderness'. Instead he speaks out of a long tradition of civic republicanism and communitarian thought. The extent to which the leadership paradigm advanced in this book can lead policy theorists back to an appreciation of this tradition will be considered in Chapter 9.

9 Conclusion

9.1   THE FOCUS ON POLICY PARADIGMS

The primary subject of study in this book has been the conceptual frameworks that shape both the understanding policymakers have of the appropriate role of the state in a mixed economy and the principles and rules that guide them in the formulation, implementation and evaluation of public policy. The term 'policy paradigm' has been used to define these conceptual frameworks.

The concept of a paradigm has a wide currency in the both the natural and social sciences. It is usually understood to refer to an organizing framework, an intellectual map, to guide students and practitioners in a particular field. It includes the set of assumptions and research questions that they share in common as well as the language they use to identify what are, for them, the salient features of a complex reality. The scope and limits of a particular paradigm usually come most sharply into focus at the time of a paradigm shift, since during the often long periods of paradigm stability they are, by and large, implicit and taken for granted.

The claim that an alternative conceptual framework constitutes a new paradigm and that its process of dissemination marks a paradigm shift is often controversial. This has certainly been the case with the purported shift from a market failure paradigm to a government failure paradigm discussed in Chapters 2 and 3. Thus, while two of the major contributors to the development of government failure theories were quick to characterize their research as revolutionary (Buchanan and Tullock, 1962, p.11), others pointed out that they were simply engaged in extending the conventional neoclassical toolkit into a new area of application (Mueller, 1975, p.395; Khalil, 1987, p.114). It has also been pointed out that many of the problems that government failure theorists have been highlighting since the 1970s had already been acknowledged by welfare economists long before this time (Cullis and Jones, 1992, p.466).

This book attempts to circumvent these controversies by distinguishing a 'policy paradigm' from a theoretical paradigm. In Chapter 5 it was argued that policy advisers play an important 'brokering' role in screening out ambiguities and fine distinctions in the course of constructing a policy paradigm from related theories. This policy paradigm can then be used to circumscribe the policy agenda and to generate the principles to guide policy formulation and the rules to govern policy evaluation.

The shift from one policy paradigm to another is therefore likely to be much more discontinuous and to come closer to the punctuated equilibrium pattern that Gersick (1991) observed with regard to paradigm shifts in other contexts, than a theoretical paradigm shift. It is therefore highly risky (both for policy advisers – since it disturbs the mutual equilibrium of trust that they have established with the 'old establishment' (Easton, 1997) and for incumbent governments since it is surrounded by *ex ante* uncertainty about its distributional consequences), in that it departs from the centrist position associated with the Downsian consensus and may create an opportunity for a coalition of minorities opposed to comprehensive reform to win the next election. The commitment by the various members of the type of reformist network that formed in New Zealand in the 1980s can be attributed largely to the opportunities such change agents had for driving through reform and avoiding blame for the type of policy failures associated with the predecessor market failure paradigm.

Chapter 5 thus presented what was essentially a private interest perspective on radical policy reform. If the book had concluded with this chapter then the claim could have been made that it augmented public choice theory by suggesting a solution to one of its notable anomalies: that is, its failure to predict the radical public sector reforms that have been introduced in many countries over the last two decades despite the clear influence that the government failure paradigm had on their design. However, once the significance of policy leadership is acknowledged within a particular discipline like economics, it would seem to be incumbent upon theorists working in that discipline to formulate a theory of how such leadership can be exercised. This was the main focus of concern in Chapters 6 to 8.

9.2   LEADERSHIP OR GOVERNANCE

Chapter 6 argued that it is possible to derive from the considerable body of interdisciplinary inquiry into leadership an organizing framework that can address the anomalous neglect of this phenomenon by both the market failure and government failure paradigms. This interdisciplinary literature returns repeatedly to the issues of the significance, distinctiveness and legitimacy of the behaviours that have been claimed to constitute leadership.

These issues are all strikingly relevant to the political economy of recent policy reform. However, the nascent literature in this area has tended to focus mainly on the significance of the 'strong', 'visionary', 'autonomous' or 'coherent' policy leadership that is required to push through a comprehensive reform programme. Chapter 7 sought to expand this focus by discussing the distinctive way in which these traits could be developed within and collectively supplied by a reformist leadership network.

It should nevertheless be pointed out, though, that the leadership literature does not provide the only organizing framework for examining and explaining the role of policy leadership in effecting radical policy change. This issue can also be examined through the lens of the 'governance paradigm' that has developed within the field of public administration from an amalgam of institutional economics, organizational studies, development studies, political science and Foucauldian-inspired critical theory (Jessop, 1995).

Areas of Overlap Between Governance and Leadership Theories

There are significant areas of overlap between the governance paradigm and the theory of policy leadership presented in Chapter 7. Both attempt to move away from the normative, formal, constitutional understanding of the government as a 'unitary state directed and legitimated by the doctrine of ministerial responsibility' toward an attempt to understand the complex reality of governing in practice where it is often the case that 'there are many centres and diverse links between many agencies of government at local, regional, national and supranational levels' (Stoker, 1998, p.19). From a governance perspective, the main concern is with whether governments can develop new tools and techniques to steer and guide policymaking without recourse to commands or the use of their authority. This also constitutes one of the chief concerns of the policy leadership theory presented in Chapter 7. Extensive reference, particularly in Chapter 5, has been made to New Zealand's reform experiment since this has been widely hailed as a model for other governments to follow because it shows how a small reformist network can take over the reins of policymaking and steer the policy process in an intentional direction.

In wrestling with the issue of how governments can effectively steer and guide the policy process, the governance literature has highlighted a number of important developments in contemporary processes of governing. Firstly, it has drawn attention to the trend toward a blurring of boundaries between the public and private sector which 'finds substance in the rise of a range of voluntary or third-sector agencies variously labelled voluntary groups, non-profits, non-governmental organizations, community enterprises, co-ops, mutuals and community-based organizations' (Stoker, 1998, p.21). To steer policy in a particular direction, governments must play a catalytic role co-opting these non-government organizations into the process of implementing policy.

Secondly, the growing importance of partnerships between government and non-government organizations has led to a power dependence between the institutions involved in the collective activity of governing. Stoker (ibid., p.22) suggests that it is possible to distinguish three such relationships: (i) principal–agent relationships in which one party (the principal) hires or contracts with another (the agent) to perform a particular task; (ii) inter-organizational negotiation which 'involves organizations in negotiating joint projects in which by blending their capacities they are better able to meet their own organization's objectives'; and (iii) systemic co-ordination that 'goes a step further by establishing a level of understanding and embeddedness that organizations develop a shared vision and joint-working capacity that leads to the establishment of a self-governing network.'

It can be argued that the New Zealand reformist network has been able to achieve this degree of systemic co-ordination. Accordingly it exemplifies a third trend in modern governance which is for policymaking to be directed by 'autonomous self-governing networks of actors' (ibid., p.23). Stone (1989, p.4) uses the term 'regime' to describe 'an informal yet relatively stable group with access to institutional resources that enable it to have a sustained role in making governing decisions.' Elsewhere, the concept of a 'policy conspiracy' (Wallis, 1997) has been used, not in a pejorative sense, but to describe the ideal-type of a network that attempts to achieve this type of stability by developing within its membership a first order commitment to advance a particular policy quest and second order commitment to advance one another into positions from which they can exert leverage over the policy process.

Although the concerns of the governance literature can be addressed by a leadership paradigm, it tends to have a broader focus. It is not just concerned with the question of governing and its primary focus is not only upon determining that type or style of policy leadership that is most effective in realizing the intentions of the agents who occupy the commanding heights of the policy process. The distinctive issues that come into view when the focus is on leadership rather than governance must now be considered.

Some Distinctive Concerns of Policy Leadership Theory

Chapter 8 made it clear that while a reformist network that achieves internal cohesion and external articulation can play a significant role in advancing paradigmatic policy reform, it can, by its very effectiveness, call forth rival sources of leadership. These can arise both from 'reactionary' networks committed to resist the further advance of reform processes and from networks of pragmatists committed to sustain a policy learning capacity and ensure that these processes do not become unbalanced by being steered too far and too fast in a particular direction.

All these networks face the same problem of achieving and sustaining internal cohesion. The theory of leadership presented in Chapter 7 addresses this issue by proposing that hope is the basic emotion that is produced and reproduced in leadership networks. Following Elster's (1998) analysis of the emotions this chapter explains how hope can be influenced through the interaction that takes place between the members of these networks. They supply one another with reasons that strengthen their belief in the worth and possibility of striving together to advance their quest. They also invest emotional energy in these interactions and contribute to the process of mutual stimulation through which these reserves of passion are developed. This in turn produces an action tendency of entrepreneurial alertness and preparedness to take advantage of opportunities that arise to advance their quest and one another. These reserves of hope also counter the dissonance they experience from the inevitable accumulation of disappointments and help to sustain their commitment to the network and its quest.

From this simple theory a concept of political agency emerges that differs significantly from that advanced by public choice theorists. The main features of this concept and its implications for the relationship between economics and politics must now be considered in the concluding section of this book.

9.3 LEADING POLICY THEORISTS BACK TO POLITICS

The issue of whether agents participate in the policy process in pursuit, exclusively, of their own private interests or with mixed motives has long been a source of contention within the theory of public policy (Mansbridge, 1990). The development and growth of public choice theory has highlighted the scope and fruitfulness of the parsimonious postulate that individuals can be modelled as if they behaved like *homo economicus* – striving to maximize the present value of a well-behaved and stable expected utility function subject to the constraints imposed by scarce resources of time and wealth.

Public choice theorists are, however, finding it increasingly difficult to ignore the growing list of anomalies associated with the economic rationalist paradigm so that there are some indications that a number of leading figures in this school such as James Buchanan (1986) and Anthony Downs

(1990) have come to accept that political participation may be driven by mixed motives. These mixed motives are typically conceived in terms of various well-known dichotomies such as that between private and public interest or between *homo economicus* and *homo sociologicus.*

However, even if the reality of mixed motivation is acknowledged, there can still be an either/or understanding of how different motives affect behaviour. The motivation of agents can thus be conceived as being situation-specific. An agent can be privately interested in some situations and publicly-spirited or altruistic in others. This does, however, create a problem in understanding political behaviour since political agents often exhibit both motives at the same time in the same situations. It is this characteristic of political expression that accounts for the impression of hypocrisy that politicians often leave with citizens. This, in turn, appears to be at least one factor accounting for the low regard in which politicians are held in most established democracies nowadays.

The theory of hope and leadership advanced in Chapter 7 offers a different way of conceiving political behaviour. It conceives political agents as being both privately and publicly interested in the same situations. They will usually have a private interest in taking a particular position on a particular issue although, since politics is a repeated game, they may take a long-term view on what constitutes this interest, being prepared to make short-term sacrifices, compromises and deals in pursuit of their long term interest. However, they will also have publicly interested reasons for taking the positions they do.

I would contend that perhaps the most serious anomaly within public choice theory is, not its insistence on a private interest perspective on policymaking, but its failure to appreciate the significance of rhetoric. Rhetoric is not just a smokescreen; it matters. It affects political behaviour and it affects the outcomes of political processes. It does this by either reducing or increasing the dissonance political agents derive from their commitments. The significance of rhetoric has long been appreciated by Albert Hirschman and Chapter 8 of this book argued that the type of rhetorical patterns he identified with political struggles over the advance of citizenship could also be discerned in the debates that have surrounded the advance of the New Public Management.

If public choice is viewed as a movement to lead policy theory from politics to economics, to depict the political realm as a marketplace where politicians buy votes by selling policies, then the first step in a counter movement would be to formulate a distinctive concept of *homo politicus.* Dissonance theory could be a useful point of departure for this concept since it captures 'a fundamental feature of human beings' which is that 'they have an image of themselves as *acting for a reason*' (Elster, 1998, p.66).

The realism of this view is confirmed by a number of studies of legislator behaviour in the United States Congress (Muir 1982; Maass 1983; and Vogler and Waldman 1985) – an institution that has long been regarded as a model of 'pork barrel' politics. In citing these studies Mansbridge (1990) reports that they found *inter alia* that many legislators 'can learn, want to learn, and often act upon what they have learned', that 'they want not to look stupid, to matter and to make good public policy' that they 'deliberate to reach agreement on the standards of common life at least as much as they aggregate particular self interests' and that there are many instances where they 'appeared genuinely concerned with what they call in private a "bad bill" or in public 'legislation detrimental to the long-term well-being of the American people (p.14).'

It would therefore seem to be an inescapable feature of political life that politicians are engaged in a quest for 'good reasons' to rationalize the positions by which they identify themselves in the political space. Moreover, it is in this space that they are exposed to the reasons articulated by their interlocutors and it is this exposure that can strengthen or weaken their commitments. A concept of *homo politicus* may thus be formulated from a hermeneutical perspective that views agents as being in a world of imperfectly understood meanings that they are striving to bring to clearer definition so that they can enhance their understanding of what is significant, what matters to them (Taylor, 1985).

From this perspective, the expression of political 'hypocrisy' could be viewed as a sign that there is still hope in the political process. It is only those agents who lose hope in politics, who cease striving to formulate a response to their interlocutors, who give up the attempt to be reasonable and to offer reasons for their commitments to 'outsiders' who do not share them. This despair is evident in the discourse of conspiracy theorists and the 'hate groups' that mobilize around ideologies of conspiracy. They have ceased trying to be 'reasonable' and focus their rhetoric on arousing and strengthening the hatred against 'the system' that they shared with other members.

Once policy theorists return to an appreciation of the legitimate role of politics, normative questions must arise regarding the standards for evaluating politics and political discourse. Chapter 8 presents two similar concepts of 'good politics'. In the first place, Hirschman has suggested the need for 'democracy friendly dialogue' in which political protagonists move away from the 'rhetorics of intransigence' that typifies debates about paradigmatic policy changes. Secondly, Benjamin Barber has advocated a notion of 'autonomous politics' in which all participants are left with the impression that they have engaged in a 'reasonable process' irrespective of its outcomes. Both concepts can also be applied to evaluate the legitimacy of leadership. It is suggested that a leadership network will come closest to the type of 'moral leadership' analyzed by Burns (1978) to the degree that it is able to 'internalize good politics' without losing its distinctive identity.

These concepts of good politics belong to a long tradition. This has been characterized as the tradition of civil republicanism. It finds contemporary expression in the communitarian thought of MacIntyre (1981), Sandel (1982) and Taylor (1985) as well as in the writings of advocates of discursive or participatory democracy such as Barber. It lies beyond the scope of this book to conduct a detailed investigation of this tradition. It will suffice, nevertheless, to say that this is an important tradition in political thought. It is therefore hoped that if the theory of leadership presented in this book leads policy theorists back to politics, it will also lead them back to a more serious consideration of this tradition.

References

Aaron, H. J. (1994), 'Public Policies, Values and Consciousness', *Journal of Economic Perspectives*, Vol. 8(2), pp.3–21.

Akerlof, G. and Dickens, W. (1982), 'The Economic Consequences of Cognitive Dissonance', *American Economic Review*, Vol. 72(3), pp.599–617.

Akerloff, G. A. (1970), 'The Market for "Lemons": Qualitative Uncertainty and the Market Mechanism', *Quarterly Journal of Economics*, Vol. 72(2), pp.388–400.

Alchian, A. and Demsetz, H. (1972), 'Production, Information Costs and Economic Organisation', *American Economic Review*, Vol. 62(4), pp.777–95.

Alchian, A. and Demsetz, H. (1973), 'The Property Rights Paradigm', *Journal of Economic History*, Vol. 33(1), pp.16–27.

Alford, J. (1993), 'Towards a New Public Management Model: Beyond Managerialism and Its Critics', *Australian Journal of Public Administration*, Vol. 52(2), pp.135–48.

Allen, D. (1991), 'What Are Transactions Costs?', *Research in Law and Economics*, Vol. 14(3), pp.1–18.

Arrow, K. (1970), 'The Organisation of Economic Activity: Issues Pertinent to the Choice of Market Versus Non-Market Allocation', in R. H. Haverman and J. Margolis (eds), *Public Expenditure and Policy Analysis*, Markham, Chicago, pp.43–51.

Aucoin, P. (1990), 'Administrative Reform in Public Management: Paradigms, Principles, Paradoxes and Pendulums', *Governance*, Vol. 3(2), pp.115–37.

Bailey, S. J. (1995), *Public Sector Economics: Theory, Policy and Practice*, Macmillan, London.

Bairoch, P. (1993), *Economics and World History*, Harvester Wheatsheaf, London.

Balcerowicz, L. (1994), 'Common Fallacies in the Debate on the Transition to a Market Economy', *Economic Policy*, Vol. 4(1), pp.18–30.

Barber, B. (1984), *Strong Democracy: Participatory Politics for a New Age*, University of California Press, Berkeley.

Barber, B. (1995), *Jihad vs McWorld*, Random House, New York.

Barzel, Y. (1982), 'Measurement Costs and the Organisation of Markets', *Journal of Law and Economics*, Vol. 25(1), pp.27–48.

Barzelay, M. (1992), *Breaking Through Bureaucracy: A New Vision for Managing in Government*, University of California Press, San Francisco.

Bass, B. M. (1990), *Bass and Stogdill's Handbook of Leadership*. Free Press, New York.

Bates, W. (1996), *Will a Coherent Economic Strategy Be Possible Under Proportional Representation?* Business Roundtable, Wellington.

Bator, F. (1958), 'The Anatomy of Market Failure', *Quarterly Journal of Economics*, Vol. 72(2), pp.311–400.

Baumgartner, F. R. and Jones, J. R. (1993), *Agendas and Instability in American Politics*, University of Chicago Press, Chicago.

Baumol, W. J. (1952), *Welfare Economics and the Theory of the State*, Harvard University Press, Cambridge, Mass.

Baumol, W. J., Panzar, J. C. and Willig, R. D. (1982), *Contestable Markets and the Theory of Industrial Structure*, Harcourt Brace, New York.

Becker, G. S. (1981), *Treatise on the Family*, University of Chicago Press, Chicago.

Bekke, H., Perry, J. and Toonen, T. (eds), *Civil Service Systems in Comparative Perspective*, Indiana University Press, Bloomington.

Bendor, J. (1990), 'Formal Models of Bureaucracy: A Review' in N. B. Lynn and A. Wildavsky (eds), *Public Administration: The State of the Discipline*, Chatham, London, pp.373–417.

Bennis, W. and Nanus, B. (1985), *Leaders*, Harper and Row, New York.

Berger, L. A. (1989), 'Economics and Hermeneutics', *Economics and Philosophy* Vol. 5(3), pp.209–33.

Blair, R. D. and Rubin, S. (1980), *Regulating the Professions*, Lexington Books, Washington.

Blau, P. M. (1964), *Exchange and Power in Social Life*, John Wiley and Sons, New York.

Bollard, A. (1994), 'New Zealand', in Williamson, J. (ed.) *The Political Economy of Policy Reform*, Institute for International Economics, Washington D.C.

Boston, J. (1985), 'Inherently Governmental Functions and the Limits of Contracting Out', in J. Boston (ed.), *The State Under Contract*, Bridget Williams, Wellington, pp.78–111.

Boston, J. (1989), 'The Treasury and the Organization of Economic advice: Some International Comparisons', in B. Easton (ed.), *The Making of Rogernomics*, Auckland University Press, Auckland.

Boston, J. (1991), 'The Theoretical Underpinnings of Public Sector Restructuring in New Zealand', in J. Boston, J. Martin, J. Pallot and P. Walsh (eds), *Reshaping the State*, Oxford University Press, Auckland, pp.1–26.

Boston, J. (1992), 'The Treasury : Its Role, Philosophy and Influence', in H. Gold, (ed.), *New Zealand Politics in Perspective*, Longman Paul, Auckland.

Boston, J., Martin, J., Pallot, J. and Walsh, P. (1996), *Public Management: The New Zealand Model*, Oxford University Press, Auckland.

Boulding, K. E. (1978), *Ecodynamics*, Sage, New York.

Bozemann, B. (1987), *All Organisations are Public*, Jossey-Bass, San Francisco.

Breton, A. and Wintrobe, R. (1982), *The Logic of Bureaucratic Conduct*, Cambridge University Press, Cambridge.

Broadbent, J. and Laughlin, R. (1997), 'Evaluating the New Public Management Reforms in the UK: a Constitutional Possibility?', *Public Administration*, Vol. 75, pp.487–507.

Bromley, D. W. (1989), *Economic Interests and Institutions*, Basil Blackwell, Oxford.

Bryson, J. and Crosby, B. (1992), *Leadership for the Common Good: Tackling Problems in a Shared Power World*, Jossey-Bass, San Francisco.

Buchanan, A. (1979), 'Revolutionary Motivation and Rationality', *Philosophy and Public Affairs*, Vol. 9, pp.71–3.

Buchanan, J. M. (1975), *The Limits of Liberty: Between Anarchy and the Leviathan*, Chicago University Press, Chicago.

Buchanan, J. M. (1978), 'From Private Preferences to Public Philosophy: The Development of Public Choice', in Institute of Economic Affairs, *The Economics of Politics*, Institute of Economic Affairs, Reading 18, London, pp.1–18.

Buchanan, J. M. (1980), 'Rent-Seeking and Profit Seeking', in J. M. Buchanan, R. D. Tollison and G. Tullock, (eds), *Toward a Theory of the Rent-Seeking Society*, Texas University Press, College Station, pp.3–15.

Buchanan, J. M. (1983), 'The Achievements and Limits of Public Choice in Diagnosing Government Failure and in Offering Bases for Constructive Reform', in H. Hanusch, (ed.), *Anatomy of Government Deficiencies*, Springer-Verlag, New York, pp.18–41.

Buchanan, J. M. (1986), *Liberty, Market and State*, Harvester Press, Brighton.

Buchanan, J. M. (1994), *The Economics and Ethics of Constitutional Order*, University of Michigan Press, Ann Arbor.

Buchanan, J. M. and Tullock, G. (1962), *The Calculus of Consent: Logical Foundations of Constitutional Democracy*, University of Michigan Press, Ann Arbor.

Burns, J. M. (1978), *Leadership*, Harper and Row, New York.

Callebaut, W. (1993) (ed.), *Taking the Naturalist Turn*, University of Chicago, Chicago.

Calvert, R. (1992), 'Leadership and its Basis in Problems of Social Co-ordination', *International Political Science Review*, Vol. 13(1), pp.7–24.

Carlyle, T. (1841), *Heroes and Hero Worship*, Adams, Boston.

Casson, M. C. (1991), *Economics of Business Culture: Game Theory, Transactions Costs and Economic Performance*, Clarendon Press, Oxford.

Castles, F. G. (1993), *Families of Nations: Patterns of Public Policy in Western Democracies*, Dartmouth Press, Aldershot.

Chang, H. J. (1994), *The Political Economy of Industry Policy*, Macmillan, London.

Chang, H. J. and Rowthorn, R. (1995), 'Introduction', in H. J. Chang and R. Rowthorn (eds), *The Role of the State in Economic Change*, Clarendon Press, Oxford, pp.1–30.

Chhibber, A. (1997), 'The State In A Changing World', *Finance and Development*, Vol. 34(3), pp.17–20.

Citizen's Electoral Council of Australia, (1997), 'Nazi Reforms Rip Up New Zealand – Australia Next', *The New Citizen*, Vol. 4(7), p.1.

Coase, R. H. (1937), 'The Nature of the Firm', *Economica*, Vol. 4, November, pp.386–405.

Coase, R. H. (1960), 'The Problem of Social Cost', *Journal of Law and Economics*, Vol. 3(1), pp.1–44.

Coase, R. H. (1964), 'The Regulated Industries: Discussion', *American Economic Review*, Vol. 62(4), pp.777–95.

Coase, R. H. (1992), 'The Institutional Structure of Production', *American Economic Review*, Vol. 82(4), pp.713–19.

Collins, R. (1993), 'Emotional Energy as the Common Denominator of Rational Social Action', *Rationality and Society*, Vol. 5(2), pp.203–20.

Colomer, J. (1995), 'Leadership Games in Collective Action', *Rationality and Society*, Vol. 7(2), pp.225–46.

Cullis, J. and Jones, P. (1992), *Public Finance and Public Choice*, McGraw Hill, New York.

Dahlman, C. J. (1979), 'The Problem of Externality', *Journal of Law and Economics*, Vol. 22(1), pp.141–62.

Damasio, A. R. (1994), *Descartes' Error*, Putnam, New York.

Davis, G. and Gardner, M. (1995), 'Who Signs the Contract? Applying Agency Theory to Politicians', in J. Boston (ed.), *The State Under Contract*, Bridget Williams, Wellington, pp.140–59.

De Alessi, L. (1983), 'Property Rights, Transactions Costs, and X-Efficiency: An Essay in Economic Theory', *American Economic Review*, Vol. 73(1), pp.64–81.

Deane, P. (1978), *The Evolution of Economic Ideas*, Cambridge University Press, Cambridge.

Delorme, C. D., Kamerchen, D. R. and Mbaku, J. M. (1986), 'Rent-Seeking in the Cameroon Economy', *American Journal of Economics and Sociology*, Vol. 45(4), pp.413–23.

Demsetz, H. (1969), 'Information and Efficiency: Another Viewpoint', *Journal of Law and Economics*, Vol. 82(4), pp.713–19.

Derthick, M. and Quirk, P. J. (1985), *The Politics of Regulation*, Brookings Institute, Washington, D. C.

Dollery, B. E. and Leong, W. H. (1998), 'Measuring the Transaction Sector in the Australian Economy, 1911–91', *Australian Economic History Review* (forthcoming).

Dollery, B. E. and Wallis, J. L. (1997), 'Market Failure, Government Failure, Leadership and Public Policy', *Journal of Interdisciplinary Economics*, Vol. 8(2), pp.113–26.

Douglas, R. O. (1993), *Unfinished Business*, Random House, Auckland.

Downs, A. (1957), *An Economic Theory of Democracy*, Harper Row, New York.

Downs, A. (1967), *Inside Bureaucracy*, Little Brown, Boston.

Downton, J. V. (1973), *Rebel Leadership: Commitment and Charisma in the Revolutionary Process*, Free Press, New York.

Drucker, P. (1993), *Post Capitalist Society*, Butterworth, Oxford.

Dunham, D. and Kelegama, S. (1997), 'Does Leadership Matter in the Economic Reform Process? Liberalization and Governance in Sri Lanka, 1989–93', *World Development*, Vol. 25(2), pp.179–90.

Dunleavy, P. (1985), 'Bureaucrats, Budgets and the Growth of the State: Reconstructing an Instrumental Model', *British Journal of Political Science*, Vol. 15(2), pp.299–338.

Dunleavy, P. (1989a), 'The Architecture of the British State: Part I, Framework for Analysis', *Public Administration*, Vol. 67(3), pp.249–75.

Dunleavy, P. (1989b), 'The Architecture of the British State: Part II, Empirical Findings', *Public Administration*, Vol. 67(4), pp.391–417.

Dunleavy, P. (1991), *Democracy, Bureaucracy and Public Choice: Economic Explanations in Political Science*, Harvester-Wheatsheaf, New York.

Dunleavy, P., Reddan, N., King, D. and Margetts, H. (1992). *The Structure of Federal Agencies in Australia compared with the UK: A Bureau-Shaping Analysis*, Mimeo, Canberra.

Easton, B. (1994), 'How Did the Health Reforms Blitzkreig Fail?', *Political Science*, Vol. 46(2), pp.1–12.

Easton, B. (1997), *The Commercialisation of New Zealand*, Auckland University Press, Auckland.

Eggertsson, T. (1990), *Economic Behaviour and Institutions*, Cambridge University Press, Cambridge.

Ekeland, R. B. and Tollison, R. D. (1982), *Mercantilism as Rent-Seeking Society: Economic Regulation in Historical Perspective*, Texas University Press, College Station.

Elster, J. (1993), 'Intuition and Judgement', in W. Callebaut (ed.), *Taking the Naturalist Turn*, University of Chicago Press, Chicago, pp.202–203.

Elster, J. (1998), 'Emotions and Economic Theory', *Journal of Economic Literature*, Vol. 36(1), pp.47–74.

Etzioni, A. (1988), *The Moral Dimension*, The Free Press, New York.

Evans, L., Grimes, A., Wilkinson, B. and Teece, D. (1996), 'Economic Reform in New Zealand 1984–1995: The Pursuit of Efficiency', *Journal of Economic Literature*, Vol. 34(4), pp.1856–902.

Farrell, M. J. (1957), 'The Measurement of Productive Efficiency', *Journal of the Royal Statistics Society*, Vol. 120 (Part III), pp.253–82.

Fernandez, R. and Rodrik, D. (1991), 'Resistance to Reform: Status Quo Bias in the Presence of Individual-Specific Uncertainty', *American Economic Review*, 81(5), pp.1146–55.

Festinger, L. (1957), *A Theory of Cognitive Dissonance*, Stanford University Press, Stanford, CA.

Frank, R. and Cook, P. (1995), *The Winner-Take All Society*, Free Press, New York.

Frankfurt, H. G. (1971), 'Freedom of the Will and the Concept of a Person', *Journal of Philosophy*, Vol. 68(1), pp.5–20.

Frant, H. (1991), 'The New Institutional Economics: Implications for Policy Analysis', in D. L. Weimer (ed.), *Policy Analysis and Economics*, Kluwer, London, pp.111–25.

Frey, B. S. (1994), 'How Intrinsic Motivation is Crowded Out and In', *Rationality and Society*, Vol. 6(3), pp.334–52.

Frijda, N. H. (1994), *The Emotions*. Cambridge: Cambridge University Press, 1986.

Frohlich, N., Oppenheimer, J. and Young, O. (1971), *Political Leadership and Collective Goods*, Princeton University Press, Princeton.

Fromm, E. (1968), *The Revolution of Hope: Towards a Humanized Technology*, Harper and Row, New York.

Furubotn, E. G. and Richter, R. (1992), 'The New Institutional Economics: An Assessment', in E. G. Furubotn, (ed.), *New Institutional Economics*, Edward Elgar, London, pp.1–32.

Gal, R. and Manning, F. J. (1987), 'Morale and its Components: A Cross-national Comparison', *Journal of Applied Social Psychology*, Vol. 17(4), pp.369–91.

Gemmill, G. and Oakley, J. (1992), 'Leadership: An Alienating Social Myth', *Human Relations*, Vol. 45(2), pp.113–30.

Gersick, C. J. G. (1991), 'Revolutionary Change Theories: a Multilevel Exploration of the Punctuated Equilibrium Paradigm', *Academy of Management Review*, Vol. 30(2), pp.90–109.

Haggard, S. and Kaufman, R. (1992), *The Politics of Economic Adjustment*, Princeton University Press, Princeton.

Hall, P. A. (1993), 'Policy Paradigms, Social Learning and the State', *Comparative Politics*, Vol. 25(3), pp.275–96.

Halligan, J. (1996) (eds), *Public Administration under Scrutiny*, Centre for Research in Public Sector Management, Australian National University, Canberra.

Hann, R. W. and Bird, J. A. (1990), 'The costs and benefits of regulation: Review and Synthesis', *Yale Journal on Regulation*, Vol. 8(1), pp.233–78.

Harmon, M. and Mayer, R. (1986), *Organisation Theory for Public Administration*, Little Brown, Boston.

Hayek, F. A. (1973), *Law, Liberty and Legislation*, University of Chicago Press, Chicago.

Hayek, F. A. (1974), *The Pretense of Knowledge*, Nobel Memorial Lecture, *Les Prix Nobel en 1974*, Stockholm.

Heclo, H. (1978), 'Issue Networks and the Executive Establishment', in A. King, (ed.), *The New American Political System*, American Enterprise Institute, Washington D.C.

Hirschman, A. O. (1982), *Shifting Involvements: Private Interests and Public Action*, Princeton University Press, Princeton.

Hirschman, A. O. (1985), 'Against Parsimony', *Economics and Philosophy*, Vol. 1(1), pp.7–21.

Hirschman, A. O. (1991), *The Rhetoric of Reaction*, Bellknap Press, Cambridge MA.

Hjern, B. and Hull, C. (1982), 'Implementation Research as Empirical Constitutionalism', *European Journal of Political Research*, Vol. 10(2), pp.105–16.

Hodgson, G. (1988), *Economics and Institutions*, Polity Press, Cambridge.

Hofstadter, R. (1965), *The Paranoid Style in American Politics and other Essays*, Vintage Books, New York.

Hood, C. (1990), 'De-Sir Humphreying the Westminster Model of Bureaucracy: A New Style of Governance', *Governance*, Vol. 3(1), pp.205–14.

Hood, C. (1991), 'A Public Administration for all Seasons?', *Public Administration*, Vol. 69(1), pp.3–19.

Hood, C. (1994), *Explaining Economic Policy Reversals*, Open University Press, Buckingham.

Hood, C. (1996), 'Exploring Variations in Public Management Reform of the 1980s', in H. Bekke, J. L. Perry and T. Toonen (eds), *Civil Service Reforms in Comparative Perspective*, Indiana University Press, Bloomington, pp.268–87.

Hood, C. and Jackson, M. (1992), 'The New Public Management: A Recipe for Disaster?', in D. Parker and J. Handmer (eds), *Hazard Management and Emergency Planning*, James and James, London, pp.246–58.

Hood, C. C. (1994), 'Emerging Issues in Public Administration', *Public Administration*, Vol. 73(2), pp.165–83.

Hood, C. C. and Jackson, M. J. (1991), *Administrative Argument*, Aldershot, Dartmouth.

Howell, J. M. (1988), 'Two Faces of Charisma', in J. A. Conger and R. N. Kanungo, *Charismatic Leadership*, Jossey Bass, San Francisco.

Howlett, M. and Ramesh, M. (1995), *Studying Public Policy: Policy Cycles and Policy Subsystems*, Oxford University Press, Oxford.

Hubbard, A. (1992), 'The Players', *New Zealand Listener*, Vol. 5, pp.14–16.

Ingraham, P. W. (1996), 'Evolving Public Service Systems', in J. L. Perry (ed.), *Handbook of Public Administration*, Jossey-Bass Publishers, San Francisco, pp.375–91.

James, W. (1880), 'Great Men, Great Thoughts and Their Environment', *Atlantic Monthly*, Vol. 46, pp.441–59.

Jensen, M. C. and Meckling, W. H. (1976), 'Theory of the Firm: Managerial Behaviour, Agency Costs, and Ownership Structure', *Journal of Financial Economics*, Vol. 3(3), pp.305–60.

Jessop, B. (1995), 'The Regulation Approach and Governance Theory: Alternative Perspectives on Economic and Political Change', *Economy and Society*, Vol. 24(3), pp.307–33.

Keleher, S. R. (1988), 'The Apotheosis of the Department of the Prime Minister and Cabinet', *Canberra Bulletin of Public Administration*, Vol. 54(1), pp.9–12.

Kelley, D. M. (1972), *Why Conservative Churches Are Growing: A Study in the Sociology of Religion*, Harper and Row, New York.

Kelman, H. C. (1958), 'Compliance, Identification and Internalization: Three Processes of Attitude Change', *Journal of Conflict Resolution*, Vol. 2(2), pp.51–60.

Kelsey, J. (1995), *The New Zealand Experiment: A World Model for Structural Adjustment*, Auckland University Press, Auckland.

Kerich, A., Furton, W. H. and Schmitz, A. (1987), 'The Cost of a Licensing System Regulation: An Example from Canadian Prairie Agriculture', *Journal of Political Economy*, Vol. 95, February, pp.160–78.

Kernaghan, K. (1993), 'Reshaping Government: The Post-Bureaucratic Paradigm', *Canadian Journal of Public Administration*, Vol. 36(4), pp.636–44.

Khalil, E. L. (1987), 'Sir James Steuart vs Professor James Buchanan: Critical Notes on Modern Public Choice', *Review of Social Economy*, 45(2), pp.113–22.

Kingdon, J. W. (1984), *Agendas, Alternatives and Public Policies*, Little Brown, Boston.

Kingdon, J. W. (1995), *Agendas, Alternatives, and Public Policies*, Little, Brown, Boston.

Kolm, S. C. (1977), *Modern Theories of Justice*, MIT Press, Cambridge.

Krueger, A. O. (1974), 'The Political Economy of the Rent-Seeking Society', *American Economic Review*, Vol. 64(2), pp.291–303.

Krueger, A. O. (1993), *Political Economy of Policy Reform in Developing Countries*, MIT Press, Cambridge, MA.

Kuflik, A. (1984), 'The Inalienability of Autonomy', *Philosophy and Public Affairs*, Vol. 4(3), pp.271–98.

Kuhn, T. (1962), *The Structure of Scientific Revolutions*, University of Chicago Press, Chicago.

Kuhn, T. S. (1970), *The Structure of Scientific Revolutions*, University of Chicago Press, Chicago.

Kuran, T. (1990), 'Private and Public Preferences', *Economics and Philosophy*, Vol. 6(1), pp.1–26.

Kymlicka, W. (1989), *Liberalism, Community and Culture*, Clarendon Press, Oxford.

Lakatos, I. (1971), 'History of Science and Its Rational Reconstruction', in R. Buck and R. Cohen (eds), *Boston Studies in the Philosophy of Science*, Norton, New York, pp.98–115.

Lakatos, I. (1976), 'Falsificationism and the Methodology of Scientific Research Programmes', in S. G. Harding (ed.), Can Theories Be Refuted?, Reidel, Boston, pp.236–52.

Lane, J. E. (1995), *The Public Sector: Concepts, Models and Approaches*, Sage, London.

Le Grand, J. (1991), 'The Theory of Government Failure', *British Journal of Political Sciences*, Vol. 21(4), pp.739–77.

Leibenstein, H. (1966), 'Allocative v. X-efficiency', *American Economic Review*, Vol. 56(2), pp.394–407.

Levinthal, D. (1988), 'A Survey of Agency Models of Organisations', *Journal of Economic Behaviour and Organisation*, Vol. 9(1), pp.153–85.

Levy, B. (1997), 'How Can States Foster Markets?', *Finance and Development*, Vol. 34(3), pp.21–3.

Lindholm, C. (1990), *Charisma*, Basil Blackwell, Oxford.

Lipsey, R. and Lancaster, K. (1956), 'The General Theory of the Second Best', *Review of Economic Studies*, Vol. 24(1), pp.11–32.

Lipsky, M. (1973), *Street Level Bureaucracy*, Russell Sage, New York.

Loury, G. (1994), 'Self-Censorship in Political Discourse', *Rationality and Society*, Vol. 6(4), pp.428–61.

Lucas, R. E. (1973), 'Some International Evidence on Output-Inflation Targets', *American Economic Review*, Vol. 63(2), pp.326–34.

Maass, A. (1983), *Congress and the common good*, Basic Books, New York.

MacIntyre, A. (1981), *After Virtue: A Study in Moral Theory*, Duckworth, London.

Maloney, J. (1994), 'Economic Method and Economic Rhetoric', *Journal of Economic Methodology*, Vol. 1(2), pp.253–67.

Mansbridge, J. J. (1990), *Beyond Self-interest*, University of Chicago Press, Chicago.

March, J. and Olsen, J. (1984), 'The New Institutionalism: Organizational Factors in Political Life', *American Political Science Review*, Vol. 78(4), pp.734–49.

March, J. and Olsen, J. (1989), *Rediscovering Institutions*, Free Press, New York.

Marsh, D. and Rhodes, R. A. W. (1992), *Policy Networks in British Governments*, Oxford University Press, Oxford.

Martin, J. (1991), 'Ethics', in Boston, J. (ed.), *Reshaping the State: New Zealand's Bureaucratic Revolution*, Oxford University Press, Oxford.

Matthews, R. C. O. (1986), 'The Economics of Institutions and the Sources of Growth', *Economic Journal*, Vol. 96(4), pp.903–18.

McCloskey, D. (1983), 'The Rhetoric of Economics', *Journal of Economic Literature*, Vol. 21, pp.481–517.

McManus, J. C. (1972), 'The Theory of the Multinational Firm', in G. Paquet (ed.), *The Multinational Firm and the National State*, Collier-Macmillan, London, pp.63–72.

Meindl, J. R. and Ehrlich, S. B. (1987), 'The Romance of Leadership', *Academy of Management Journal*, Vol. 30(2), pp.90–109.

Migue, J. L. and Belanger G. (1974), 'Towards a General Theory of Managerial Discretion', *Public Choice*, Spring, pp.27–47.

Mitchell, W. C. and Simmons, R. T. (1994), *Beyond Politics, Westview Press, San Francisco.*

Moe, T. M. (1984), 'The New Economics of Organisation', *American Journal of Political Science*, Vol. 28(4), pp.739–77.

Moon, J. (1995), 'Innovative Leadership and Policy Change: Lessons From Thatcher', *Governance*, Vol. 8(1), pp.1–25.

Mueller, D. C. (1975), *Public Choice*, Cambridge University Press, Cambridge.

Mueller, D. C. (1989), *Public Choice II*, Cambridge University Press, Cambridge.

Muir, W. K. (1982), *Legislature: California's school for politics*, University of Chicago Press, Chicago.

Musgrave, R. A. and Musgrave, P. B. (1984), *Public Finance in Theory and Practice*, McGraw-Hill, Singapore.

Nethercote, J. R. (1989), 'The Rhetorical Attacks of Management: Reflections on Michael Keating's Apologia', *Australian Journal of Public Administration*, Vol. 48(3), pp.363–67.

New Zealand Treasury (1987), *Government Mangement: Briefing to the Incoming Government*, Government Printer, Wellington, New Zealand.

Niskanen, W. A. (1968), 'The Peculiar Economics of Bureaucracy', *American Economic Review*, Vol. 57(2), pp.293–305.

Niskanen, W. A. (1971), *Bureaucracy and Representative Government*, Aldine-Atherton, Chicago.

Niskanen, W. A. (1975), 'Bureaucrats and Politicians', *Journal of Law and Economics*, Vol. 18(4), pp.617–43.

Niskanen, W. A. (1987), 'Bureaucracy', in C. K. Rowley (ed.), *Democracy and Public Choice: Essays in Honour of Gordon Tullock*, Basil Blackwell, Oxford, pp.78–95.

North, D. C. (1979), 'A Framework for Analysing the State in Economic History', *Explorations in Economic History*, Vol. 16(3), pp.249–59.

North, D. C. (1984), *Structure and Change in Economic History*, Norton, New York.

North, D. C. and Thomas, R. P. (1973), *The Rise of the Western World*, Cambridge University Press, Cambridge.

Nozik, R. (1974), *Anarchy, Utopia and State*, Basil Blackwell, Oxford.

Nutley, S. and Osborne, S. P. (1994), *The Public Sector Management Handbook*, Longmans, London.

O'Dowd, M. C. (1978), 'The Problem of "Government Failure" in Mixed Economies', *South African Journal of Economics*, Vol. 46(4), pp.360–70.

Olson, M. (1965), *The Logic of Collective Action*, Harvard University Press, Cambridge MA.

Olson, M. (1982), *The Rise and Decline of Nations*, Yale University Press, New Haven.

Ordeshook, P. C. (1986), *Game Theory and Political Theory*, Cambridge University Press, Cambridge.

Orzechowski, W. (1977), 'Economic Models of Bureaucracy: Survey, Extensions and Evidence', in T. E. Borcherding (ed.), *Budgets and Bureaucrats*, Duke University Press, Durham, pp.229–59.

Osborn, D. and Gaebler, T. (1992), *Reinventing Government*, Addison-Wesley, New York.

Papandreou, A. A. (1994), *Externality and Institutions*, Clarendon Press, Oxford.

Peacock, A. T. (1979), *The Economic Analysis of Government*, Martin Robertson, Oxford.

Peltzman, S. (1976), 'Towards a More General Theory of Regulation', *Journal of Law and Economics*, Vol. 19(2), pp.211–40.

Perry, J. L. (1996) (eds), *Handbook of Public Administration*, Jossey-Bass, San Francisco.

Perry, J. L. and Rainey, H. G. (1988), 'The Public-Private Distinction in Organisation Theory: A Critique and Research Strategy', *Academy of Management Review*, Vol. 13(2), pp.201–17.

Peters, G. B. and Savoie, D. J. (1994), 'Civil Service Reform: Misdiagnosing the Patient', *Public Administratration Review*, Vol. 54(5), pp.418–25.

Peters, G. B. (1996a), *The Future of Governing: Four Emerging Models*, University Press of Kansas, Lawrence.

Peters, G. B. (1996b), 'Models of Governance for the 1990s', in D. F. Kettl and H. B. Milward (eds), *The State of Public Management*, John Hopkins Press, Baltimore, pp.15–46.

Peters, T. J. and Austin, N. K. (1985), *A Passion for Excellence: The Leadership Difference*, William Collins, Glasgow.

Pfeffer, J. (1977), 'The Ambiguity of Leadership', *Academy of Management Review*, Vol. 2(2), pp.104–12.

Pigou, A. C. (1920), *The Economics of Welfare*, Macmillan, London.

Plosser, C. L. (1987), 'Fiscal policy and term structure', *Journal of Monetary Economics*, Vol. 20(2), pp.343–67.

Plowden, W. (1994), *Ministers and Mandarins*, Institute for Public Policy Research, London.

Polaschek, R. (1958), *Government Administration in New Zealand*, Oxford University Press, London.

Pollitt, C. (1993), *Managerialism and the Public Services*, Blackwell, Oxford.

Popper, K. (1959), *The Logic of Scientific Discovery*, Routledge and Kegan Paul, London.

Popper, K. (1969), *Conjectures and Refutations*, Routledge and Kegan Paul, London.

Posner, R. A. (1977), *Economic Analysis of Law*, Little Brown, Boston.

Pressman, J. and Wildavsky, A. (1973), *Implementation*. University of California Press, Berkeley.

Prosser, C. I. (1989), 'Understanding Real Business Cycles', *Journal of Economic Perspectives*, Vol. 3(3), pp.51–78.

Przeworski, A. (1991), *Democracy and the Market: Political and Economic Reforms in Eastern Europe and Latin America*, Cambridge University Press, Cambridge.

Rabin, M. (1994), 'Cognitive Dissonance and Social Change', *Journal of Economic Behaviour and Organisation*, Vol. 23(2), pp.177–94.

Raelin, J. A. (1986), 'The Clash of Cultures: Managers and Professionals', Harvard Business School Press, Boston.

Ranson, S. and Stewart, J. (1994) (eds), *Management for the Public Domain*, Macmillan, London.

Rawls, J. (1971), *A Theory of Justice*, Harvard University Press, Cambridge, Mass.

Rees, R. (1985a), 'The Theory of Principal and Agent: Part I', *Bulletin of Economic Research*, Vol. 37(2), pp.1–26.

Rees, R. (1985b), 'The Theory of Principal and Agent: Part II', *Bulletin of Economic Research*, Vol. 37(2), pp.75–95.

Rhodes, R. A. W. and Marsh, D. (1992), 'New Directions in the Study of Policy Networks', *European Journal of Political Research*, Vol. 21(3), pp.181–205.

Rodrik, D. (1995), 'The Dynamics of Political Support for Reform in Economies in Transition', *Journal of Japanese International Economics*, Vol. 5(1), pp.37–58.

Rodrik, D. (1996), 'Understanding Economic Policy Reform', *Journal of Economic Literature*, Vol. 34(1), pp.9–41.

Romer, T. and Rosenthal, H. (1979), 'Bureaucrats vs. Voters: On the Political Economy of Resource Allocation by Direct Democracy', *Quarterly Journal of Economics*, Vol. 93(3), pp.563–87.

Rousseau, J. J. (1968), *The Social Contract*, Cranston (ed.), Penguin Books, London.

Rutherford, M. (1996), *Institutions in Economics: The Old and the New Institutionalism*, Cambridge University Press, Cambridge.

Sabatier, P. (1986), 'Top-down and Bottom-up Approaches to Implementation Research', *Journal of Public Policy*, 1 Vol. 6(1), pp.21–48.

Sabatier, P. (1988), 'An Advocacy Coalition Framework of Policy Change and the Role of Policy-Oriented Learning Therein', *Policy Sciences*, Vol. 21(2), pp.129–68.

Sabatier, P. A. (1988), 'An Advocacy Coalition Framework of Policy Change and the Role of Policy-Orientated Learning Therein', *Policy Sciences*, Vol. 21, pp.129–68.

Sabatier, P. A. and Jenkins-Smith, H. C. (1993) (eds), *Policy Change and Learning An Advocacy Coalition Approach*, Westview Press, Boulder.

Sampson, A. (1995), *Company Man: The Rise and Fall of Corporate Life*, Harper Collins, London.

Samuels, W. J. (1972), 'Interactions between legal and economic policies', *Journal of Law and Economics*, Vol. 14(2), pp.435–50.

Samuelson, P. A. (1954), 'The Pure Theory of Public Expenditure', *Review of Economics and Statistics*, Vol. 36, November, pp.378–89.

Sandel, M. (1982), *Liberalism and its Critics*, New York University Press, New York.

Saunders, P. (1993), *Welfare and Inequality*, Cambridge University Press, Melbourne.

Schick, A. (1996), *The Spirit of Reform: Managing the New Zealand State Sector in a Time of Change*, State Services Commission, Wellington, New Zealand.

Schneider, F. (1991), 'A European Public Choice Perspective', *Public Choice*, Vol. 71(2), pp.197–200.

Schumpeter, J. A. (1943), *Capitalism, Socialism and Democracy*, Allen and Unwin, London.

Self, P. (1993), *Government by the Market?: The Politics of Public Choice*, Macmillan, London.

Self, P. (1995), 'The Consequences of Reorganising Government on Market Lines', *Australian Journal of Public Administration*, Vol. 54(3), pp.339–45.

Sen, A. (1977), 'Rational Fools: A Critique of the Behaviour Foundations of Economic Theory', *Philosophy and Pubic Affairs*, Vol. 6(4), pp.317–44.

Shackle, G. (1973), *An Economic Querist*, Cambridge University Press, Cambridge.

Shubik, M. (1975), 'The General Equilibrium Model is Not Complete and Not Adequate for the Reconciliation of Micro and Macroeconomic Theory', *Kyklos*, Vol. 28(3), pp.545–73.

Simon, H. (1983), *Reason in Human Affairs*, Basil Blackwell, Oxford.

Sinclair, A. (1989), 'Public Sector Culture: Managerialism or Multiculturalism', *Australian Journal of Public Administration*, Vol. 48(4), pp.732–41.

Smith, J. E., Carson, K. P. and Alexander, R. A. (1984), 'Leadership: It Can Make A Difference', *Academy of Management Journal*, Vol. 27(6), pp.765–76.

Snyder, C. R. (1994), *The Psychology of Hope*, The Free Press, New York.

Spicer, B., Emanuel, D. and Powell, M. (1995), *Transforming Government Enterprises*, Centre for Independent Studies, Sydney.

Spicer, B., Emanuel, D. and Powell, M. (1996), *Transforming Government Enterprises*, Centre for Independent Studies, St Leonards, Australia.

Stern, K. S. (1996), *A Force Upon the Plain: The American Militia Movement and the Politics of Hate*, Simon and Schuster, New York.

Stigler, G. C. (1971), 'The Theory of Economic Regulation', *Bell Journal of Economics*, Vol. 2(1), pp.137–46.

Stigler, G. J. and Becker, G. S. (1977), '*De Gustibus Non Est Disputandum*', *American Economic Review*, Vol. 67(2), pp.76–90.

Stoker, G. (1998), 'Governance as Theory: Five Propositions', *International Social Science Journal*, Vol. 25(1), pp.17–28.

Stone, C. (1989), Regime Politics, Lawrence University Press, Kansas.

Strange, S. (1988), *States and Markets*, Pinter, London.

Stretton, H. and Orchard, L. (1994), *Public Goods, Public Enterprise, Public Choice*, St. Martin's Press, New York.

Sutherland, S. (1989), 'Hope' in Vesey, G. (ed.), *The Philosophy in Christianity*, Cambridge University Press, Cambridge.

Sylvia, R. and Hutchison, T. (1985), 'What Makes Ms Johnson Teach? A Study of Teacher Motivation', *Human Relations*, Vol. 17(3), pp.143–54.

Taylor, C. (1985), *Philosophy and the Human Sciences*, Cambridge University Press, Cambridge.

Taylor, C. (1985), *The Self and Modern Identity*, Cambridge University Press, Cambridge.

Terry, L. D. (1995), *Leadership of Public Bureaucracies: The Administrator as Coordinator*, Sage, Thousand Oaks.

Thynne, I. (1996), 'Public Administration in Troubled Waters: Organisations, Management and a New Oceania', *Australian Journal of Public Administration*, Vol. 55(2), pp.47–53.

Tillich, P. (1956), *Dynamics of Faith*, Allen and Unwin, London.

Tollison, R. D. (1982), 'Rent-Seeking: A Survey', *Kyklos*, Vol. 35(4), pp.575–602.

Tullock, G. (1967), 'The Welfare Costs of Tariffs, Monopolies, and Theft', *Western Economic Journal*, Vol. 5(2), pp.224–32.

Tullock, G. (1975), *The Vote Motive*, Institute for Economic Affairs, London.

Vining, A. R. and Weimer, D. L. (1991), 'Government Supply and Production Failure: A Framework Based on Contestability', *Journal of Public Policy*, Vol. 10(1), pp.1–22.

Vining, A. R. and Weimer, D. L. (1996), 'Economics', in D. F. Kettl and H. B. Milward (eds), *The State of Public Management*, Johns Hopkins Press, Baltimore, pp.92–117.

Vira, B. (1997), 'The Political Coase Theorem: Identifying Differences between Neoclassical and Critical Institutions', *Journal of Economic Issues*, Vol. 31(3), pp.761–89.

Vogler, D. L. and Waldman, S. R. (1985), *Congress and democracy*, Congressional Quarterly Press, Washington DC.

von Mises, L. (1962), *Bureaucracy*, Arlington House, Westport.

Wallis, J. L. (1996), 'Economics, Hope and Leadership', *Journal of Interdisciplinary Economics*, Vol. 7(4), pp.255–76.

Wallis, J. L. (1997), 'Conspiracy and the Policy Process: a Case Study of the New Zealand Experiment', *Journal of Public Policy*, Vol. 17(2), pp.47–75.

Weisbrod, B. A. (1978), 'Problems of Enhancing the Public Interest: Toward a Model of Governmental Failures', in B. A. Weisbrod, J. F. Handler and N. K. Komesar (eds), *Public Interest Law*, University of California Press, London, pp.30–41.

West, E. G. (1990), *Adam Smith and Modern Economics*, Edward Elgar, Aldershot.

Williamson, J. (1994), *The Political Economy of Policy Reform*, Institute for International Economics, Washington.

Williamson, O. E. (1979), 'Transaction-Cost Economics: The Governance of Contractual Relations', *Journal of Law and Economics*, Vol. 22, October, pp.233–61.

Williamson, O. E. (1985), *The Economic Institutions of Capitalism*, Free Press, New York.

Williamson, O. E. (1989), 'Review of Markets or Governments: Choosing Between Imperfect Alternatives', *Journal of Economic Literature*, Vol. 27(1), pp.92–3.

Wilson, J. Q. (1980), *The Politics of Regulation*, Basic Books, New York.

Wolf, C. (1979a), 'A Theory of Nonmarket Failure: Framework for Implementation Analysis', *Journal of Law and Economics*, Vol. 22(1), pp.107–39.

Wolf, C. (1979b), 'A Theory of Non-Market Failures', *Public Interest*, No. 55, pp.114–33.

Wolf, C. (1983), '"Non-market Failure" Revisited: The Anatomy and Physiology of Government Deficiencies', in H. Hanusch, (ed.), *Anatomy of Government Deficiencies*, Springer-Verlag, New York, pp.138–51.

Wolf, C. (1987), 'Market and Non-Market Failures: Comparison and Assessment', *Journal of Public Policy*, Vol. 6(1), pp.43–70.

Wolf, C. (1989), *Markets or Governments: Choosing Between Imperfect Alternatives*, MIT Press, Cambridge.

World Bank Development Report (1997), *The State in a Changing World*, Oxford University Press, Oxford.

Wright, V. (1994), 'Reshaping the State: The Implications for Public Administration', *West European Politics*, Vol. 17(3), pp.102–37.

Yeatman, A. (1987), 'The Concept of Public Management and the Australian State in the 1980s', *Australian Journal of Public Administration*, Vol. 46(4), pp.339–53.

Yeatman, A. (1997), 'The Reform of Public Management: An Overview', in M. Considine and M. Painter (eds), *Managerialism: The Great Debate*, Melbourne University Press, Melbourne, pp.173–88.

Index

Aaron, Henry, xiii
accountability of public agencies, 163, 165
action tendencies, 181
Adler, Alfred, 124
administrative failure, 37
administrative values, New Public
    Management, 84–6
adverse selection
    agency theory, 70
    market failure, 19–20
advisers, *see* policy advisers
agency failure, 41
    leadership, 130–1
agency theory
    New Institutional Economics, 68–71;
        public sector, 73, 74, 75, 76
    New Public Management, 81–2
agglomeration, industrial, 17–18
Aid to Families with Dependent Children
    (USA), 22
airline deregulation, Australia, 11
Akerloff, G. A., 19–20, 147
Alchian, A., 63
Alexander, R. A., 119
Alford, J., 86
Allen, D., 66
allocative efficiency, 12, 31
    government failure, 50, 51, 54
    New Institutional Economics, 65
    Paretian approach, 13–14
    Pigouvian approach, 12–13
Arrow, Kenneth, 66
asset specificity, 52, 67
asymmetric information
    agency theory, 70
    government failure, 57
    market failure, 19–20
    between politicians and policy advisers,
        97
Aucoin, P., 156
Austin, N. K., 136
Australia
    airline deregulation, 11
    Commonwealth Public Service, 87
    competition, limited, 17
    fiscal federalism, 11
    government expenditure, 24
    Medicare, 22
    New Public Management, 157, 159

    policy advisers, 96
autocratic policy leadership, 128
Automobile Association, 129
autonomous politics, 176–7
autonomous state theories, 34
Ayres, Clarence, 62

Bailey, S. J., 82
Bairoch, Paul, 15–16
Balcerowicz, L., 95
Barber, Benjamin, 176, 177, 180, 181, 182,
    189–90
Barzel, Y., 66
Barzelay, M., 77, 156
Bass, B. M., 118, 119, 122
Bates, Winton, 175–6, 178
Bator, Francis, 9, 23
Baumgartner, F. R., 6
Baumol, William J., 9, 52
Becker, Gary S., 132, 147–8
Bekke, H., 79
Belanger, G., 40
Bendor, J., 40
Bennis, W., 136, 151
Berger, L. A., 134, 137
bilateral bargaining, 67
Blair, R. D., 43
Blau, P. M., 121
Bolger, Jim, 110
Bollard, A., 114
bonding costs, 69
Boston, J.
    generic managerialism, 77
    New Institutional Economics, 63, 71,
        74
    New Public Management, 81, 88
    New Zealand Treasury, reinvention, 108,
        109
    paradigmatic policy change, 101
    public choice theory, 44–5
    state, role of, 60
Boulding, Kenneth, 10, 72
bounded rationality, 63–4
Bozemann, B., 71
Breton, A., 40
Brittan, Samuel, 108
Broadbent, J., 162, 168
Bromley, D. W., 65
Bryson, J., 116

derived externalities, 48–9
Derthick, M., 6
desperate predicament thesis, 167–8, 173
Dickens, W., 147
disabled people, 'dignified' employment, 48
disappointment *vs* leadership, 149–51
dissonance reduction, leadership as
    mechanism of, 146–7, 171–3
  Beckerian theory of leadership, 147–8
  disappointment *vs* leadership, 149–51
  homo politicus, 188
Dollery, B. E., 37, 39, 68
Douglas, Roger, 110, 111–12, 113, 115
Downs, Anthony, 26, 39, 40, 102, 187–8
Downton, J. V., 120
drought relief programmes, 11
Drucker, P., 113
Dunham, D., 125–6
Dunleavy, P., 40, 104, 166
dynamic efficiency, 14–15, 65

Easton, B., 94, 95
  policy paradigms, 184
  Treasury, New Zealand, 114, 174, 179;
    Business Roundtable and 'New
    Executive', 112–13, 114; Coalition
    of Public Health, 173; policy
    evaluation, 100; politics of leadership,
    153; reactionary rhetorical criticisms
    of New Public Management, 173;
    reactive control role, 99; reinvention,
    108; 'Troika' and 'blitzkreig', 111,
    174
economic efficiency, 10–11
  allocative, *see* allocative efficiency
  dynamic/intertemporal efficiency, 14–15,
    65
  New Institutional Economics, 64–5
  Paretian approach, 13–14
  Pigouvian approach, 12–13
  productive efficiency, 11–12, 65
economic rationalist model, New Public
    Management, 83–4
economic theories of leadership, 129–32
economic theory of regulation, *see* capture
    theory of regulation
education subsidies, 18
efficiency, *see* economic efficiency
Eggertsson, T., 61, 66
Ehrlich, S. B., 119
Ekeland, R. B., 42
Elster, J.
  emotion theory, 8, 138–9, 144, 146, 181,
    187

hope, 140, 141, 143
incoherent intention, 139–40
leadership, 137, 146–7, 188
social sciences and natural sciences, 3
emotion theory, 138–9, 144, 181, 187
enforcement failure, 37
equity criteria, 21–3
ethical considerations, 21–3
Etzioni, A., 137
Evans, L., 111
exchange system, 10–11
exploitation theories of the state, 34
externalities
  derived, 48–9
  market failure, 17–18
externalization of politics, 179, 182

falsifiability, principle of, 3
Farrell, M. J., 11
Fernandez, R., 104
Fernyhough, John, 114
Festinger, Leon, 146
'Fewer Civil Servants but a Better Civil
    Service' programme (Holland), 88
France, 58, 88
Frank, R., 113–14
Frankfurt, H. G., 133
Frant, H., 63, 75
Frey, B. S., 131, 163
Frijda, N. H., 144
Frohlich, N., 129
Fromm, Erich, 144
fundamentalist religion, 180, 181
Furtan, 35
Furubotn, E. G., 62–3, 64, 66
futility of resistance theorem, 168, 172
futility thesis, 155, 164–6, 168, 172
  progressive counterpart, 168

Gaebler, T., 78, 156, 159, 172
Gal, R., 119
gaming operators, 17
Gandhi, Mahatma, 124
Gardner, M., 70
Gemmill, G., 119
general equilibrium approach to allocative
    efficiency, 13–14
generic managerialism (GM), xiv, 62,
    77–86
  criticisms, 86–7
Gersick, C. J. G., 95, 106, 184
Gibbs, Alan, 114
Gore, Al, 88
governance, 184–7

DATE DUE

			Printed in USA

HIGHSMITH #45230